BUILDING AND USING
A SOLAR-HEATED GEODESIC GREENHOUSE

Building and Using
a Solar-Heated
GEODESIC GREENHOUSE

John Fontanetta
Al Heller

GARDEN WAY PUBLISHING
Charlotte, Vermont 05445

Back cover:
The Fordham dome has been a model for others, built at three other sites. The sites, from top to bottom, are: Fordham University, Bronx, New York; Gateway National Park, Jamaica, New York; West 46th Street, Manhatten, New York; and Washington, D.C.

Copyright © 1979 by John Fontanetta and Alvis S. Heller

All rights reserved. No part of this book may be reproduced without permission in writing from the publisher, except by a reviewer who may quote brief passages or reproduce illustrations in a review with appropriate credit; nor may any part of this book be reproduced, stored in a retrieval system, or transmitted in any form or by any means — electronic, photocopying, recording, or other — without permission in writing from the publisher.

Illustrations by Robert Vogel

Photographs by the authors

Printed in the United States
First printing, October 1979

Library of Congress Cataloging in Publication Data

Fontanetta, John, 1957–
  Building and using a solar-heated geodesic greenhouse.

   Includes index.
   1. Solar greenhouses — Design and construction.
2. Geodesic domes — Design and construction. 3. Greenhouse gardening.   I. Heller, Al, 1950–   joint author.   II. Title.
SB46.F66   631.5'44   79-20849
ISBN 0-88266-161-2

To
Anthony Fontanetta

In Memory of
Gloria Fontanetta

Contents

Introduction

Chapter 1:
The Solar-Heated, Food-Producing Dome 1

An effective design. Other advantages. Easy assembly. Insulating cover. Raising food. Retaining heat.

Chapter 2:
Choosing a Site 7

Siting considerations. Changing paths of the sun. Solar altitude and azimuth. Surveying the sun and site obstructions. Finding true south. How much sunlight is needed. Degree days.

Chapter 3:
Selecting and Ordering Materials 17

Insulation: above-ground and underground. The dome frame. Protecting wood. Securing posts. Hardware. Glazing. Water heat storage. Solar energy–absorbing paints. Ordering: Sun-Lite storage and aquaculture container. Scotchrap 50 tape. Monsanto "602." Insulation. Polyethylene film for underground insulation. Lumber. Fifty-five and thirty-gallon drums. Hardware.

Chapter 4:
Woodworking 34

Getting started. Equipment needed. Frame parts. Preparing work surface. Building jigs. Cutting long struts. Cutting short struts. Cutting hub struts. Cutting base hub struts. A jig for drilling holes. Possible measurement problems. Drilling strut holes. Cutting plywood hub plates. Preserving wood. Assembling hubs. Drilling holes for outer plates.

Chapter 5:
Site Preparation — 53

Laying out the base. Closing the circle. Site leveling. Preparing the garden bed. Digging trenches for underground insulation. Installing the securing posts. Installing underground polyethylene. Drainage ditch. Securing base hubs to posts. Attaching underground polyethylene to the frame.

Chapter 6:
Erecting the Dome Frame — 71

A frame with four levels. Rules for strut-hub assembly. Level two assembly. Keeping frame segments secure. Level four assembly. Top level placement. Completing the dome frame. Misaligned base hubs. Misplaced struts. Framing the door and vent. Building the door and vent.

Chapter 7:
Covering the Dome — 89

Covering procedures. Terms of attachment. Covering level four. Covering level three. Cutting film. Covering level two. Installing fiberglass. Installing the inner covering. Covering the door and vent. Hanging the door and vent.

Chapter 8:
Maintaining and Operating Your Dome — 113

Temperature maintenance, winter heating. Setting up water storage: Using thirty and fifty-five gallon drums, using drums and one-gallon containers, using drums and a 725-gallon tank. Reducing infiltration. Temperature requirements. Other ways to maintain temperatures. Summer cooling. Spring and fall. General upkeep. Cleaning the glazing. Replacing film. Replacing struts and hubs. Handling emergencies.

Chapter 9:
Raising Food in the Dome — 132

Gardening. Intensive gardening. Organic vs. conventional gardening methods. Soil preparation. Setting up garden beds: wide-row with steps, wide-row with paths, conventional row. Seedlings. Gearing your garden to the seasons. Looking after your garden: planting, cultivation, pollination, companion planting, watering, insect control. The FUSES team winter garden. The FUSES team summer garden. Gardening references. Aquaculture.

Chapter 10:
Using the Dome to Earn and Save Money   152

Selling vegetables. Growing seedlings for sale. Using the dome for home heat. Using the dome to pre-heat water. Community gardens. Educational aid. A cover for swimming pools and hot tubs.

Chapter 11:
Domes of Other Sizes   159

Frame. Materials: lumber, underground polyethylene, above-ground covering, insulation. An example.

Appendix   165

Appendix 1: Solar Altitude and Azimuth
Appendix 2: Degree Days Across the United States
Appendix 3: The Nature of Sunlight
Appendix 4: The Time it Takes to Build Your Dome
Appendix 5: Vegetables for Different Seasons
Appendix 6: Organic Methods of Insect Control

Glossary   183

Acknowledgments   189

Index   191

Introduction

Four out of every ten American families garden, but many are able to grow fresh vegetables only four or five months a year due to unfavorable climates.

At Fordham University in New York City, we developed what we regard as a successful solution to this problem: a low-cost, solar-heated geodesic greenhouse.

This was the work of an interdisciplinary research group known as the Fordham Urban Solar EcoSystem (FUSES) team. The research project was co-founded by Don Devey and myself.

We selected the classic geodesic dome structure, made famous by R. Buckminster Fuller, because it may be adapted easily for year-round vegetable gardening.

As development and improvisation of the design progressed, we kept these questions in mind: Is this geodesic greenhouse practical? Is it energy efficient? And, is it easy to use?

We are confident the answer to these questions is an unequivocal, "Yes."

The 23-foot-diameter structure described in this book can be built by virtually anyone, without special carpentry skills. Common hand tools are all that is needed to cut the dome's basic parts and framing into proper sizes.

The sturdy, 11½-foot-high dome is covered with a double layer of resilient, specially reinforced polyethylene, designed to withstand harsh weather.

Inside the Fordham dome, gardens produced up to $25 worth of fresh vegetables per month in just 65 square feet of space. (The remainder was used for research and raising fish.)

If more of the 416-square foot interior were used, vegetable production could easily triple. With reasonable care and attention — about 15 minutes a day — you could produce and sell enough vegetables to pay back the cost of constructing the dome within one year. The Fordham dome was built for less than $480.

How is this possible? The key to successful year-round gardening rests with the dome design, its insulation and its ability to retain heat. Because the dome has many surfaces, it receives sunlight for longer periods of the day than conventional greenhouses.

Because the dome is insulated, both above and below ground, and because its north-facing walls are lined with water drums, it retains the earth's and the sun's heat effectively. And, all this is achieved with low-cost, readily available, scientifically proven materials.

In 1978, the FUSES team received a grant from the National Science Foundation to help test materials. After two years of operation, the dome has withstood the test of harsh weather, and the materials have proven their durability.

The FUSES dome has served as a prototype for four similar domes built in New York City. Members of the FUSES team have consulted on the construction of these domes and have assembled for exhibition a temporary dome in Washington, D.C.

This versatile structure has several other uses, in addition to serving as a greenhouse. It may be adapted to serve as a source of supplementary home heat, to preheat water for a hot-water system and, with the necessary tanks, to raise fish. The dome also may be built to various sizes.

As director of the FUSES research team, I've been pleased to see the expanding number of dome applications and the ever-widening interest in the project. Schools, national parks, community groups, food cooperatives and even prisons have asked to learn more about the dome.

Many inquiries were prompted by news reports on the FUSES project appearing in *The New York Times, The New York Daily News, New York* magazine, the Gannett newspapers, CBS-TV and other news media.

Soon after its conception, the FUSES team expanded to include James McGurk, Barbara Ann Tomascovick Devey and, later, more than a dozen others joined the project. Together, we've been a team with varied interests

Charles Crawford of CBS-TV interviews John Fontanetta, left, and Donald Devey, co-founders of the FUSES project. At center, is Barbara Ann Devey, another FUSES team member.

and fields of study, including agriculture, biology, physics, sociology and community relations.

Our intent was to focus our diverse points of view on a single objective: to design, build and operate a greenhouse structure that would be affordable for anyone.

Now, we want to make this dome available to anyone interested in producing his or her own fresh food twelve months a year. For this reason, Al Heller, a writer and photographer, and I have written this book. It's the best way we know of to bring the dome in to your backyard, to help you enjoy successful, low-cost greenhouse gardening.

John Fontanetta

ABOUT THE AUTHORS

JOHN FONTANETTA is an honors graduate of Fordham University and has conducted solar energy studies for the past three years. He's a medical student at Cornell University. He's also a consultant and lecturer and has constructed geodesic greenhouses in New York and Washington, D.C.

AL HELLER, a writer and photographer, has also edited business and technical publications. He is assistant public relations director at Fordham University.

Chapter 1: The Solar-Heated, Food-Producing Dome

The dome-shaped, geodesic greenhouse is an ideal passive solar energy collector. Unlike conventional greenhouses with V-shaped roofs, the dome has many surfaces, facing many different angles. This means that, as the sun passes overhead, it's almost constantly striking one or more dome surfaces nearly directly. And this continuous, uniform lighting and heating supports vigorous vegetable growth.

Figure 1-1. Dome receives direct morning, midday and afternoon sun. Northern-facing surfaces are insulated.

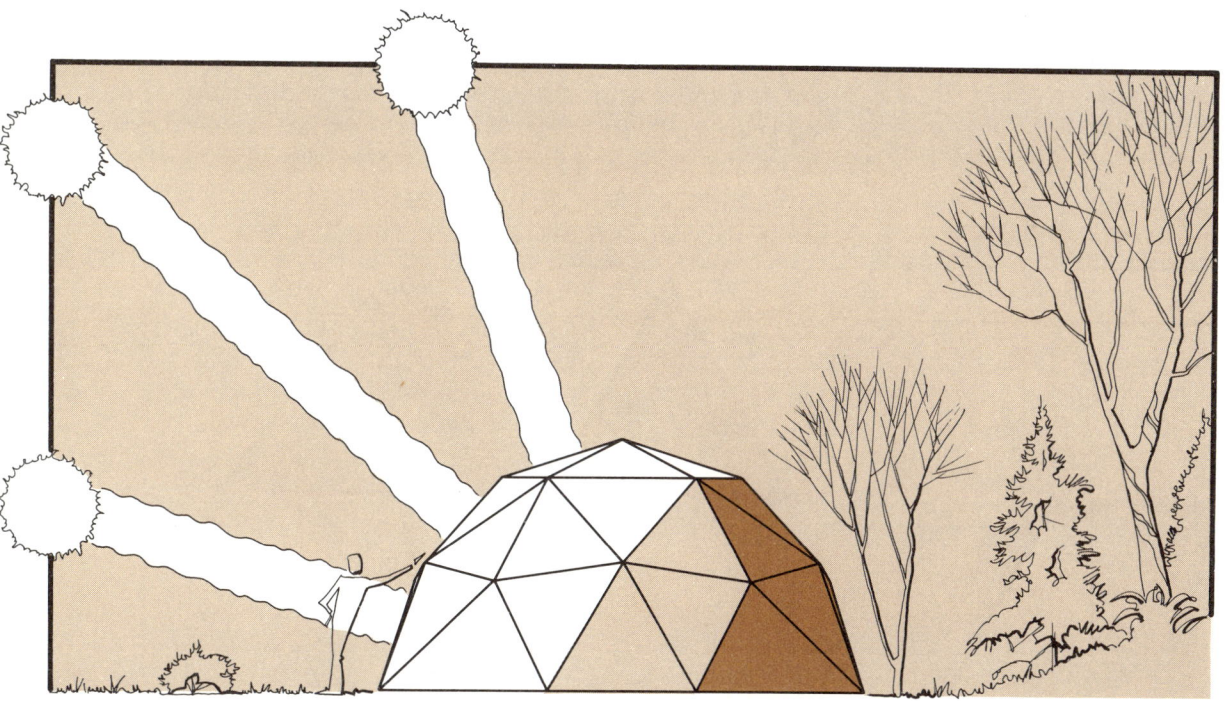

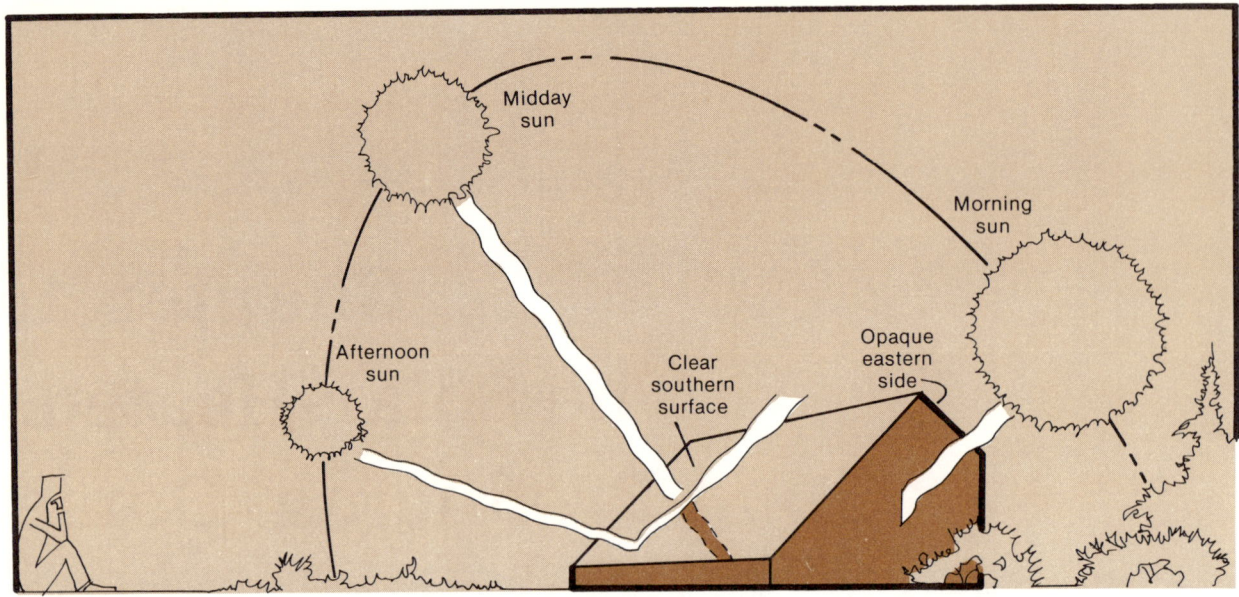

Figure 1-2. Some conventional designs restrict or reflect sunlight.

AN EFFECTIVE DESIGN

Because the geodesic greenhouse receives and retains solar energy effectively, it's not uncommon to walk inside to temperatures in the 70s while outside temperatures are below freezing. And there are other reasons to use the 11½-foot high geodesic greenhouse described in these pages. The dome has an inherently rigid design and it can be built of sturdy, but low-cost, materials. A cement foundation is not necessary; five wooden posts secure the dome to the ground.

The dome's inherent strength is derived from its basic component, the triangle. A triangle's angles won't shift under stress and, therefore, stress is distributed along the triangle's entire surface rather than concentrated at its joints. Joints of rectangular structures sometimes **do** shift under stress, resulting in distortion and structural instability unless extra bracketing is used.

Figure 1-3. A triangle's angles won't shift under stress; rectangles without support will.

OTHER ADVANTAGES

There are other advantages to the dome, built at Fordham University by the Fordham Urban Solar Eco-System (FUSES) research team. For example, the 23-foot diameter was selected as a dimension because it results in minimum waste when the wood components and polyethylene covering are cut to proper sizes. (Of course, the dome can be built to other dimensions.) Its frame is made of 2 x 2-inch lumber struts instead of 2 x 4s, which are heavier and more costly. The struts are bolted together, in "tinkertoy" fashion, at plywood hubs.

EASY ASSEMBLY

All components of the frame can be cut, drilled, painted and even partially assembled off-site, then brought to the dome site for final assembly. This means you can set up lumber and equipment in your basement or garage, then work on it at your own pace without worrying about backyard clutter or possible theft of materials.

Wood used in the dome is preserved with redwood stain to protect against rot. The only wooden parts not coated with redwood stain are the 4 x 4-inch securing posts, anchored in the ground to keep the structure steady. The

The Fordham dome.

posts are **walmanized,** a process that effectively protects wood against decay. The posts need this added protection because they are embedded in soil permanently.

INSULATING COVER

The dome frame is covered with a double layer of strong, plastic film called **Monsanto "602,"** a resilient, clear polyethylene material specially treated for long life. It's inexpensive, compared to the price of most greenhouse coverings, and it's easy to secure to the dome frame. The double layer of film creates a two-inch "dead air space" over the entire structure; this space retards heat loss the same way storm windows do.

The "602" feels tough and stands up to harsh winter weather. A skeptic trying to poke a hole through it might sprain a finger instead. And that's not an exaggeration!

If you're a six-footer, you have to bend down to step through the door of the Fordham dome because it is built into one of the dome's lower triangles. But, once inside, you immediately feel a sense of roominess. And heat.

RAISING FOOD

The half-sphere is filled with warm, moist air and the healthy scent of soil and vegetable plants. Straight ahead and to the left are dense lettuce and spinach plants. On either side of semicircular pathways, there are trellises of peas with alternating beds of beets, radishes and other thriving vegetables.

To the right, there's a tall, cylindrical, fiberglass tank for raising fish, another of the dome's possibilities. If you're lucky, you may see some silvery shadows flitting about; these are some of the 150 tropical African fish known as **tilapia aurea.** You may even glimpse a lizard darting by the tank to a meal, perhaps an unwanted insect or garden pest.

The garden's high productivity is largely the result of using the French Intensive gardening method, whereby closely spaced plants are grown in raised beds of loose soil. The raised beds provide an optimum balance of air, moisture and bacteria, an ideal growing medium. Plant roots need not be as developed as they are in conventional gardens and this means more plants may be packed into smaller spaces. At Fordham, we've found that yields in these intensive plots are **four times greater** than in most backyard gardens.

The dome door opens to a winter garden of fresh vegetables. Fiberglass insulation is packed between the two film layers on the dome's northern sides.

New York magazine writer Veronica McNiff took a look at the Fordham garden and later reported that, "plants jostle one another with rude health, presenting a thicket of bright leaves and blossoms. . . ." WCBS/TV health and science editor Charles Crawford called it "one of the most luscious-looking vegetable gardens you'll ever see: peas, lettuce, carrots, onions, collards, cabbage and beets . . . and they are delicious."

RETAINING HEAT

Vegetables can continue to grow year-round, thanks to the dome's ability to retain solar heat. Fiberglass insulation is packed between the two layers of film covering the dome's northern surfaces. Foil on the inside surface of the insulation reflects sunlight back toward the dome garden.

Insulation is also used underground. Two sheets of polyethylene film envelop a two-foot thick circle of soil beneath the dome's base to protect the earth inside from freezing temperatures. The film joins the dome's above-ground covering, creating a waterproof, draftproof

5

6

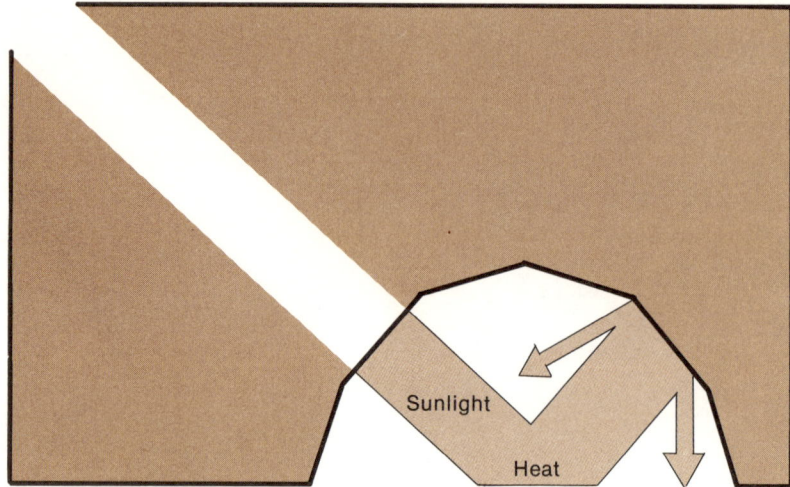

Figure 1-4. Sunlight passes through clear surfaces and warms garden. Foil-backed insulation reduces heat loss and reflects sunlight toward garden.

shell. Inside, the large fish tank and black 55-gallon drums filled with water absorb solar energy during the day and release this heat during dark or overcast periods.

In most regions of the country, you can enjoy growing vegetables year-round in the dome, with solar energy as your only source of heat. In regions of extreme cold or extensive cloud cover, a small auxiliary heater may be needed. But, the need for a heat source other than the sun is minimized by the dome because it uses solar energy so effectively. If you haven't made up your mind about the greenhouse design best suited for you, examine other designs as well as the dome. We believe the geodesic greenhouse will fare well when compared with other structures.

Chapter 2: Choosing a Site

Think twice, then think again, about your dome site. Where you locate the dome largely determines its effectiveness as a food producer and the amount of time and effort needed to build and operate it properly.

With a little forethought, long, inconvenient walks to and from your residence usually can be avoided. At Fordham, for example, the selected dome site was a 300-yard walk from where the researchers lived. And water was supplied through a 100-foot garden hose attached to a spigot behind a row of bushes. With proper planning, inconveniences like these can often be avoided.

SITING CONSIDERATIONS

Building Codes

Before choosing a site, check the local building codes. Generally, there won't be restrictions against erecting domes, but some communities have unusual codes that you should review carefully to assure that your structure complies.

Proximity to Home

Since you may visit the dome nearly every day, why not locate it nearby? This will shorten walks through winter snows and make it easier to check the dome frequently. It's also less expensive to locate the dome near water, utility and supply sources.

Land Characteristics

Areas with poor drainage or steep slopes are not suitable dome sites. Avoid flood plains. To judge an area's

7

suitability, check it after heavy rains. Do many puddles develop? Does it remain wet for extended periods? If so, select another site.

The effectiveness of the dome's underground insulation will be significantly reduced in wet terrain. Also, cold water might leach into the dome, lowering its temperature and resulting in poor gardening soil. Poor drainage also creates a need for extensive soil preparation before gardening.

Although steep grades are unsuitable, domes may be built on slight slopes of about five degrees or less. If a steep slope is the only alternative, the dome site must be leveled, or nearly leveled, before construction.

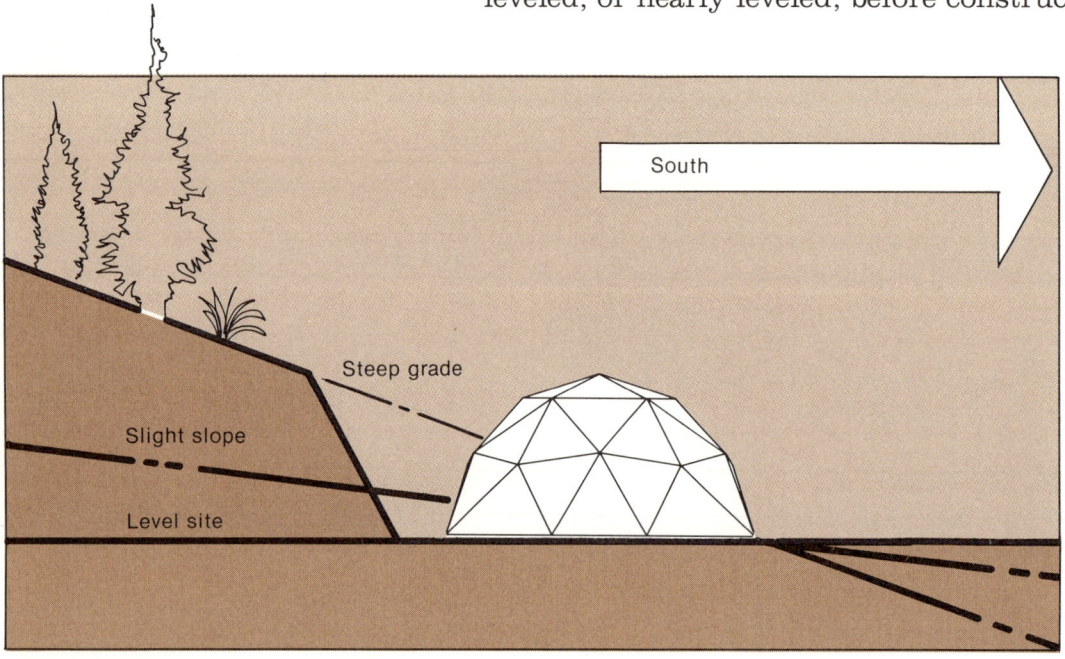

Figure 2-1. Steep grades must be leveled; slight slopes are acceptable; level sites with plentiful sunlight are preferable.

Naturally, if more than one site has ample sunlight, choose the one requiring the least leveling. However, if a site has enough sunlight but requires some leveling because of small mounds or depressions, choose it over a level site that receives less sun. (See "Site Leveling," Chapter 5.)

Wind Barriers

Wind barriers, such as fir and pine trees (which do not lose leaves in the fall), buildings and hedges, offer good protection for the dome. These should be on the dome's

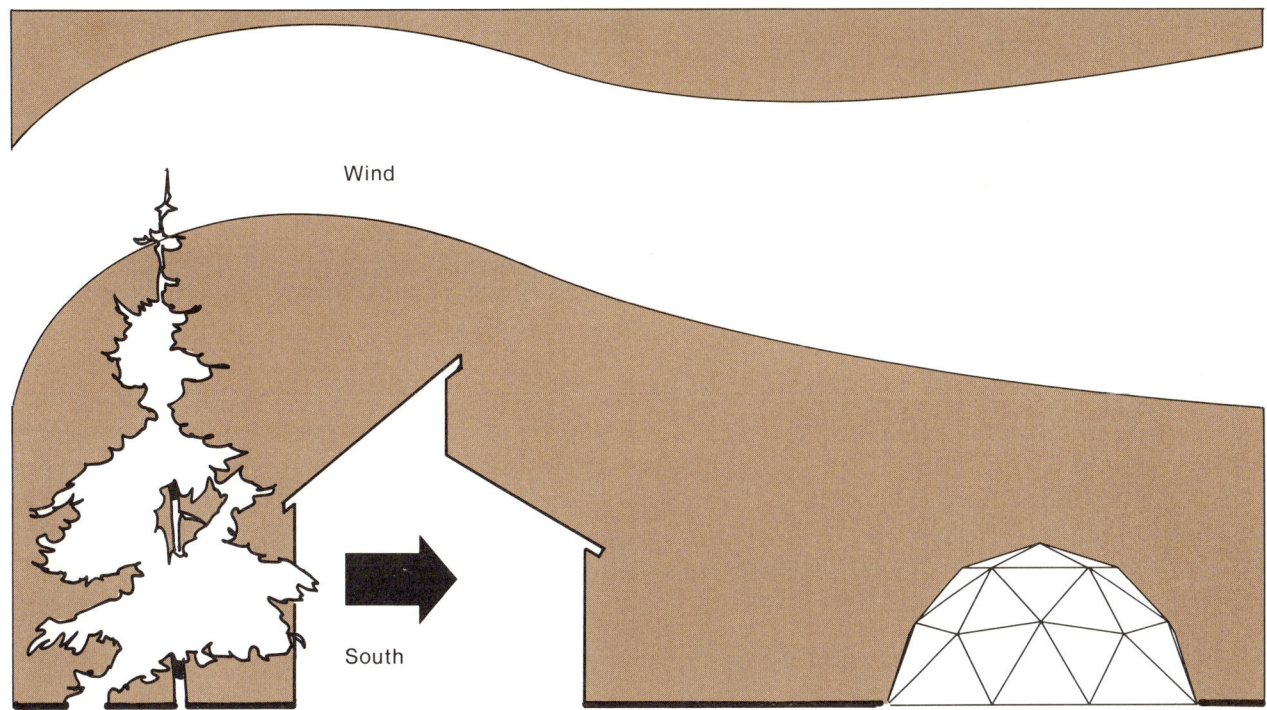

Figure 2-2. Wind barriers help protect the dome, even if the dome is as far as 100 feet downwind of the barrier.

upwind side, to either the north or northwest or points in between. Barriers 20 feet high will help protect the dome even if the dome is more than 100 feet downwind of the barrier. These barriers do not keep sunlight from the dome because its northern side is fiberglass insulated and only diffuse sunlight, of little value as a heat source, would enter from this direction anyway.

Sunlight

Far and away, the most important siting consideration is sunlight: the dome's exposure to it must be maximized. To do this, locate the dome so shading from barriers or obstructions is minimal and so the dome's clear, uninsulated surfaces are perpendicular to as much direct sunlight as possible.

The dome, of course, depends on the sun's energy for heat and its plants need sunlight to grow. A location with a totally unobstructed southern exposure is ideal. One with a few obstructions may be acceptable if sufficient sunlight strikes the dome.

CHANGING PATHS OF THE SUN

When selecting a greenhouse site, it's important to keep in mind that the sun's path varies with the season and time of day. The sun's position changes constantly. By knowing the sun's paths or positions, you can avoid shady areas and select sites with the most direct, intense sunlight. The sun's hourly and monthly positions are presented in tables at the back of the book (see Appendix 1).

Remember that the amount of energy transmitted to a spot on the earth during different seasons depends more on the angle at which the sun's rays reach that spot than on the actual intensity of these rays. When the sun is low in the sky, as in winter, its energy is distributed over a larger surface area of the earth, reducing its effect; when the sun is higher in the sky, its energy is more concentrated.

To understand this better, aim a flashlight directly on top of a table; then angle the light so it hits the table at a slant. This simulates the sun at its peak altitude, when its rays are most concentrated, and at lower altitudes, when its rays dissipate.

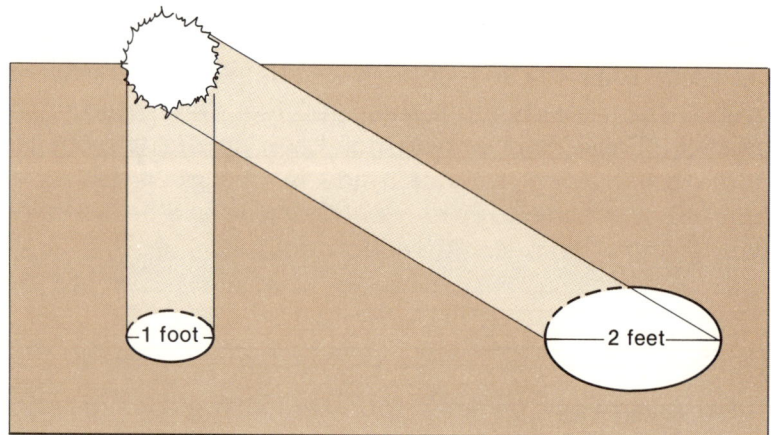

Figure 2-3. When held directly above a spot, a flashlight beam is more concentrated than when the flashlight is slanted. The same principle applies to the sun.

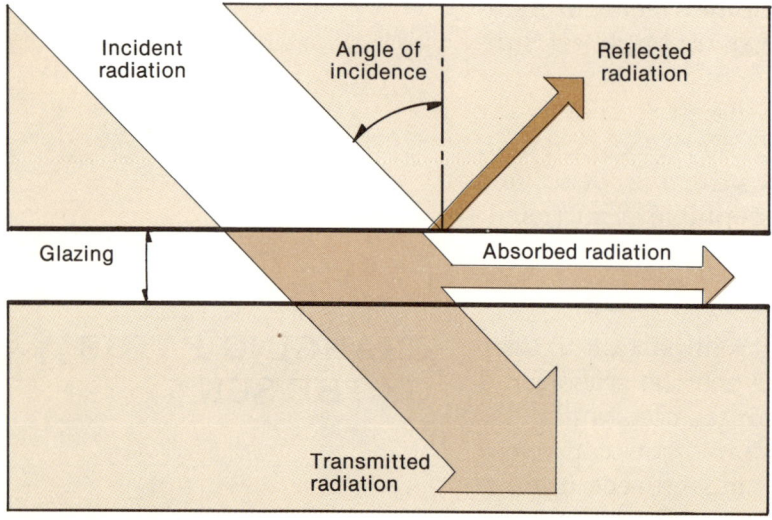

Figure 2-4. When sunlight (incident radiation) strikes greenhouse glazing, most radiation is transmitted through; some is absorbed; and some is reflected. The greater the angle at which the sunlight strikes the surface (angle of incidence), the more sunlight that is reflected and the less transmitted.

When the clear surfaces of a solar greenhouse are perpendicular to the sun's rays, the greenhouse receives concentrated, intense sunlight. The farther from perpendicular (or the greater the **angle of incidence**), the less concentrated the light becomes. And as the angle of incidence increases, the amount of sunlight **reflected** by the surfaces also increases, depriving the greenhouse of solar energy. This is a physical characteristic of all clear surfaces.

Solar Altitude and Azimuth

Two terms commonly used to express the sun's position are: **solar altitude**, the angle in a vertical plane between the sun and the earth's horizon; and **solar azimuth**, the angle in a horizontal plane between the sun and true south. These angles change continually as the earth spins on its axis and rotates about the sun.

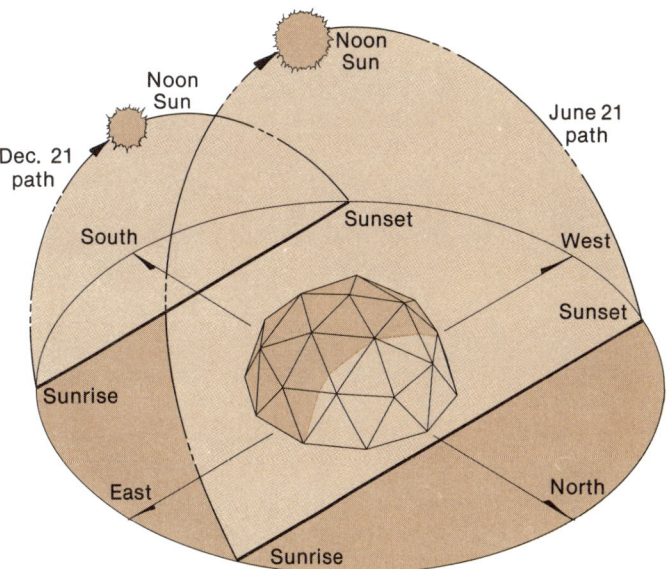

Figure 2-5. In December, the sun's path and noon altitude are lower than they are in June.

For example, at noon December 21 — in the New York area and at other locations near 40° north latitude — the sun's **altitude** is about 27°. At noon June 21, the angle is about 73°, meaning, of course, that the sun is much higher in the sky in June than in December.

The sun's **azimuth,** or angle between its position and true south, also changes constantly. For example, on

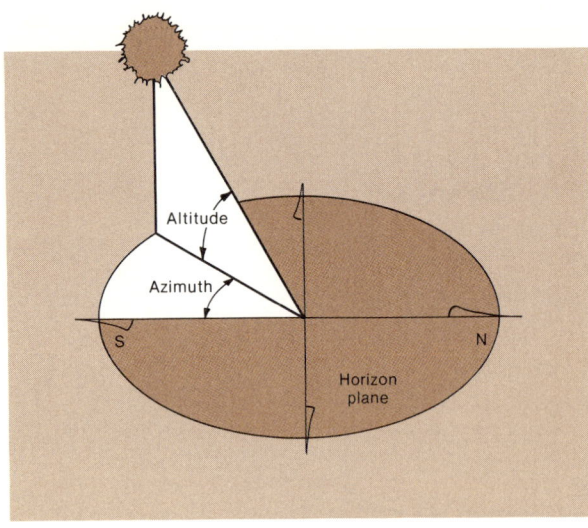

Figure 2-6. Solar altitude is the vertical angle between the horizon and the sun. Azimuth is the horizontal angle between the sun and due south.

March 21 at 40° north latitude, the sun rises at an azimuth of 80° east of south, moves to an azimuth of 0° at noon and sets at an azimuth of 80° west of south.

SURVEYING THE SUN AND SITE OBSTRUCTIONS

By knowing the altitude and azimuth for both the sun and obstructions on the south side of the dome site, you can determine the amount of shading a site will receive. The altitude and azimuth, or, in effect, the height and width, of trees, buildings, hedges or other obstructions may be determined by using a protractor and a simple, homemade device.

A Surveying Device

To make the device, screw a one-foot long furring strip or other thin piece of wood into a corner of a carpenter's level. Acting as a pivot, the screw allows the angle between the wood strip and the level to be adjusted. The

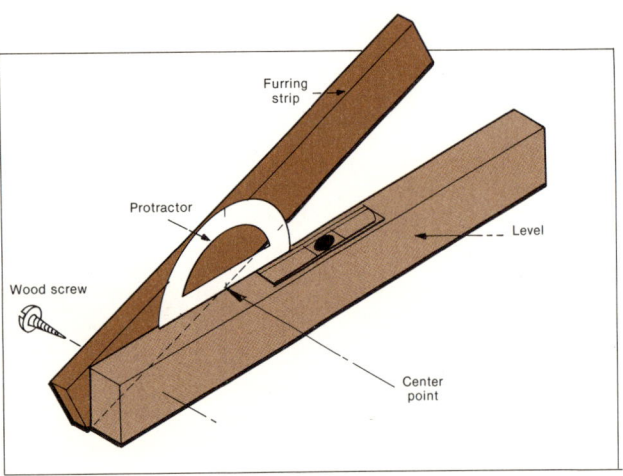

Figure 2-7. Sun surveying device, made of a carpenter's level and one-foot long furring strip.

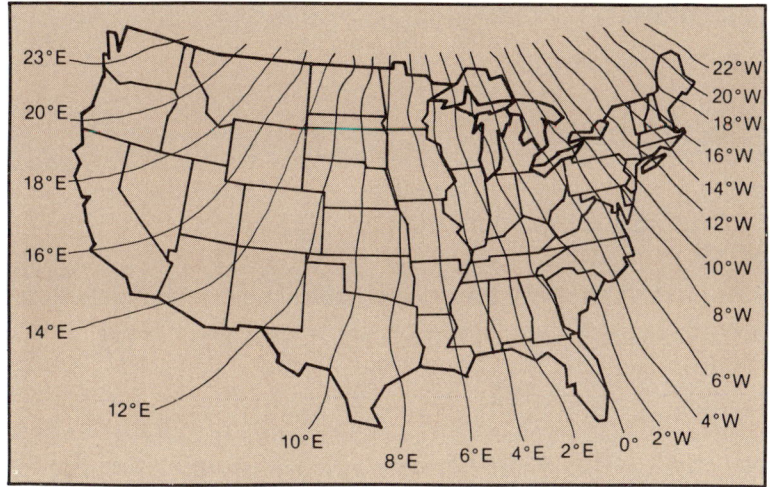

Figure 2-8. To find true south from your dome site, take a compass reading and then adjust it as necessary, using the correction indicated in the United States map at left. Find the curved vertical line for your location, determine the deviation and apply it to your site. For example, the magnetic deviation for New York is 10° west. This means the compass points 10° west of true north in the New York area; and, conversely, the compass points 10° east of true south. When a magnetic compass indicates south in New York, true south is 10° to the right.

screw must also be tight enough, however, to avoid inadvertent shifting of the strip.

Before you can complete an accurate survey, you need to know the point of the 0° azimuth from your proposed site. This point or direction is **true** south, not magnetic south read off a compass.

When you sit down in the middle of your proposed site to conduct the sun survey, take the tables (Appendix 1), surveying device, protractor, pen and paper. Find true south and mark it on the ground with a stick; then mark off 65° east of true south and 65° west of true south. Since no significant winter sun is available at azimuths beyond 65°, you can ignore obstructions outside these markings.

Obstructions within the 65°—0°—65° range may cause significant shading and must be taken into account when determining whether a proposed site offers sufficient year-round sunlight. For example, trees and tall buildings might make the site undesirable.

Figure 2-9. Set stakes as shown to prepare for survey of obstructions on south side of dome site.

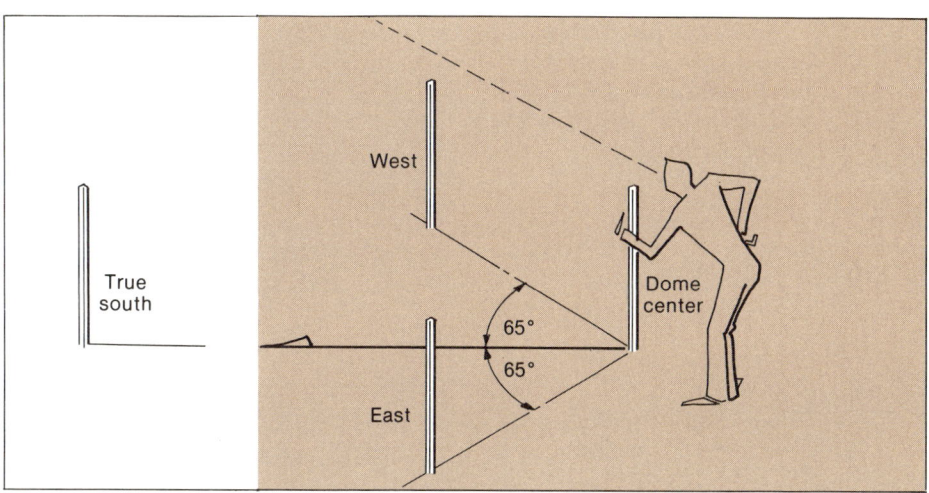

13

Charting Obstructions

To chart these obstructions, hold the surveying device to your eye so the bubble in the carpenter's level is centered, indicating that it is level with the horizon. (It may be easier to ask another person to check the bubble for you.)

Sighting along the furring strip, adjust the angle between the level and the strip so the top of any obstruction within the 65°—0°—65° range is aligned with the strip. Hold this angle, measure it with the protractor and record it: this is the solar altitude of the obstruction, the angle in a vertical plane it forms with the horizon. A one-story house might form a 28° angle, while a two-story house might form an angle of 40°.

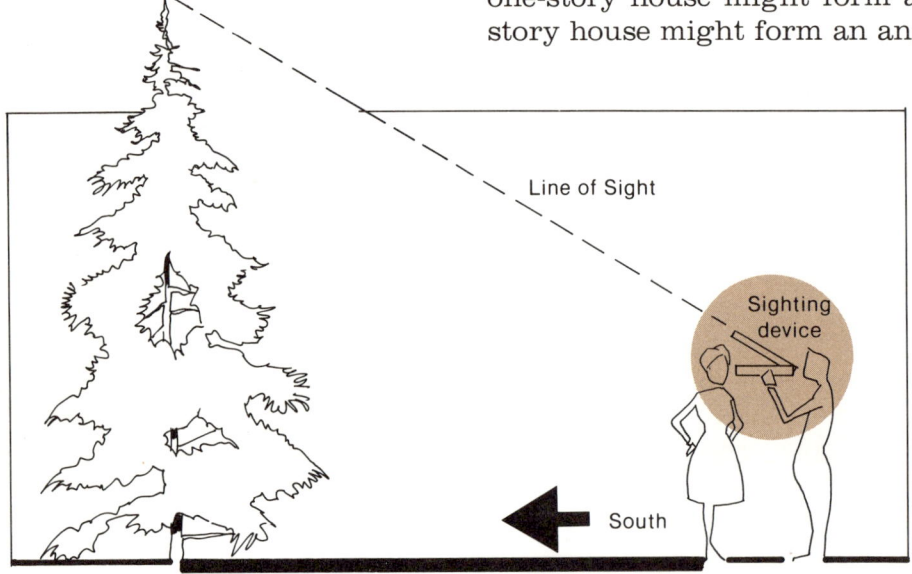

Figure 2-10. Ask a friend to ensure that carpenter's level remains level while you align furring strip with top of obstruction.

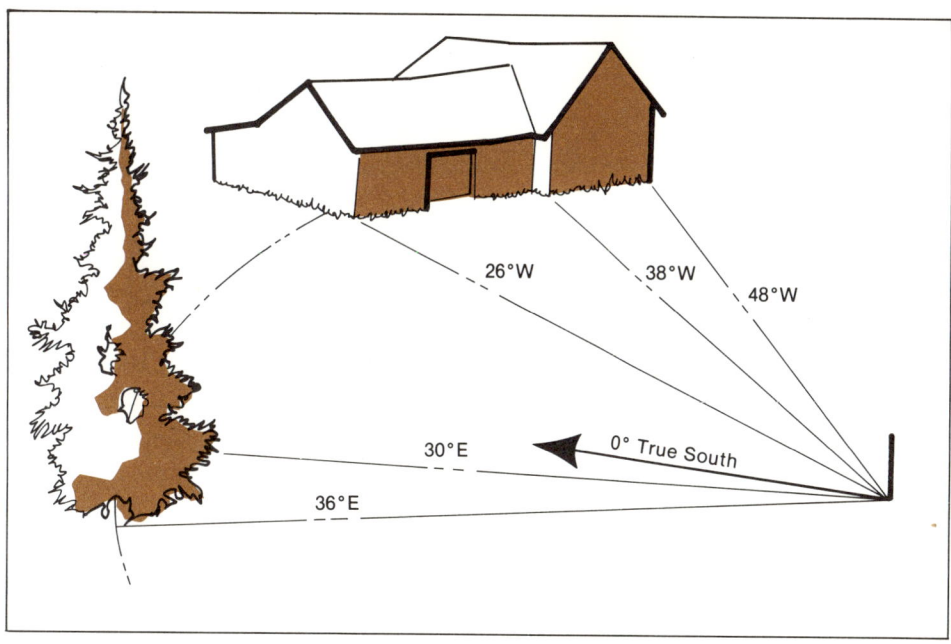

Figure 2-11. Azimuths for obstacles within the 65-0-65-degree range must also be determined. When obstacle altitudes and azimuths are matched with solar altitudes and azimuths found in tables, shading can be determined.

Now, using the ground as a horizontal plane, determine the angle range between true south (the 0° azimuth) and the beginning and end of each obstruction. For example, a tree may be sited between azimuths 18° and 36° east of south.

Record the azimuth of each obstruction next to its solar altitude. Every obstruction within the 65°—0°—65° range must have its solar altitude and azimuth recorded; these readings, when matched against the sun tables in Appendix 1, indicate the amount of obstruction to the dome's sunlight at different times of the year.

If, for example, at 40° north latitude, the top of a tree has a solar altitude of 40° and its azimuth is 35° to 40°, the sun tables show a dome facing this obstruction will likely be shaded from 9:30 to 10 A.M., October to March. If the tree is deciduous, it poses a minimal shading problem because it won't have leaves during this period.

If there are no obstructions, of course, a survey is not needed and the site is ideal.

HOW MUCH SUNLIGHT IS NEEDED?

There is no standard amount of sunlight needed to operate a dome because local climatic conditions vary from place to place. Sunshine, temperature and wind are among the variables; and obstructions causing partial shading may or may not present a problem. Nonetheless, a few generalizations apply:

In most parts of the United States, temperatures needed to support a thriving dome vegetable garden throughout the winter are attainable using only solar

15

DEGREE DAY

Degree day is a measurement originally used by oil companies to anticipate consumer need for oil in various parts of the country. It is the number of degrees between 65°F., assumed to be the average home temperature, and the mean temperature of a particular day. For example, if the mean temperature in New York City on December 20 is 30°F., then the number of degree days for that day is 35.

The four-page chart in Appendix 2 gives monthly degree days for various locations in the United States.

heat. In areas of the country having mild to cold winters, characterized by 900 to 1,300 degree days in January (see Appendix 2), the dome can do well on solar heat alone even if it is subject to minimal shading. In areas of harsh winters (over 1,300 degree days in January), the dome may need a small auxiliary heater to help maintain required temperatures. This need will be determined by sky clearness, altitude and other environmental factors.

Auxiliary Heating

The dome uses solar energy efficiently, and it also uses auxiliary heating well; and since this extra heat is needed infrequently, it should cost no more than $50 a year. Someone building a dome in a harsh climate who chooses not to supplement the sun's heat can still have a year-round garden, though it will grow slowly during the coldest weeks of winter. This is discussed more extensively in the section "Maintaining Temperatures in the Dome" in Chapter 8.

Shading

Your concern now is to determine the amount of shading your dome can withstand without impairing its performance. Your garden needs to be **unshaded** at least six hours a day, including a minimum of three hours between 9 A.M.–3 P.M. when sunlight is most intense. More sunlight results in a more productive garden.

Except for these plant lighting needs, there is no minimum amount of sunlight required to operate the dome. Of course, any shading the dome receives will be evident in its lower average temperatures, which may cause a need for extra heating. So choose a site that has the greatest amount of available sunlight, especially at mid day. By referring to the last column of the solar altitude and azimuth tables in Appendix 1, you can see that a dome shaded for two early morning hours often receives more radiant energy than one shaded for an hour at noon.

Chapter 3: Selecting and Ordering Materials

This chapter describes materials used in the dome, tells why they were chosen and explains how to order them. At the end of the chapter, materials are listed in the proper sequence for timely ordering. It's a good idea to check the availability of materials at least six weeks in advance of the time you plan to start construction. Generally, materials are readily available and are both inexpensive and durable. Information on cutting and assembling dome parts follows in later chapters.

INSULATION

Insulation is simply a barrier to the loss of heat. It can be made of many materials, or it can be simply an air vacuum. Fiberglass, commonly used in walls, attics or other places about the home, is a good insulator. A 3½-inch-thick section has an R-value of 11, the same high rating as 10 feet of concrete. The greater the R-value, the better the insulator. R-values are an indication of the resistance (R) a material offers to the flow of heat through it. A two-inch dead air space, similar to the space between a home window and a storm window, has an approximate R-value of 1.

The flow of heat through a material, known as the process of conduction, is expressed in this formula:

$$H_L = \frac{1}{R} \times (A) \times (\Delta T)$$

H_L = heat loss measured in Btus per hour
R = effectiveness of material used as insulator
A = area through which heat is lost
ΔT = the difference between inside and outside temperatures

Each factor helps determine the amount of heat loss from a structure. The larger the surface area of outer walls through which heat is lost, the greater the heat loss. The greater the difference between inside and outside temperatures, the greater the heat loss. And, as already indicated, insulation having high R-values performs the best and results in the least amount of heat loss.

Above-Ground Insulation

It makes sense to insulate greenhouse walls with materials having the greatest R-values. But, obviously, it's impossible to use materials like fiberglass insulation on south walls and at the same time provide sunlight for plant growth.

The only alternative, therefore, is to use a double layer of glazing with an insulative dead air space between layers. Double layers of clear or translucent materials such as polyethylene allow sunlight to enter while preventing direct contact of the cold outer layer with the warm air inside the dome.

Fiberglass insulation **is** appropriate for the dome's northern-facing walls. A 3½-inch thick section of foil-backed fiberglass insulation is packed between the layers of glazing on the dome's northerly sides. This insulation not only slows heat loss, but the foil backing on the fiberglass reflects sunlight that would otherwise be lost back toward the garden.

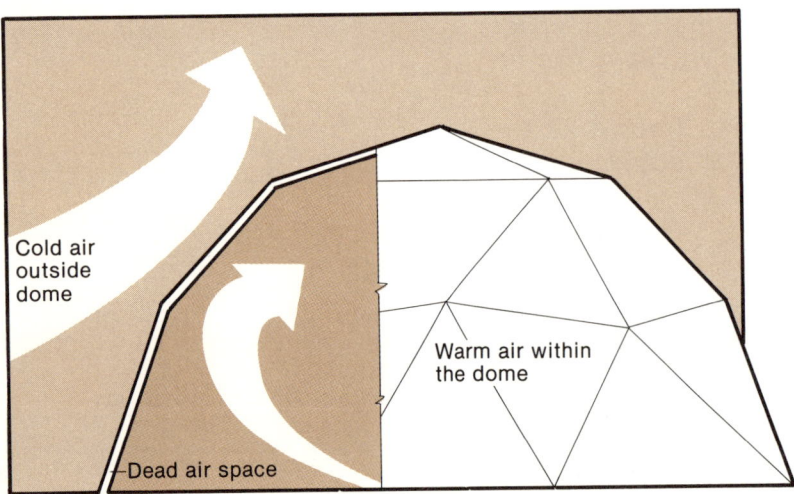

Figure 3-1. A two-inch dead air space between a double layer of polyethylene insulates the dome's southern walls.

The dome door, opened to the left, and northern-facing walls are packed with fiberglass insulation.

For some time, it was commonly thought that insulation on the north side of a greenhouse blocked diffused sunlight, an important source of energy in the winter when there are fewer hours of sunlight and the sun is lower in the sky. But researchers at Brace Research Institute of McGill University, Montreal, found compensating features in such materials.

They demonstrated that reflective material on the northern side of a structure increases available sunlight about 10 percent by redirecting the sun's rays toward interior surfaces. Obviously, plants would benefit from this increased light.

Some solar greenhouse designers recommend large amounts of insulation for northern walls, including materials almost six times more effective than fiberglass. But the FUSES team at Fordham found that a level is reached quickly where adding extra insulation to the dome's northern side decreases heat loss very little. This is because the southern clear surfaces of the dome, comprising about 45 percent of the entire structure, have an approximate R-value of 1. Most heat loss (88 percent)

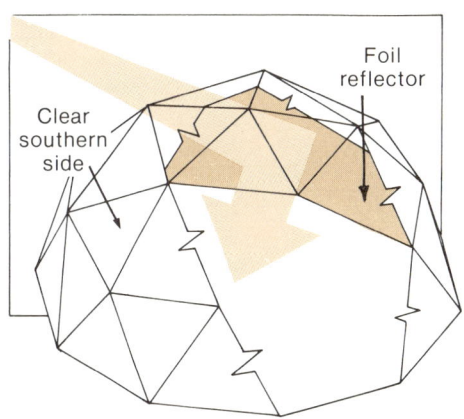

Figure 3-2. The foil-backed fiberglass reflects sunlight back toward the garden bed.

takes place through this side, making it economically impractical to add extra insulation to the northern sides. If you double the fiberglass insulation on the northern sides, you reduce heat loss by only about 6 percent — not 50 percent — and extra or larger struts to support the added insulation would be required.

Underground Insulation

The dome's underground insulation is made from a $30 roll of standard polyethylene film with a thickness of either four or six mils. Like other materials selected for the dome, this film is less expensive than the material often recommended by greenhouse designers: two-inch thick sheets of polyethylene or polystyrene. Enough of these rigid foam sheets to insulate the dome would cost at least $200.

The single roll of standard polyethylene film is laid vertically into two 2½-foot deep circular trenches, dug on either side of the dome's frame. Once the film is in place, the trenches are refilled with dirt. The underground film "fences," set two feet apart, create an envelope of soil that insulates against heat loss from the warm earth inside the dome to the cold ground outside.

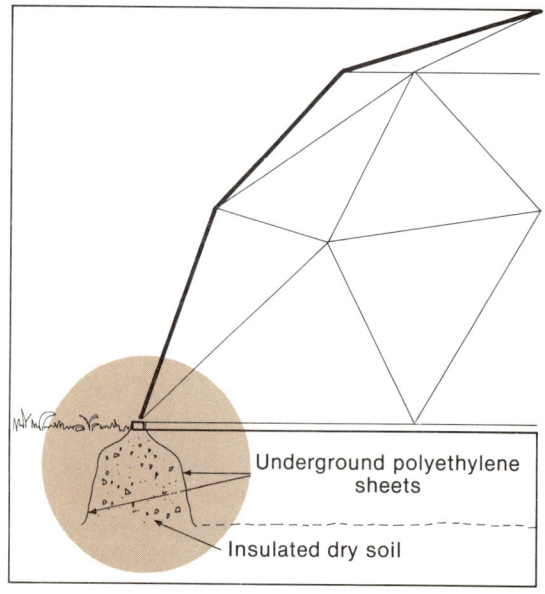

Figure 3-3. A cross-section of the underground film in place. Sheets from a roll of film are placed in trenches, then the trenches are refilled, creating an envelope of dry soil that insulates the dome below the surface.

Soil is a good insulator when kept dry, in this instance by polyethylene film. Two feet of dry soil have an approximate R-value of 44, although the value may vary depending upon the soil type. Therefore, the film is a good, low-cost way to provide more than enough underground insulation for the dome.

Trenches for the polyethylene are dug to a depth of 2½ feet. In most regions, frost does not penetrate below this depth and temperatures below 2½ feet remain at least 50°F. throughout the year. Only a small amount of heat is lost at deeper levels beneath the polyethylene.

THE DOME FRAME

The dome frame is made of wood, another material selected because of its low cost and ease of handling. Wooden parts may be cut and assembled off-site, meaning the chances of vandalism — or simply clutter at the worksite — are reduced. Working at home also allows you to proceed at your own pace.

The frame struts are wooden 2 x 2s, a lightweight material well suited for the dome. They weigh less than conventional 2 x 4s often used in construction; and this feature eliminates the need for a heavy foundation to support the structure. The 2 x 2s also create an insulating dead-air space between the dome's two layers of glaz-

Two geodesic dome frames at Gateway National Park in New York. The frame struts are lightweight 2 x 2s.

ing. (A larger insulating space, which allows more air movement and does not keep the air as "dead," is not significantly more effective than a two-inch space.)

When you purchase 2 x 2s, you actually receive struts measuring 1½ x 1½ inches; 2 x 2 is the pre-finished measurement. If possible, buy perfectly square 2 x 2s. Avoid 2 x 4s that have been "ripped" or sawn in half, since ripping may produce dimensions other than 1½ x 1½ inches.

Although aluminum conduit, a popular greenhouse framing material, is also light and sturdy, it has some disadvantages that make it unsuitable for the dome: special equipment is needed to work with conduit; polyethylene glazings may not be attached to it easily; it's thin (¾ of an inch) and this makes it difficult to form a dead-air space; and it costs three times as much as wood.

Any standard, construction-grade lumber is suitable for the dome; don't hesitate to buy whatever your local supplier has in stock. Strong softwoods like Douglas fir are preferred because they bolt together easily and don't splinter under pressure. But softer woods like white fir are also adequate. A complete list of lumber needed for the dome follows at the end of the chapter.

PROTECTING WOOD

It makes sense to buy 4 x 4-inch securing posts that have been walmanized (placed in a pressurized salt solution). Many lumberyards do not carry this specially treated wood, but it's worth the extra effort to try and find it. Tests have shown walmanized wood can stand in soil for 10 years with no sign of rot or deterioration.

However, walmanized wood also loses some of its strength and ability to hold nails, so **don't** buy walmanized wood for the remainder of the dome. Choose another preservative. The dome framework **must be preserved** because of the frequently high temperatures and humidity inside the structure.

The framework preservative should be inexpensive, it should protect the wood from rot adequately, and it should be **non-toxic to plants and animals.** Even though the wood struts are between two layers of polyethylene, high humidity and condensation cause a slight drip, and leaking toxic preservatives could be harmful to both plants and the people eating them. Creosote and Woodlife

SELECTING AND ORDERING MATERIALS

23

are among the preservatives to **avoid** because of their high toxicity.

Probably the best preservative for the dome is redwood stain, which protects wood from water penetration. Both latex and oil-based redwood stains sell for about $8 per gallon. Latex redwood stain dries quickly and can be cleaned from brushes and hands easily with water.

But **oil-based redwood stain is recommended** because it penetrates wood more deeply than latex, and therefore provides longer-lasting protection. Plastic solutions are also available that may be used as penetrating preservatives, but these are expensive and some are toxic.

SECURING POSTS

The dome frame is anchored securely to the ground with five 4 x 4-inch posts. (Actually, they measure 3½ x 3½ inches.) No cement foundation or footings are needed because the structure is inherently rigid. The length of the posts may vary. Although the Fordham dome has three 5-foot and two 3-foot long posts, you may be able to

Figure 3-4. Five securing posts, three or five feet long, hold the dome in place.

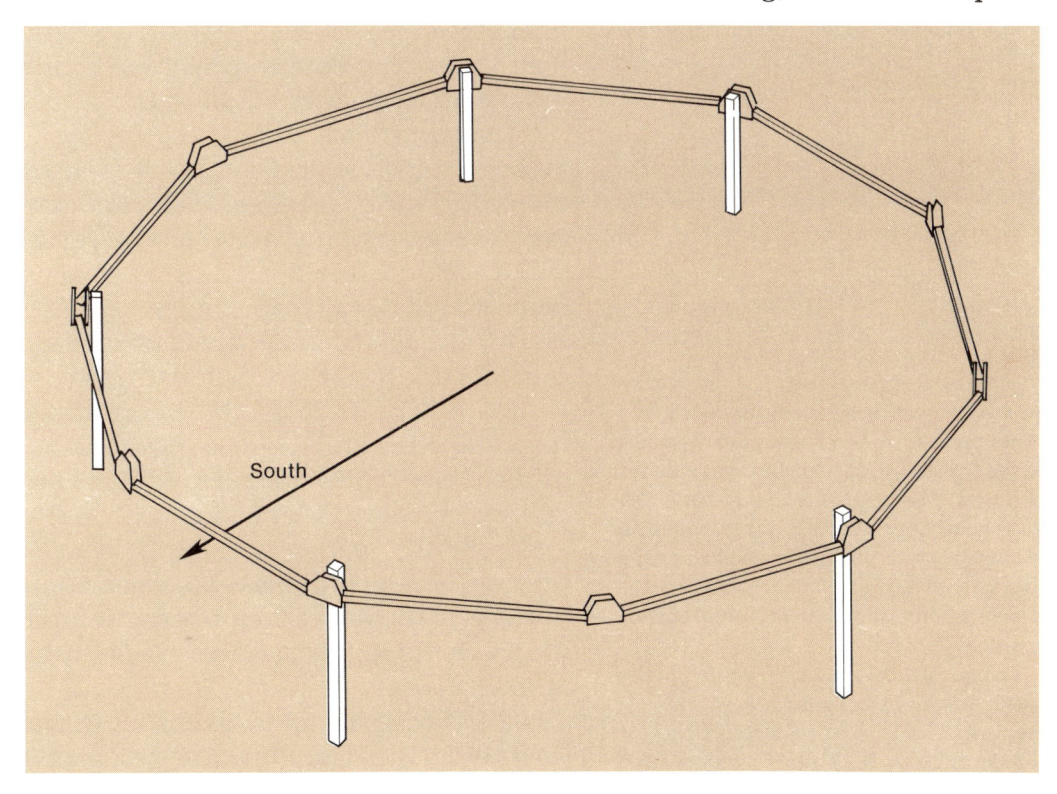

secure your dome with only two 5-foot and three 3-foot posts if the dome is sheltered from heavy winds.

On the other hand, if your dome is in an open area or near the ocean, you'll need more stability. Use either three 5-foot and two 3-foot posts or five 3-foot posts with cement footings. Using cement is not recommended if you haven't had experience working with it.

HARDWARE

Although the dome is exposed to all kinds of weather and inside the humidity's high, expensive, **rust-proof** nuts, bolts, screws and other hardware are not needed. Low-cost, **rust-resistant** hardware, such as common roofing nails, nickel-plated nuts, bolts and screws, are satisfactory. Only a few dome parts, the vent and door hinges, are subject to rust-inducing abrasion.

GLAZING

The dome frame is covered with a double layer of **Monsanto "602,"** a clear, resilient polyethylene film specially treated to resist harmful ultraviolet light. The polyethylene is taped to the dome struts and other parts with two-inch wide **Scotchrap 50 Tape;** then the tape is stapled, using a heavy-duty staple gun.

Monsanto "602" is not only resistant to the sun's high energy, ultraviolet light, but it is durable. The Fordham dome covering has been in place for two years with little yellowing and only a few minor repairs.

The "602" on the dome's southern, exterior walls is expected to last three to four years; the northern exterior and southern interior walls, six to eight years; and the northern interior walls, indefinitely.

The "602" should not be confused with standard polyethylene which is a poor greenhouse glazing because it discolors and weakens quickly. The useful lifespan of standard polyethylene is usually only six months.

The "602" was selected over glass and high-quality translucent fiberglass, two other popular glazings with longer lifespans. Glass is fragile and costly, about 55 cents per square foot. Fiberglass costs about the same as glass, making it about 15 times more expensive than "602." Fiberglass is more difficult than polyethylene to install on the triangles of a geodesic dome.

In comparison, the "602" costs about 2½ cents per

WHY USE TAPE?

When using a relatively thin — albeit sturdy — film like "602," an effective way to secure it to the dome's frame must be found. The reason for this can be seen by stapling together two sheets of paper, then pulling them apart. It's done easily because the staple tears one of the sheets in pulling. Something like this can happen to "602" joined to the frame when under stress from weather or abuse.

To prevent this, tape is applied to the "602" in the spots where it will be stapled. The tape adds strength to these surfaces, making it much harder to separate or damage them.

Scotchrap 50 Tape secures the polyethylene glazing, Monsanto "602," to the dome and accentuates its form.

square foot in 4 mil thickness for use as the dome's inner layer, and 4 cents per square foot in 6 mil thickness for use as its outer layer. If damaged or discolored, the "602" can be replaced or repaired easily using techniques described in Chapter 8.

Light transmission, which is important to healthy vegetable growth, is high with **Monsanto "602."** Two layers of this material transmit 73 percent of the available sunlight, according to a study in *American Vegetable Grower* magazine. By comparison, the study shows, one-day-old glass transmits 62 percent, while two layers of fiberglass transmit 77 percent. After two years, the "602" transmitted 70 percent, a deterioration of only 3 percent.

Scotchrap 50 Tape

Scotchrap 50 tape, a tough vinyl tape often used for wrapping metal steam pipes, is used to hold in place and seal the "602" before it is stapled. This durable, waterproof tape acts as a reinforcement, preventing the "602" from ripping at points where it is stapled. It secures the polyethylene and acts as a waterproof seam. The tape also joins the "602" to the underground polyethylene, giving the dome an uninterrupted above-ground and underground waterproof shell.

The polyethylene and tape should be stapled with an

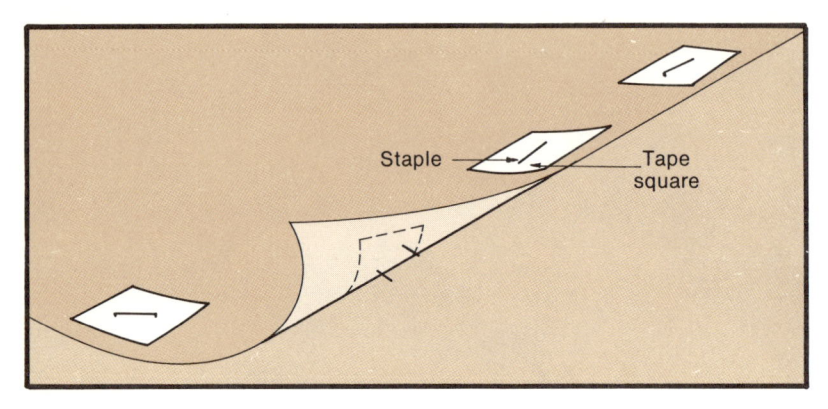

Figure 3-5. Tape is applied to the polyethylene film at points where it is stapled, adding strength and making it difficult to tear the film.

Arrow T50 stapling gun or a gun of similar quality. A good staple gun may be purchased for about $12. You'll need four boxes of staples (about 1,250 staples each), costing about $1.50 a box.

WATER HEAT STORAGE

The amount of solar energy available to heat the dome changes continually. Because of this, there's a need to store the sun's energy for periods of cloudiness and at night.

The best heat storage medium for the money is water, which is readily available and twice as effective as rock, another often-used medium. Water stored in the dome is heated by sunlight; and, when outside temperatures cool, the water releases its heat to keep the dome warm.

The best containers for water storage are either small or have a shape that gives the water a large surface area relative to its volume. This is so because the only water that can transfer its heat to a colder surface (in this case,

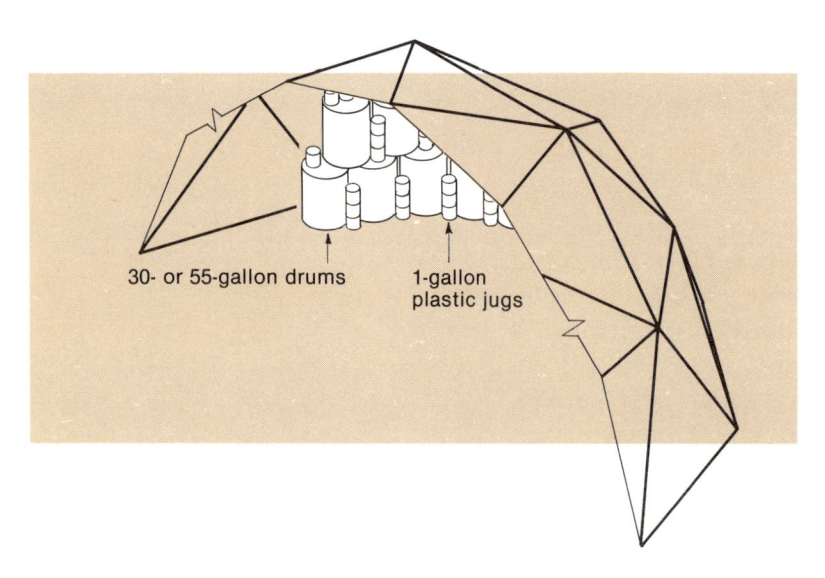

Figure 3-6. Water drums and jugs are used to store heat in the dome; these are lined up near the dome's northern walls.

SELECTING AND ORDERING MATERIALS

27

the dome) is water in direct contact with the container's surface. So, the greater the surface area, the quicker the heat transfer.

Some researchers suggest using one-pound honey cans or containers of similar size. These would be ideal for storing heat if you could obtain 1,000 or so, but that may be difficult. One-gallon plastic milk containers are also ideal, but they may be hard to acquire in large quantities and they are not easily stacked.

Cylindrical 55- and 30-gallon drums are not quite as effective as the small containers for storing heat, but they're easy to stack and most often can be acquired free from dumps or disposal areas of large institutions.

One solution is to obtain enough drums to store the amount of water needed to heat the dome, then supplement these with as many one-gallon jugs as you can acquire. You might ask friends to save their empty one-gallon milk containers for you; these can be nestled above and between the drums.

Heat storage requirements vary depending upon the locale, but two to three gallons of water per square foot of floor space is a good rule of thumb; this means that most domes will require 900 to 1,200 gallons of water. Figure 3-7 and the section in Chapter 8 on installing drums will help you determine the requirements for your location.

The Fordham dome has 55-gallon drums and a 725-gallon fish tank for water storage. This giant heat sink is effective: even on bitter winter nights, temperatures are

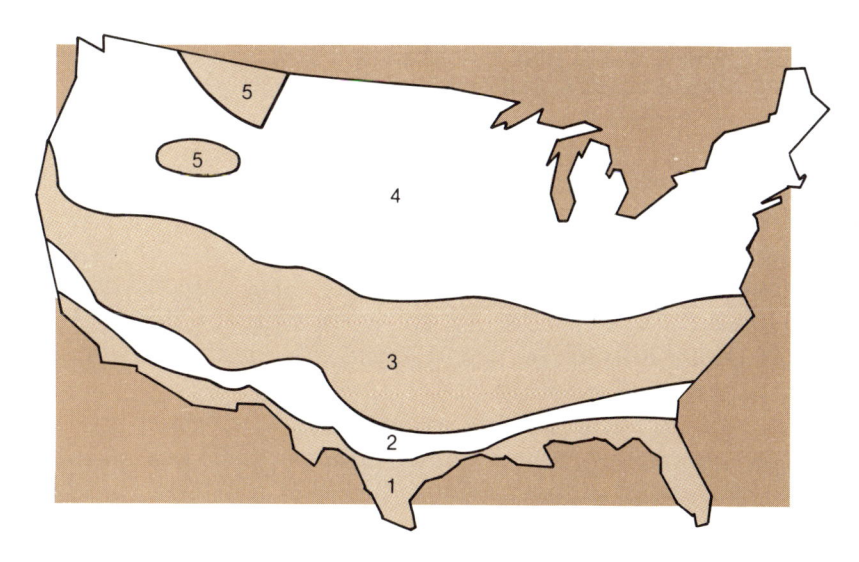

Figure 3-7. In zone 1, no heat storage is needed for the 23-foot diameter dome. As a general guide, these other volumes of heat storage are appropriate: zone 2, 416 gallons; zone 3, 832 gallons; zone 4, 1248 gallons; and zone 5, 1664 gallons.

warm enough for the vegetable garden. If you do not plan to raise fish, store water in drums and as many one-gallon plastic jugs as you can obtain. The large fish tank is not ideal as a primary heat storage container: it uses a lot of gardening space, and its relatively small surface area gives it a heat storage ability equal to just three or four 55-gallon drums.

It makes no difference what was in the drums earlier because you'll fill them with water, seal them and never reopen them. Start collecting drums at least a few weeks before construction. (They fit in the trunks of many cars.)

Solar Energy–Absorbing Paints

The side of each drum that will be exposed to the sun should be painted flat black before the drum is placed in the dome. The one-gallon plastic containers should not be painted, but the water inside should be mixed with enough flat black paint to make the liquid opaque. Dark colors absorb solar energy better than light colors and transfer more heat to the water.

Special solar energy paints cost $18–$50 per gallon, but you needn't pay such a steep price. **Martin's** flat black latex paint performs as well as other brands costing more than twice as much, according to laboratory tests at Fordham.* **Martin's** paint sells for about $8.

Steel brush lightly over any rusted spots on the containers before painting. The paint has no foul odors. After using it, brushes and stray spots can be cleaned with water. Two coats of Martin's paint is enough.

ORDERING MATERIALS

In acquiring materials, it's important to time your orders properly. The time of year and where you live determine if you'll have a two-day or six-week wait for items. Anticipating this can help you make the construction process go more smoothly.

A general rule: Decide exactly when to place orders based on the information here, but check the availability

---

*These test results were published in *Popular Science,* May 1979.

SELECTING AND ORDERING MATERIALS

of all materials at least six to seven weeks before construction. With this knowledge, you can prepare an appropriate purchasing schedule and avoid construction delays. Remember, prices quoted here are from early 1979, so don't be surprised if they've increased.

Items listed in this chapter are for a dome measuring 23 feet in diameter. Those listed first should be ordered first, since they are likely to take the longest to receive. Most local materials suppliers are listed in classified telephone directories.

Sun-Lite® storage and aquaculture container
Kalwall Corporation, Solar Components Division
P.O. Box 237
Manchester, NH 03105
Phone: (603) 668-8186

The 725-gallon container is needed only if you intend to raise fish. It is five feet high, 58 inches in diameter and weighs just 35 pounds. It costs $155 plus shipping charges. These charges vary; but the cost of shipping one container is the same as the cost for shipping four, making it worthwhile for friends and neighbors to combine orders.

For those living on the East coast, one way to reduce the shipping costs, which might be as much as $150, would be to rent a five- by eight-foot open trailer at an approximate cost of $40 per day. If transported this way, strap the tank with the **open end down** to avoid buckling and possible cracking.

Handle the tank carefully. Pick it up from the base to avoid flexing; flexing may cause it to crack. The tank will not fit through the dome door, so a dome strut will have to be removed if the tank arrives after the structure is up. To avoid this complication, order the tank at least six or seven weeks before construction.

Scotchrap 50 tape
3M Corporation (New York area branch office)
15 Henderson Drive
West Caldwell, NJ 07006
Phone: (212) 285-9600

One case of two-inch wide tape (ten rolls), costs $50 plus shipping. It's unlikely a retailer or distributor has it in stock because the tape is designed for special applications. Order the tape from a nearby 3M office at least six weeks before construction.

Monsanto "602" (polyethylene)
Monsanto Corporation
North 8th Street and Monroe Avenue
Kenilworth, NJ 07033
Toll-free number: (800) 526-4054

Two 14- x 100-foot rolls of Monsanto "602" are needed for the dome. One, for the dome's exterior wall glazing, should have a thickness of 6 mils and cost about $50. The second roll, for the dome's interior wall glazing, should be 4 mils thick and cost about $36.

If ordering directly from Monsanto, allow six weeks for delivery and expect to pay a shipping charge. Or buy "602" from a local greenhouse distributor or supplier, who may deliver it free.

Insulation
Various manufacturers and suppliers

Six 15-inch wide x 70-foot long rolls of 3½-inch thick fiberglass insulation with foil vapor barrier, costing about $85, are needed. This is a commonly used housing insulation. After insulating the dome, you should have about three-quarters of a roll for use about the home.

Finding insulation to buy may be a major problem since supplies vary depending upon locale. Order it at least six weeks before erection of the dome.

Polyethylene film for underground insulation
Various manufacturers and suppliers

One 8-foot wide roll of film in 4 or 6 mil thickness is needed. Any color can be used, but the 100-foot length is usually the smallest size available, and you'll have to buy it even though you need only 75 feet. After using what you need to encircle the dome twice (approximately 8 x 75 feet), excess can be used about the home.

The film costs about $20 and can be bought from a nearby home improvement center like **Channel** or **Rickel's**, or through mail order catalogs like **Sears** or **Montgomery Ward**. Check the film's availability at least four weeks in advance of site preparation.

Lumber
Local suppliers

A source for lumber should be found at least three weeks before you plan to start woodworking. Comparison-shop a few lumberyards in your area, since prices vary with time of year, location and dealer. Delivery time on the order should be one week or less, even if you buy walmanized wood, which is recommended only for your 4 x 4 posts.

The following items are needed:

- Fifty 12-foot lengths of 2 x 2s for struts. Any construction-grade lumber can be used, but the stronger the wood the better. White fir would be adequate; Douglas fir would be preferred.

- Three exterior grade plywood sheets, ½ inch thick, measuring 4 x 8 feet, for hubs.

- Enough 4 x 4 posts to suit the amount of securing needed for your location and environment. This wood should be walmanized, since posts embedded in the soil require the most protection from rotting. If walmanized wood is unavailable, buy posts treated with creosote.

- Thirty feet of furring strips or other suitable wood strips for use as a doorstop and to help in weatherproofing.

Good prices for these items are:

- 13 to 16 cents per linear foot for 2 x 2s of White fir or Douglas fir.

- $16 per sheet of ½-inch thick, 4- x 8-foot exterior grade plywood sheets.

- $1.05 per linear foot for 4 x 4 posts of walmanized White fir or Douglas fir.

- 10 to 15 cents per linear foot for wood strips.

55- and 30-gallon drums
Local suppliers

If you can't find free drums in nearby disposal areas, buy them reconditioned: 55-gallon drums cost about $10.50 each, 30-gallon drums about the same. But first try to convince a reconditioning company to sell you the

BUILDING AND USING A SOLAR-HEATED GEODESIC GREENHOUSE

drums in the same condition they receive them, since this will be less expensive. (To determine the number of drums needed, refer to Figure 3-7 and the section in Chapter 8 on installing drums.)

Hardware
Local suppliers

Most hardware may be purchased quickly at local hardware, lumber or supply stores, with one exception: the fender washers used with bolts to secure struts. You will need 260 of these, with 1¼- to 1½-inch diameters and holes measuring ¼ inch. Washers like these have a large surface area relative to the size of the hole, which means they press against — rather than dig into — wood.

Figure 3-8. Shown is the hardware used to secure struts to hubs. From left to right; 1/4-inch nut; lock washer; fender washer; star washer; fender washer; lock washer; and 1/4-inch bolt.

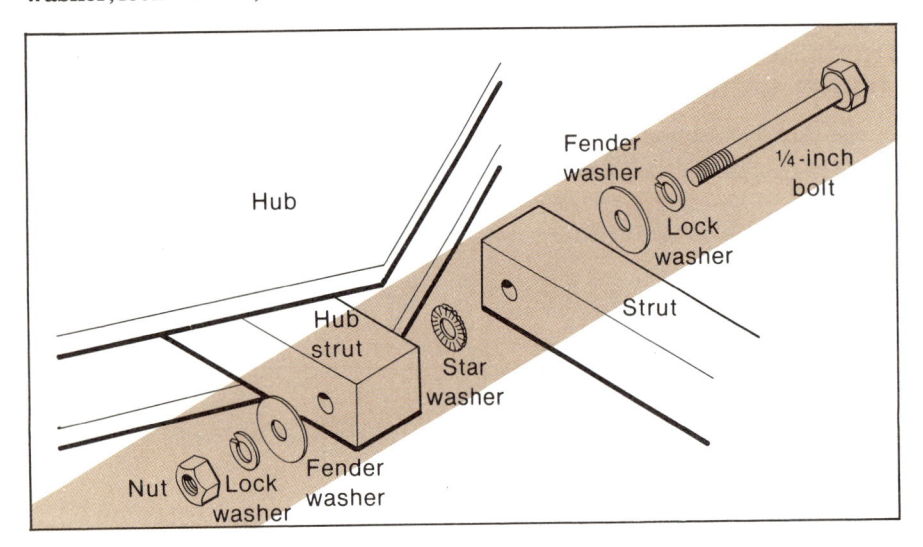

Try to find these washers five weeks in advance of construction. Comparison shop because prices vary sharply. When you locate a source, buy extras; they cost from 2 to 10 cents each. If these can't be found, use regular washers, which cost about $1.25 per pound.

Also needed are 130 nuts and bolts, but buy extras to allow for waste. The bolts ought to be 4 to 4½ inches long. They must be plated to resist rust and have hex heads if you're working with a socket set. If using other tools, or if they're unavailable, use round head or flat head bolts. Combined costs of nuts and bolts are 10 to 18 cents per set.

In addition, buy 135 large star washers or, if unavailable, 135 large lock washers for placement between bolted wood struts to prevent turning. Larger sizes are better for use on the dome; don't buy any smaller than ½-inch diameter. They cost about $1.98 per pound.

Other hardware you'll need include:

- Three boxes (or 3 pounds) of 1½-inch roofing nails
- Eighteen ⅛- x 4½-inch bolts, with nuts and washers
- Four 3-inch, rust-resistant hinges
- One 2-inch, rust-resistant hinge
- One small box (about 144 count) of 1-inch No. 8 wood screws, flat-headed
- Twenty-five 1½-inch, No. 8 wood screws
- Two 3- or 4-inch flat mending bars, with two to four holes pre-drilled in each
- Two hundred seventy ¼-inch lock washers
- Wire, hand tools
- Four boxes of ½-inch or ⅜-inch staples

Hardware needed to secure the dome frame to its securing posts is described in Chapter 5. Since the distance from the frame to the posts varies at each post, the type and amount of items needed are determined just before securing.

Chapter 4: Woodworking

By the time you complete the steps outlined in this chapter, you'll have cut and preserved the wooden parts of the dome frame and assembled the dome hubs. The frame is made of these basic parts: long 73½-inch struts, short 63½-inch struts; and base, pentagonal and hexagonal hubs. The hubs, which hold the struts together, are made of plywood plates and 7¼-inch hub struts.

Simple assembly-line techniques described in this chapter help cut the time needed to make the parts and help ensure that they are made with precision. Methods and steps are presented so they can be followed by anyone, without special skills or tools. Technical construction expertise is not required.

Woodworking is one of the two most time-consuming tasks in building your dome. Two people working together should need about 14 hours to complete it, one person alone will need a bit longer. Appendix 4 describes more fully the time needed for each step in building the dome.

Figure 4-1. Basic parts of the dome frame are short and long struts, and base, pent and hex hubs.

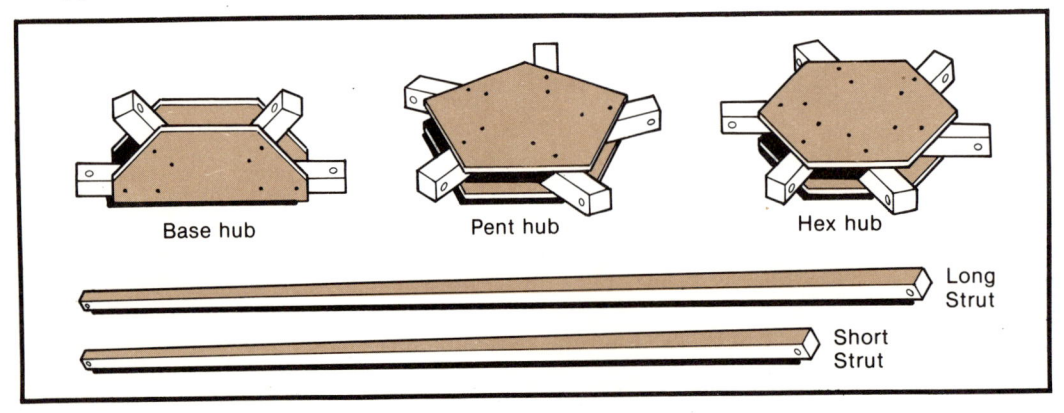

GETTING STARTED

The first step is to find a good sheltered place for woodworking, perhaps a basement or garage with enough space to allow comfortable handling of lumber up to 12-feet long and plywood sheets measuring 4 × 8 feet. Woodworking need not be done at the dome site and, because of this, you can work at your own pace at home without worrying about theft of materials.

EQUIPMENT NEEDED

The first essential item is a sturdy table at least 6½ feet long into which nails can be hammered. Lacking a picnic or work table, you can try sawhorses, but they must provide sturdy support.

You also need a saw, preferably a circular power saw, although a saber or jigsaw will work. Even a handsaw will suffice if you don't mind blisters. Two blades are recommended for the power saw: a fine-tooth plywood-cutting blade and a coarser-cut blade for cutting through other wood quickly. High-quality blades, like the Sears Craftsman line, are worth buying because of their durability and performance.

Other necessary items are:

1. A power drill with a ¼-inch bit at least 4½ inches long
2. A hammer and nails
3. A screwdriver and screws
4. A tape measure
5. Two mending bars
6. Protractor
7. Goggles

All tools are easy and safe to use as long as safety precautions are followed. Although instructions are presented here for those with little or no carpentry skills, experienced woodworkers may want to use other methods that work equally well. Precision is the key requirement, regardless of how it is achieved.

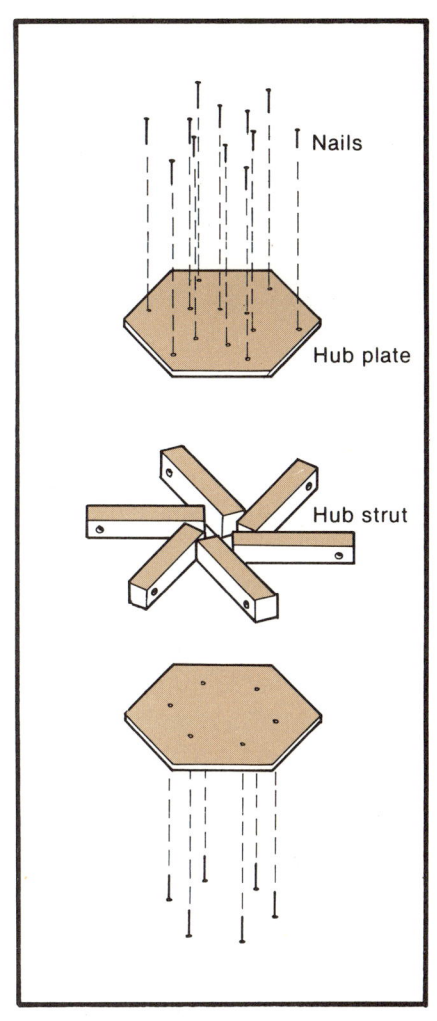

Figure 4-2. Hubs are made of hub struts sandwiched between two plywood plates.

BUILDING AND USING A SOLAR-HEATED GEODESIC GREENHOUSE

FRAME PARTS Assembly of the 23-foot-diameter dome frame is easy if struts, hubs and plates are cut to proper sizes. Upon completion of woodworking, the following parts should have been cut:

— 36 **long struts** (35 are used; 1 is extra), 2 x 2s, each 73½ inches long with a 1/4-inch hole drilled 7/8 inch inside each end and centered

— 31 **short struts** (30 are used; 1 is extra), 2 x 2s, each 63½ inches long with a 1/4-inch hole drilled 7/8 inch inside each end and centered

— 140 **hub struts**, 2 x 2s, each 7¼ inches long with a 1/4-inch hole drilled 7/8 inch inside one end and centered

— 11 **base hub struts**, 2 x 2s, each 16½ inches long with a 1/4-inch hole drilled 7/8 of an inch inside each end and centered

— 30 **hex hub plates** of 1/2-inch thick exterior grade plywood, hexagon shaped, measuring one foot from point to point

Co-author John Fontanetta describes geodesic dome frame to Phil Barnow of WNBC-TV. Note triangles formed by struts and hubs.

WOODWORKING

— 18 **pent hub plates** of 1/2-inch thick exterior grade plywood, pentagon-shaped with 11 inches from each of the top three points to the center of the base

— 30 **base hub plates** of 1/2 inch thick exterior grade plywood, shaped like half-hex plates with 2¼-inch bottom "skirts"

PREPARING A WORK SURFACE

Before cutting the lumber into the specified lengths, make a large work surface by nailing two 4 x 8-foot plywood sheets, one on top of the other, to the top of your work table. If the table is made of material that you can't nail into — or don't want to — use two or more C-clamps to hold the plywood in place. The result will be a sturdy work surface that can withstand abuse.

This task accomplished, you're almost prepared to start cutting the struts. But, since so many struts are needed of only a few different sizes, it's best to first build a construction **jig** or guide that eliminates the need to measure each piece individually. The jig increases speed and accuracy, and results in parts of uniform sizes.

BUILDING JIGS

Cut a 7-foot section from one 12-foot length of 2 x 2 for use as a guide to measure and cut other 2 x 2 lengths. Using three long finishing nails, secure the 7-foot length to the plywood. Space the nails to avoid the same grain; this will help prevent splitting. Leave the head of each nail protruding so the nails may be removed easily later.

Position the 7-foot length parallel with the plywood's 8-foot edge and in a spot where you can cut struts comfortably, using the 4-foot edge of the plywood as a guide. If right handed, this will be one foot inside the plywood's left edge; if left handed, just the opposite.

Now cut two 10-inch lengths of 2 x 2. Using two nails, secure one of these perpendicular to and touching the 7-foot length and flush with the table edge where you will cut. The 10-inch length serves as a rest area for your saw and an improved cutting guide, which is particularly useful for circular saws.

Using a tape measure, mark a spot 73½ inches in from the table's cutting edge. At this spot, nail in the other 10-inch length to use as a stop. Since each long strut will

DAMAGED LUMBER

Whenever you buy a large amount of lumber, you're bound to get some that is warped, knotted or split. Examine the wood immediately upon receipt and return any that is bad.

If you keep wood that is just slightly warped, you may be able to use these pieces for hub struts, if the warp is not noticeable. But never use them for long or short struts because the warp may cause misalignment of the dome frame. Warped struts should not be used for jigs, either, because they might cause flaws in your cutting procedures and result in imperfect cuts.

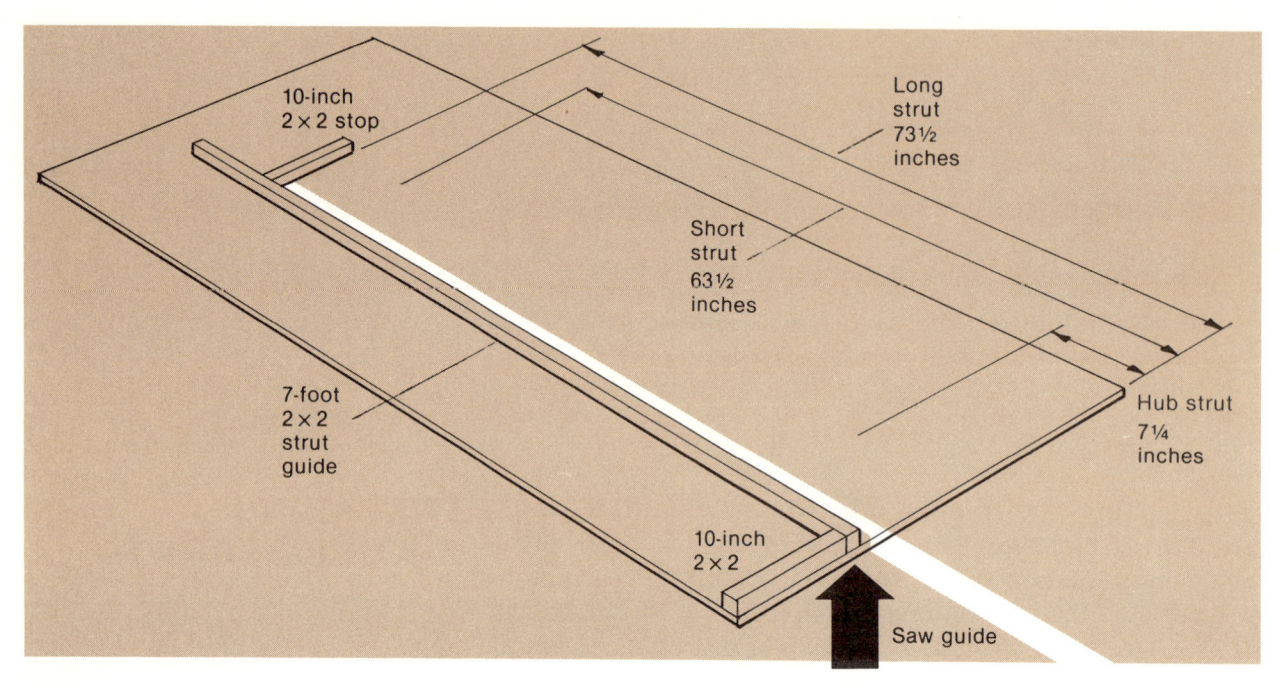

Figure 4-3. Strut cutting jig has a 10-inch 2 x 2 stop which may be positioned as necessary to cut long struts (73½ inches), short struts (63½ inches) and hub struts (7¼ inches).

be cut to this size, it's wise to recheck this distance to ensure it's exactly 73½ inches. In addition, to ensure speed and safety, be sure your jig is stable.

CUTTING LONG STRUTS

Once the jig is in place, you're ready to begin sawing. If you plan to use a power saw, be careful. **Never** lock a saw trigger in the "on" position; this is extremely hazardous if you lose control of the saw. And remember, power tools don't stop, they wind down with the blade in motion, after the trigger has been released. Always wear protective eye goggles when cutting.

First, pick up a 12-foot length of 2 x 2, place it firmly against the jig, flush against the stop 73½ inches from your cutting edge. Align the saw with the guide, hold it tightly, cut and follow through. This first cut should be perfect. But, to be sure, check the length of the 2 x 2 with a tape measure.

Wood cut within ¼ inch of the desired length is useable; if it's not within this tolerance, save it for later use and, if necessary, readjust the stop. If the strut is the correct length, continue working until all 36 struts are cut. Pile completed struts in one area, the remainders elsewhere.

Once you are comfortable cutting struts this way, try cutting two or three at a time by placing them next to each other on the work surface. Make sure they're all cut to the same length.

When placing the 12-foot lengths into the jig, you may notice knots in the wood at points where you have to cut or drill. If so, simply turn the strut around to avoid the knot. If knots interfere on the other end too, use another board and save the knotted one for later use.

CUTTING SHORT STRUTS

Before cutting the 31 short struts, reposition the stop used for the long struts. The new position should be 63½ inches from the cutting edge and, once the stop is in place, this distance should be rechecked with a tape measure.

Short struts may be cut from lengths of 2 x 2 remaining after you cut the long struts. Pick up a left-over length, which should be 70½ inches long, place it firmly against the jig, flush against the stop 63½ inches from your cutting edge. Place saw on guide, hold tightly, cut and follow through. Measure the first length to ensure it's within the 1/4-inch tolerance. If it is, continue cutting; if not, see if the stop needs readjustment.

Since there's only a 7-inch waste, the short struts may be difficult to cut without splitting or other imperfections. Make sure the guide is secure, and it's a good idea to check the length of about every third strut.

CUTTING HUB STRUTS

There are two good ways to cut the 140 7¼-inch long hub struts, using the same jig designed for the long and short struts. Either procedure solves the problem of supporting lengths up to 12 feet long while cutting short sections from them.

You may reposition the jig stop to a mere 7¼ inches from the cutting edge and use the jig as a guide for your cuts. Another person or nearby table will be needed to support the protruding length of wood.

Or, you may remove the stop, measure and mark continuous 7¼-inch segments on the jig and place each wood length in alignment with the jig markings. When ready to cut, simply slide the wood lengths from marking to marking.

Unfortunately, both methods are more error prone than the techniques used for cutting long and short struts. So, double check every jig marking and spot check every few hub struts for straightness of cuts and

POSSIBLE MEASUREMENT PROBLEMS

If possible, buy perfectly square 2 x 2s. If you bought "ripped" 2 x 4s (sawn in half) instead of 2 x 2s, your wood will not be perfectly square and this can cause a problem when nailing hub struts between their two plywood plates.

If hub struts of different measurements are sandwiched between the plates, the result is lopsided hubs.

When a 2 x 4 (with actual dimensions of 1½ x 3½ inches) is sawn in half, the result is two pieces, usually, but not always, measuring 1½ x 1$^{11}/_{16}$ inches. (One piece is 1$^{11}/_{16}$ inches wide, the saw cut (kerf) is ⅛-inch and the second piece is 1$^{11}/_{16}$ inches wide. Together, these add up to 3½ inches.) To avoid lopsided hubs, make sure you drill your holes through the 1$^{11}/_{16}$-inch side of the strut. Then, during hub assembly, the side that is 1½ inches is the side sandwiched between the plywood plates.

If the widths of your 2 x 2s vary, some pieces may not fit into the U-shaped, hole-drilling jig. To accommodate larger pieces, you may have to raise the lower mending bar. This, of course, will mean smaller pieces won't be snug, but they will be secure enough. Centering the holes is not as critical as drilling the holes straight. Angled holes will cause added stress to the dome frame during construction.

You shouldn't experience these problems if you're using 2 x 2s, though you may have a few pieces that aren't properly sized. It may be necessary to drill this wood free hand or perhaps use it for other purposes.

---

accuracy of dimensions. Each length should be within a ½-inch tolerance. Hub struts needn't be cut precisely, but must be positioned precisely during hub assembly.

By nailing an extra securing block parallel and to the right of the hub strut being cut, the wood will be held securely in place, easing the hub strut cutting procedure. And, to reduce waste, cut these hub struts first from the remaining 3-foot, 4-inch section of the 12-foot long 2 x 2 used to make the jig, then from remaining lengths of 2 x 2s used for struts and, finally, from additional 12-foot lengths.

CUTTING BASE HUB STRUTS

Using short lengths of 2 x 2s or a fresh 12-foot length, measure 16 inches from one end and cut at this point. Then double check that it measures 16 inches within a 1/4-inch tolerance. Using this piece as a guide, cut 10 more base hub struts to the same size, and make sure they're all within the allowable tolerance.

A JIG FOR DRILLING HOLES

Since each long and short strut requires two holes and each hub strut one, it makes sense to drill 274 holes, using an accurate, "assembly-line" technique. Building the jig needed to do this may take an hour or two, but it's worth the effort. The jig saves time and reduces errors and waste.

Holes **must** be drilled straight through the wood, not at angles that would result in entry and exit holes at different distances from the strut's end. If you have a drill press, you're in business; if not, build a jig to ensure the holes you drill are the holes you need.

To make the jig, start by nailing three 4-inch long sections of 2 x 2 in a U-shape. The closed end of the U should be nearest the table edge. The parallel 4-inch sections must be placed exactly the width of a 2 x 2 apart so the 2 x 2s fit snugly inside the U. The entire U should be near a table corner so working with it is easy.

Now, place a mending bar on the work table and drill a 1/4-inch hole through the center of it, if one is not predrilled. Do the same with a second mending bar. Then position one bar precisely across the top of the U-jig so the center of the 1/4-inch hole is 7/8 to 1 inch from the U's closed end.

To check the mending bar's location, take a hub strut marked in its exact center, 7/8 of an inch from its end; place it flush against the U's closed end, and look through the center hole in the mending bar to confirm that it's centered directly over the hub strut's marking.

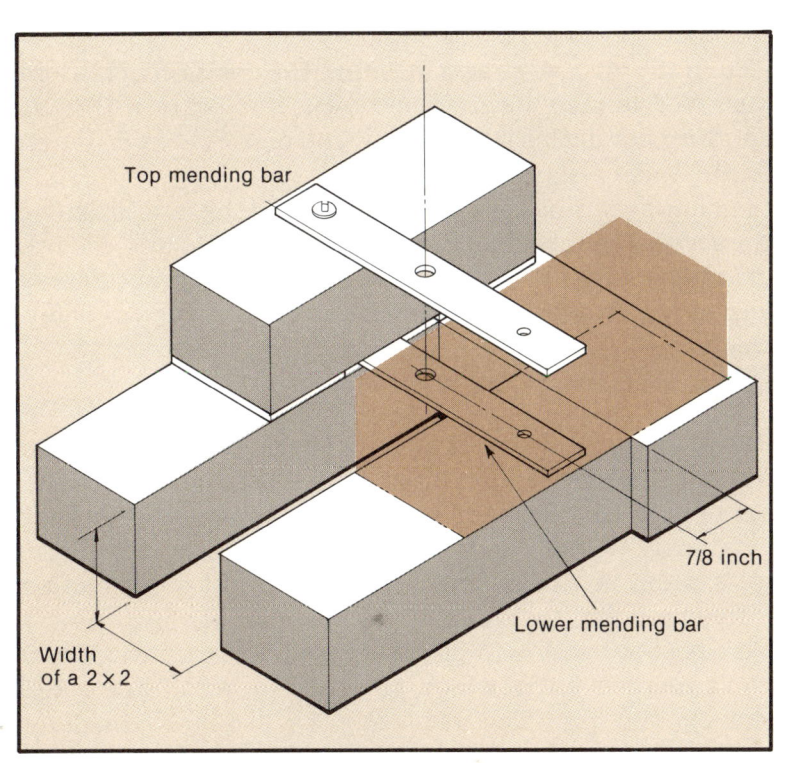

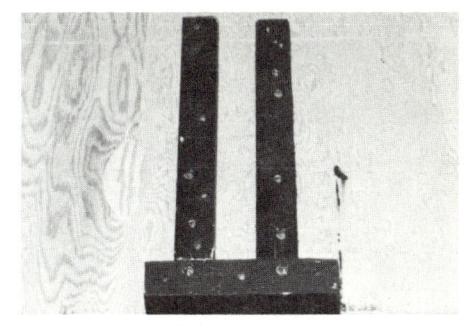

To make the jig, first nail three 4-inch long 2 x 2s in a U shape.

Position a mending bar precisely across the top of the jig.

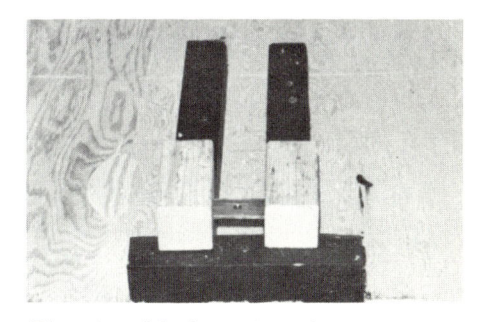

Place 2 x 2 blocks on top of mending bar (above); and place second mending bar directly above first.

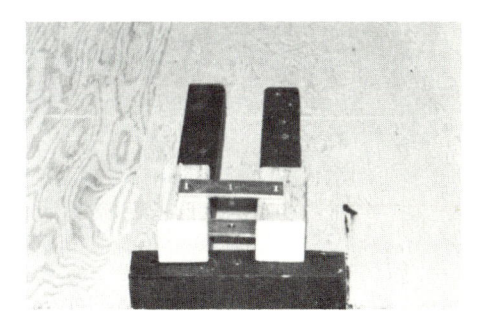

Figure 4-4. The U-shaped drilling jig, made of 2 x 2 blocks and two mending bars; notice the center of the drilling hole is 7/8 of an inch from the U's closed end.

Figure 4-5. Completed jig with strut in position for drilling. Be sure to check holes to ensure they are centered and within 7/8 to 1 inch from struts' ends.

When satisfied with the location of your mending bar, screw it in place through pre-drilled holes near its ends.

The drilling jig is nearing completion. Now you need a guide to ensure that you drill straight down, not at an angle. To make this guide, nail 2 x 2 blocks on top of the parallel portions of the U and place the second mending bar directly above the first.

Drop a drill bit through the center holes of the mending bars and adjust the top bar until the drill appears exactly perpendicular to the table top. Perpendicular may be determined by placing a carpenter's square next to the drill bit. Once satisfied with the top mending bar's position, screw it in place through pre-drilled holes near its ends. Leave the screws loose; do **not** tighten them down yet.

Insert your first hub strut into the jig, drill down through the holes in both mending bars and through the strut. Take the strut out of the jig, measure carefully to ensure the hole just drilled is 7/8 to 1 inch from the strut's end and is centered in its width. If the position of the entry hole (top surface of the strut) is within 1/8 of an inch of the desired measurements, the bottom mending bar is in place.

Turn the strut over and measure the position of the exit hole. If it is also within the 1/8-inch tolerance, the top mending bar is also in place and you can tighten it. If not, readjust as necessary.

Perhaps a simpler way to determine if the hole is drilled correctly is to insert a bolt through the hole and see if it forms a 90-degree angle with the strut. Again, it may help to use a carpenter's square or table corner as reference.

DRILLING STRUT HOLES

The drill guide is designed to ensure speedy, precise drilling. Using a ¼-inch bit at least 4 ½ inches long, drill one hole at both ends of every long, short and base hub strut and one hole near **one** end of every hub strut. All holes must be drilled precisely to prevent construction problems later.

It's best to use a drill bit designed for use on wood so it won't inadvertently widen the mending bar holes and destroy the jig. The bit must be 1/4-inch diameter throughout most of its length so it fits well through the holes of the mending bars; if narrower, it may drill sloppily.

If a high-speed metal bit is used, you'll have to replace the top mending bar a few times before all drilling is completed because the metal bit enlarges the 1/4-inch hole, causing inaccurate drilling. The top bar won't have to be realigned because the same screw holes are used to fasten the bar in place.

After drilling every five or six holes, blow sawdust from the jig to keep it from collecting. Otherwise, the strut will not fit flush against the end of the U, causing the hole to be drilled in the wrong place.

CUTTING PLYWOOD HUB PLATES

Although the dome frame requires just 20 hexagonal, 12 pentagonal and 20 base hub plates for proper assembly, additional plates are recommended for both aesthetic and structural reasons. Additional plates for the dome's outer surface improve the dome's appearance and the securing of its polyethylene covering. Therefore, it's recommended that 30 hexagonal, 18 pentagonal and 30 base hubs be cut and used.

When cutting hub plates from plywood, simplify the task by resting your power saw periodically and by using a fine-tooth plywood cutting blade. Also, be sure the plywood remains secure because loose, sagging or unsupported plywood can bind a saw, causing it to jump dangerously.

HEXAGONAL HUBS

Hexagonal (or "hex") hub plates are the easiest of the three plates to cut, so start with these while gaining experience and familiarity with the measuring, drawing and cutting procedures. These hexagon-shaped hubs have 6-inch sides and measure 12 inches from point to point.

The first step is to make a rigid cardboard template to be used as a guide for cutting and assembling the plywood hexagonal hub plates. To do this, draw a straight line, 12 inches long, and mark its center point (6 inches). Draw a second 12-inch line bisecting the first at its center and at a 60-degree angle. Repeat once more at a 120-degree angle. Connect the outer ends of the lines to form a hexagon.

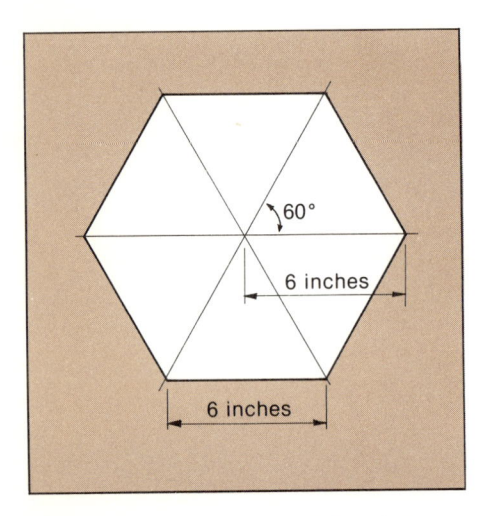

BUILDING AND USING A SOLAR-HEATED GEODESIC GREENHOUSE

Figure 4-6. Hex-hub template is a guide for cutting plywood hub plates to proper sizes. Template should measure 6 inches from center to points and center-to-point lines should form 60-degree angles.

Figure 4-7. The hex-hub template is traced on 1 x 4-foot plywood strips as shown. Thirty hexagonal hub plates are cut from the strips.

PENTAGONAL HUBS

Now take the two plywood sheets and cut off two 1 x 4-foot strips. You may cut each separately, but if your saw bite is large enough, keep the plywood nailed together, flush on all sides, and cut once through both pieces. Then secure one 1 x 4-foot strip on top of the other with five long nails and, using the hexagon-shaped template, draw four hexagons on the top strip.

Use a circular saw with a large bite to form the hexagons by cutting off excess corner triangles. (Save the triangular wedges; they'll be useable during site preparation.) Repeat the measuring, drawing and cutting steps until you have made 30 hex plates.

Straight hub plate edges and precise measurements are only cosmetic concerns. What's important is that the hub struts remain properly aligned during hub assembly.

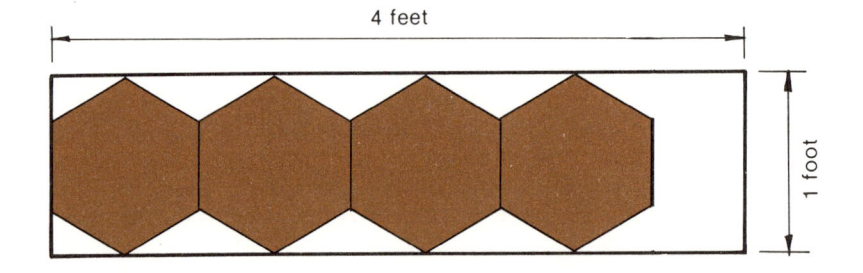

The 18 pentagon-shaped plates measure 11 inches from each point of the pentagon to the center of its opposite side. As before, draw a pentagon on rigid cardboard to use as a template.

To draw a pentagon template, choose a center point. Draw a 6-inch line out from it and, using a protractor, measure a 72-degree angle. Then draw another 6-inch line outward from the center and at 72 degrees from the first. Repeat this procedure three more times for a total of five lines. Connect the ends of the lines to form a pentagon. Cut out the cardboard pentagon; then recheck measurements.

This done, cut off two more 1 x 4-foot plywood strips, nail one on top of the other and, using the pentagon-shaped template, draw four pentagons on the top strip. Cut out these forms with your saw, and repeat these steps until you have 18 pentagon hub plates. Because there are no common lines joining them, the pent hubs will be more difficult to cut than the hex hubs.

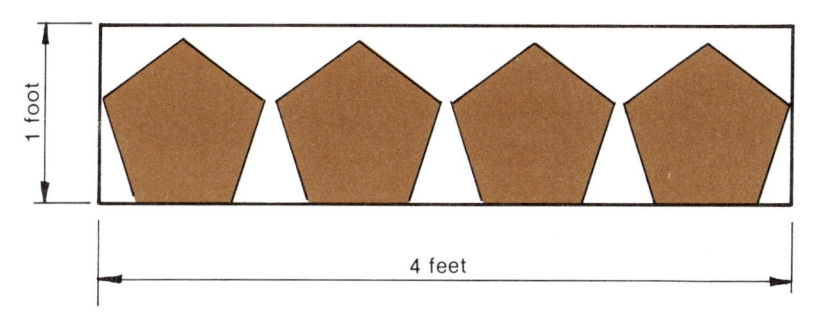

WOODWORKING

45

Figure 4-8 (above). Pentagon template is traced on 1 x 4-foot plywood strips. Eighteen pentagon-shaped hub plates are cut from plywood.

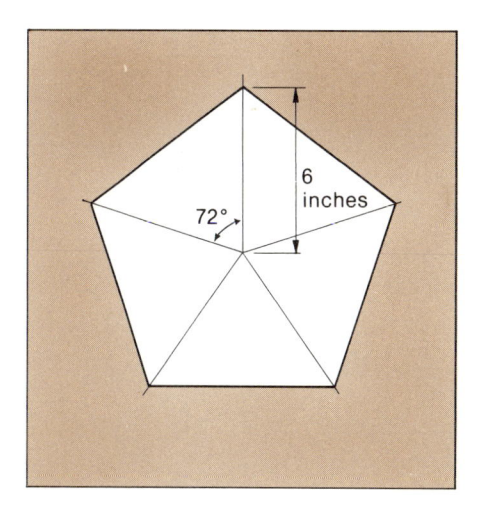

Figure 4-9 (right). Pentagon-shaped template has 6-inch center-to-point lines, forming 72-degree angles.

BASE HUBS

The 30 base hub plates are shaped like half-hex plates with 2¼-inch bottom "skirts." To make them, draw a template on rigid cardboard, (using the base hub drawing, p. 46), cut it out and confirm that its measurements are correct.

Use the base hub template to draw six outlines on the plywood strips, which are set up as before: one 1 x 4-foot section nailed securely on top of another. Cut the base plates and repeat this measuring, drawing and cutting process until you have 30 base hub plates.

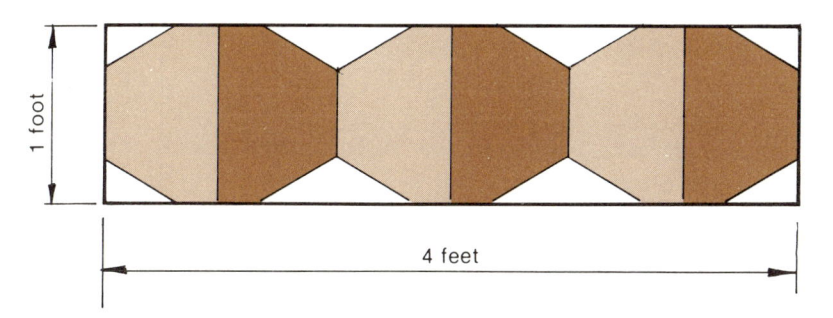

Figure 4-10. Use base-hub template on page 46 to draw six outlines on the 1 x 4-foot plywood strips, and then cut 30 base hubs.

Keep the three hub templates in good condition because you may break a hub during assembly of the dome's frame and have to make a replacement.

With woodcutting complete, the next task is to preserve each wooden piece of the frame, with the exception of the walmanized securing posts. If these were purchased without walmanization or creosote, they should be preserved as well.

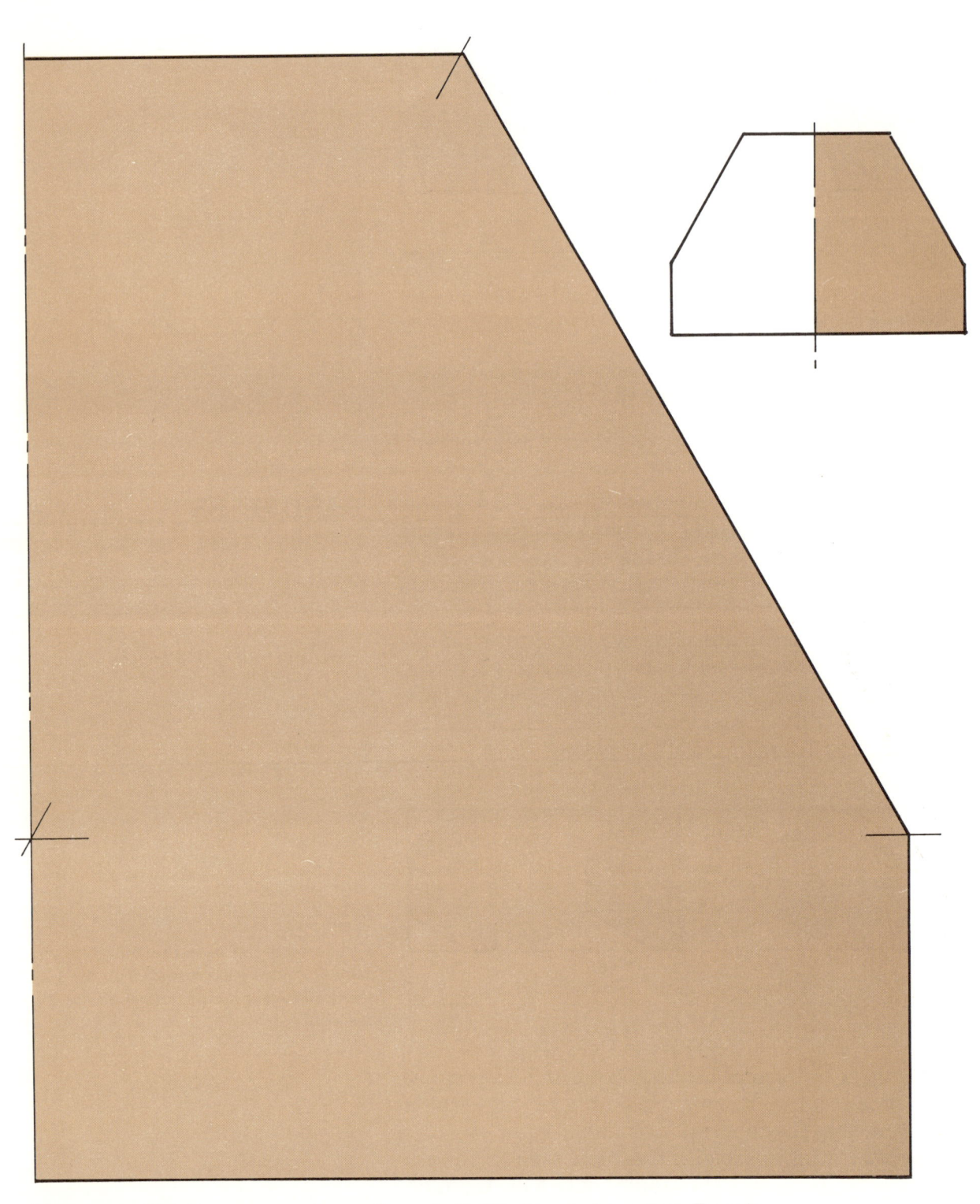

Figure 4-11. This form represents exactly one half of the base-hub template. Trace it twice, place halves together, then retrace to form a full-sized template.

46

PRESERVING WOOD

Preserving the wood components adds years to the dome's life. If it's done properly, parts will need replacement infrequently and that means a savings of time, trouble and money.

Any wood preservative that is non-toxic to plants or animals is suitable, but we suggest an oil-based redwood stain. Its advantages were mentioned in Chapter 3; its only disadvantage is the long drying time — about two hours.

To protect the wood properly, coat it at least twice and preferably three times. Allow it to dry between each coating. Coat all sides and edges of struts and plates; the edges, in particular, are vulnerable to rot and need protection.

If you have workspace outdoors, try this technique to facilitate the coating process: thread a rope through the holes in one end of the struts. Secure the rope between two trees just high enough so the struts' bottoms touch the ground. This allows you to reach nearly every surface of the wood with a paint brush and helps to steady the struts while you coat them.

ASSEMBLING HUBS

Before assembling the hubs (made up of hub struts and plates), keep these two points in mind:

- The wood must be completely dry.

- When securing hub struts to the hex, pent and base plates — the assembly process — position the struts at **precisely** the correct angles. If the angles are wrong, you won't be able to erect the dome properly.

(The ten hexagonal, six pentagonal and ten base hub **outer plates** should be set aside because they are not secured to the hubs until the dome frame is standing. Installation of these plates is described in Chapter 7.)

To ensure that struts are positioned correctly between the hub plates (like a "strut-sandwich") build another jig. As you know, jigs can enhance speed, accuracy and ease of workmanship.

TWO RULES

Here are two general rules to follow when assembling hubs:

1. The cardboard cutouts must be made correctly because it's critically important that the hub struts protrude from the hub at the correct angle. Repeatedly recheck to ensure that the hubs stay in place despite hammering and inadvertent movement.

2. Plywood plates needn't be aligned precisely with one another; visual alignment is close enough because their main function is to hold the hub struts in place. Otherwise, the plates are not critical parts of the dome frame.

ASSEMBLING HEX HUBS

Figure 4-12. To make cardboard hex hub jig, draw straight lines from point to point, then draw another parallel line ¾ of an inch to the left of first line (a). Position struts so ends are 8¼ inches from the hub center, then outline struts (b). Outline all six struts, then cut out strut-sized sections (c).

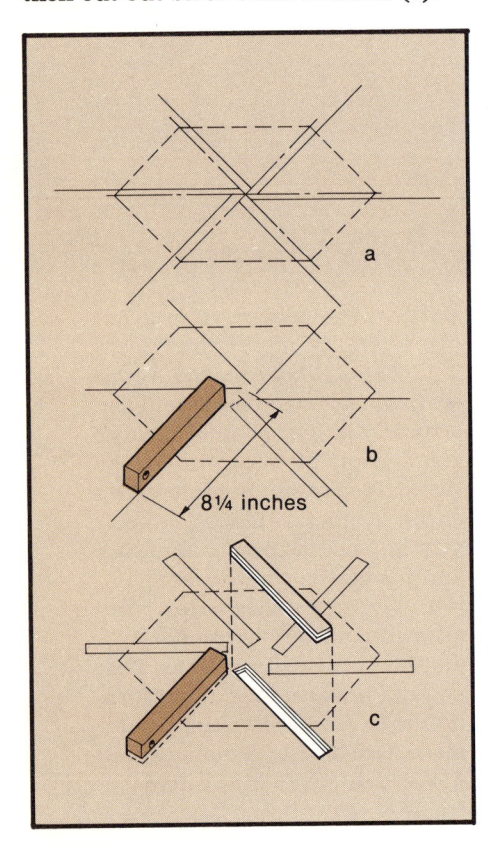

Two 2-foot square sections of heavy cardboard, at least 1/8 inch thick, are needed to make the hex hub jig. The sides of a heavy cardboard box can be used.

First, glue or tape one cardboard section on top of the other. Then, with the hexagonal template used earlier for cutting plates, outline the hexagon on the cardboard. Draw a straight line from each point of the hexagon through the center to its opposite point. Exactly 3/4 inch to the left of each line, draw another parallel line.

Ultimately, the edge of the left side of the hub struts will lie flush with the second set of lines in off-center positions. The center lines — the first set — serve as projected sight lines for the frame's long and short struts, which do not enter the hub, but must be aligned toward its center to assure adequate structural stability. Long and short struts are bolted to the hub struts, which protrude from the hub assembly.

Hub struts will have to be positioned so their ends are exactly 8¼ inches from the hub's center, and the struts' holes will have to face sideways to allow proper bolting to the long and short struts during erection of the dome frame.

To complete the jig, place a hub strut flush against the left side of one of the second set of lines, positioned as just described. Using a sharp pencil, outline the struts' position on the cardboard, making sure the line is drawn precisely, with no space between the line and strut.

Follow this same drawing procedure until all six hub struts are outlined on the cardboard. Then, using a sharp razor knife, X-acto blade or single-edge razor blade, cut along the inside edge of these lines, and remove sections of cardboard the size of the hub strut from both cardboard layers. Check to see that each hub strut fits snugly into its cutout.

If the cutout is too big, build up the jig's cardboard edges by adding masking tape; if too small, simply trim it with a blade. Once in place, make sure the strut is parallel and exactly ¾ of an inch from the first-drawn, center-aimed line, and its end is 8¼ inches from the hub's center.

When this process has been completed for all six hub struts, the jig is complete. Tape it securely to your work surface and begin assembling hubs, as follows:

Leave the struts in place in their cutouts, lay a plywood hex plate on top of them and align it with the template

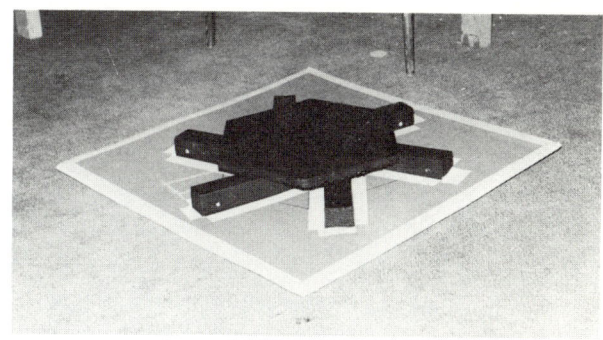

When hex hub jig is complete, place the six hub struts in their cutouts (left). Then a plywood hex plate is placed, with its best side up, on top of the hub struts and aligned with template.

below. (For aesthetic reasons, place the plate with its best side up.) Using a pencil, mark on this plate where you will hammer two nails through it into each hub strut. To avoid splitting any struts, nails should be positioned apart and staggered so they'll be hammered into different grains.

After marking 12 nail locations, remove the plate and, elsewhere on your work surface, hammer 1½-inch roofing nails through the plate until the nail points start to protrude.

Return to the struts and check again that they are in place; reposition the hub plate on top of the struts; and hammer one nail halfway into one strut. Vibrations from this hammering may cause the strut to move, so be sure it's in position before hammering the second nail. Then recheck positions of the five remaining struts and follow this procedure for them. After nailing all six struts, check again to ensure that the struts are positioned correctly in their cardboard cutouts. Reposition any that are misplaced.

Once nails have been pounded through the plate and halfway into the six struts correctly, move this unit to another work surface away from the jig and template and continue to hammer all nails their full length into the struts; this locks the hub struts into their correct positions permanently. Then, turn this unit over so the struts are on top; lay another hexagonal plywood plate on top of the unit, aligned with the bottom plate; and mark a central location for a third nail to be hammered into each of the six hub struts and through the top plate.

After marking these spots, remove the plate and, elsewhere on your work surface, hammer nails through it until their points start to protrude. (This reduces stress

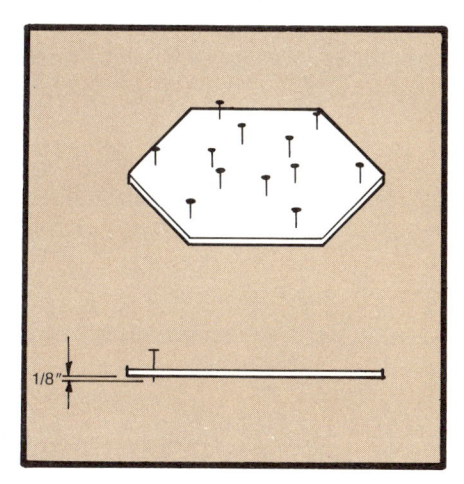

Figure 4-13. Nails should be driven through the plywood hub plates until they begin to protrude, about 1/8 of an inch.

49

on the hub.) Replace the plate, aligned atop the struts, and hammer the nails their full length into the struts. This done, you have your first completed hex hub, with only nine more to go.

ASSEMBLING PENT HUBS

Pent hubs are assembled with the same jig-building, measuring and nailing procedures as before. Using the pentagon template, the distance from the five hub struts' ends to the center of the templates remains exactly 8¼ inches. To make the pent hub jig, outline the pent template on a two-foot square double layer of heavy cardboard. Then, as in making the hex jig, draw lines from point to center, and draw parallel lines to the left of each of these. Next, place a hub strut atop the cardboard, outline and cut out its form, and, when the jig is complete, secure struts to plates the same way as during hex hub assembly.

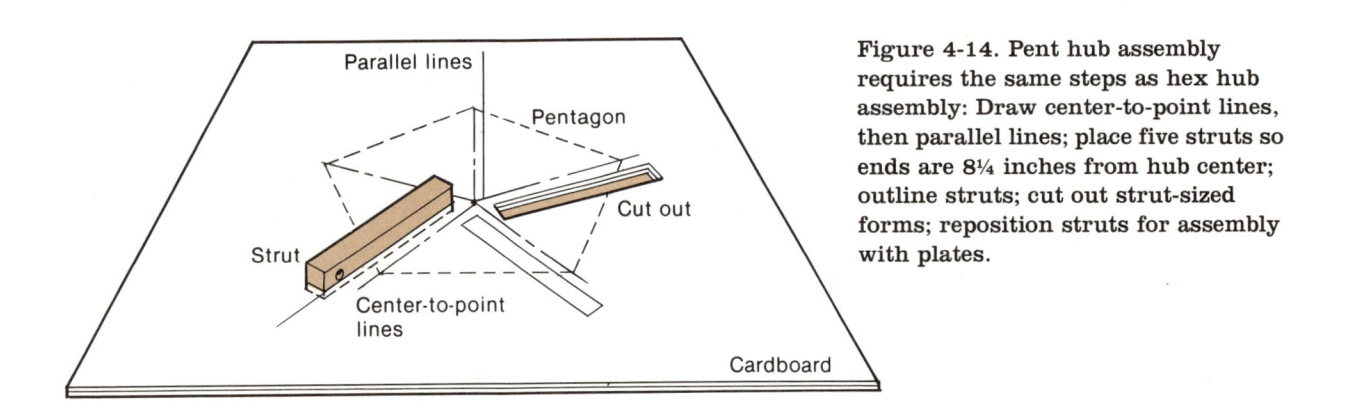

Figure 4-14. Pent hub assembly requires the same steps as hex hub assembly: Draw center-to-point lines, then parallel lines; place five struts so ends are 8¼ inches from hub center; outline struts; cut out strut-sized forms; reposition struts for assembly with plates.

ASSEMBLING BASE HUBS

Base hubs are also assembled using the same jig-building, measuring and nailing procedures as before, with three exceptions:

1. The base hub template has different dimensions from the others, though the distance from the two hub struts' ends to the center of the template is still 8¼ inches.
2. The two hub struts that protrude from the top of each base hub are set on opposite sides of the hexagon's points.

> **TROUBLE SHOOTING**
>
> If a hub strut splits because two nails were driven into the same grain, remove the strut and replace it.
>
> If hub struts shift from their proper positions during assembly, simply slide them back into their correct spots and nail them. If plates are nailed to incorrectly placed struts, remove the nails, readjust the strut and nail it in place.
>
> Some struts may vary in size, depending on how accurately you cut them. Any strut more than ½ inch too large or too small should not be used. Struts that do not fit precisely, but are within the ½-inch tolerance, should be used as follows: If the strut is too short, place it so it fills the outer part of the cutout and leaves a space on the inner part; if too narrow, place it flush against the cutout edge that is closest to the first-drawn, center-aimed line; if too wide or long, maneuver the strut gently into the space, being careful not to damage the jig.
>
> During hub assembly, cardboard edges may become torn or ragged; if so, simply repair them with masking tape.

3. A 16-inch long base hub strut is used here. It is placed across the bottom of the hub plate — centered so its holes are equidistant from the hub's center — in a way that each of the base hub strut's ends acts as a securing point for a long strut.

Except for these differences, set up the jig and secure hub struts to plates the same way as you would during hex and pent hub assembly.

Figure 4-15. Base hubs are also assembled using same procedures as before, with a few exceptions. Notice the single, 16-inch long base hub strut outline and the positions for the two smaller hub struts.

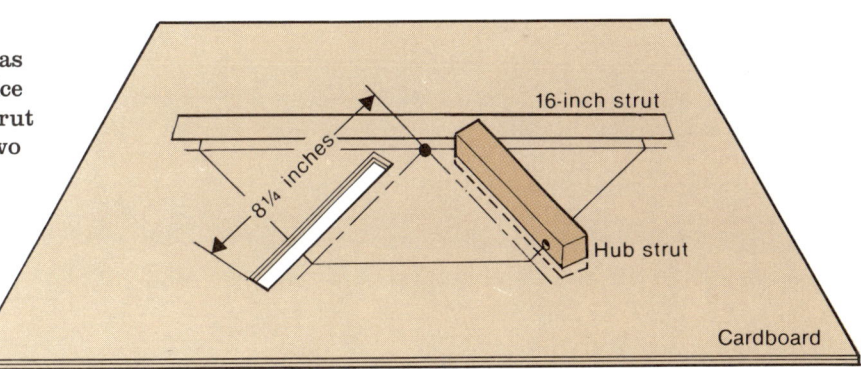

Each outer plate requires holes for a ¼-inch bolt through its center and three No. 8 screws on its outskirts. The outer plates and hubs will be joined by the center bolt, through the plate and complete hub, and the three screws, through the outer plate and just one hub plate.

To drill the bolt holes, align a plate atop a hub. Drill a ¼-inch hole through the plate's center and continue drilling through the entire hub. Since these holes must line up during later installation, it's a good idea to number each hub on both sides and each plate on one side. Holes

DRILLING HOLES FOR OUTER PLATES

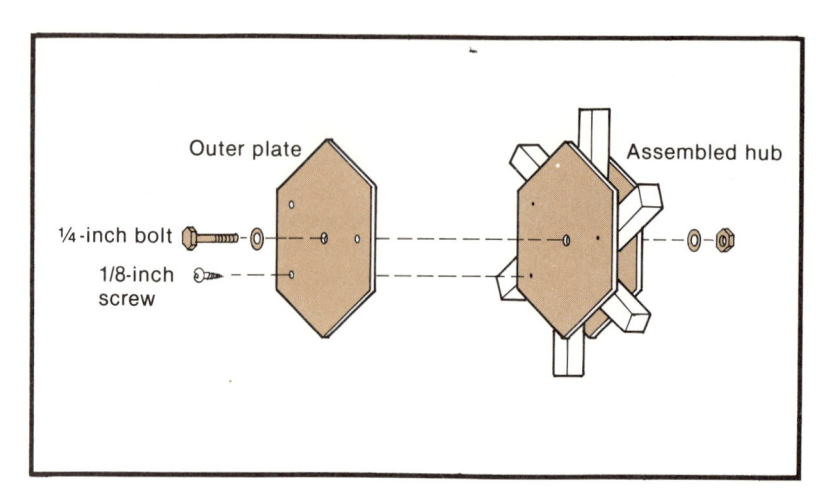

Figure 4-16. Center holes, for 1/4-inch bolts, are drilled through each outer plate and hub; three 1/8-inch holes are drilled through outer plates and just barely into top hub plates.

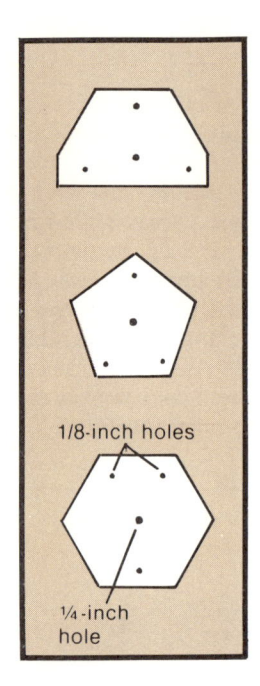

Figure 4-17. This shows positions for 1/4-inch and 1/8-inch holes on all three outer hub plates; these plates are not bolted and screwed in place until later.

for the 1-inch long No. 8 screws need to be predrilled (with a ⅛-inch bit) through outer plates and just barely into the hub's plywood plate. This will make starting the screws easy during later installation of the outer plates.

Chapter 5: Site Preparation

Preparing the dome site requires a lot of work, concentration and precision. So, make the job easier and ask a few friends for help. With the site completed, the most tedious construction work is over. Site preparation takes about 22 hours for two people.

Much of the dome's strength and rigidity depends on careful layout and placement of the dome parts to minimize structural stress. Stress results if the dome base is not placed in a nearly circular shape.

Before beginning site preparation, you'll need to have found a suitable site (Chapter 2) and to have completed the woodworking (Chapter 4).

Equipment needed to start site preparation includes: some of the small plywood wedges saved from wood-cutting; a length of bell wire; and a stake.

Hammer the stake into the soil at the exact center point of the dome site and attach to it a piece of bell wire one half the dome diameter. Although the diameter is referred to as 23 feet for convenience, it's actually a bit smaller. Your wire size should be 11 feet, 3½ inches measured from the stake to the innermost surface of each base hub. Measure the wire **after** you tie it to the stake or its length will be off by four or five inches.

Standing at the stake, determine **true** south (Chapter 2), then lay out the wire in precisely that direction. Hammer a plywood marker into the soil at the wire's end. This will mark the exact midway point between two base hubs as well as the middle of the dome's non-insulated section or southern-facing 45 percent that allows sunlight and heat to enter.

Pick up a long strut and lay it immediately inside the plywood marker so the marker bisects it. Pull the wire

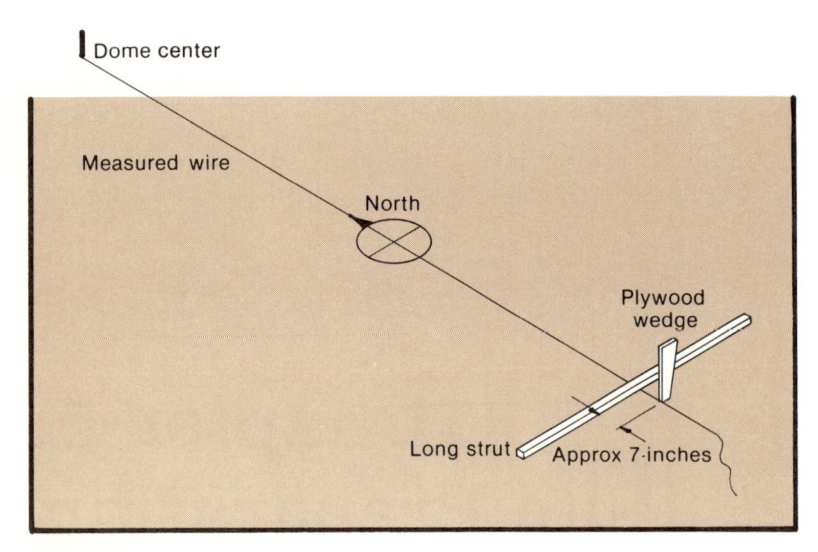

Figure 5-1. Lay long strut inside true-south marker, then pull wire toward one end of strut as shown below.

tautly from the center stake toward one end of the strut; line up the end of the strut with the end of the wire; where ends meet is the location of your first base hub. (Only the ten base hubs will line up with the end of the wire; the base struts do not. The base hubs represent points on the diameter of your imaginary circle, so do not expect the wire's end or the first plywood wedge to touch any struts.)

Connect a base hub to the strut, by inserting 1/4-inch bolts through the base hub and strut holes; make sure fender, lock and star washers are in place to keep all parts steady, but do not tighten the bolts because they are likely to need readjustment later. Then lay another long strut into position adjoining the hub.

Continue forming the circle, by pulling the wire taut and positioning hubs and struts in order until the entire base (10 long struts and 10 base hubs) is laid out and

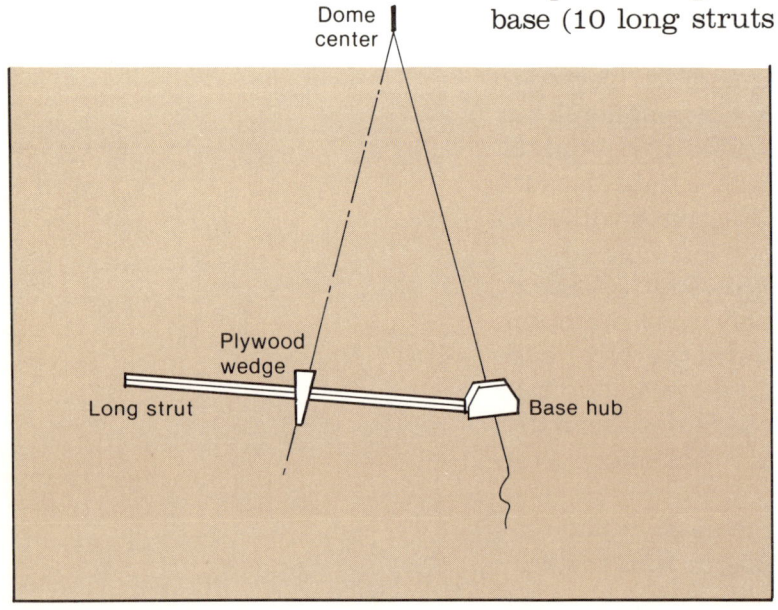

Figure 5-2. Wire at end of long strut; distance from center stake to inner surface of base hub is 11 feet, 3½ inches.

54

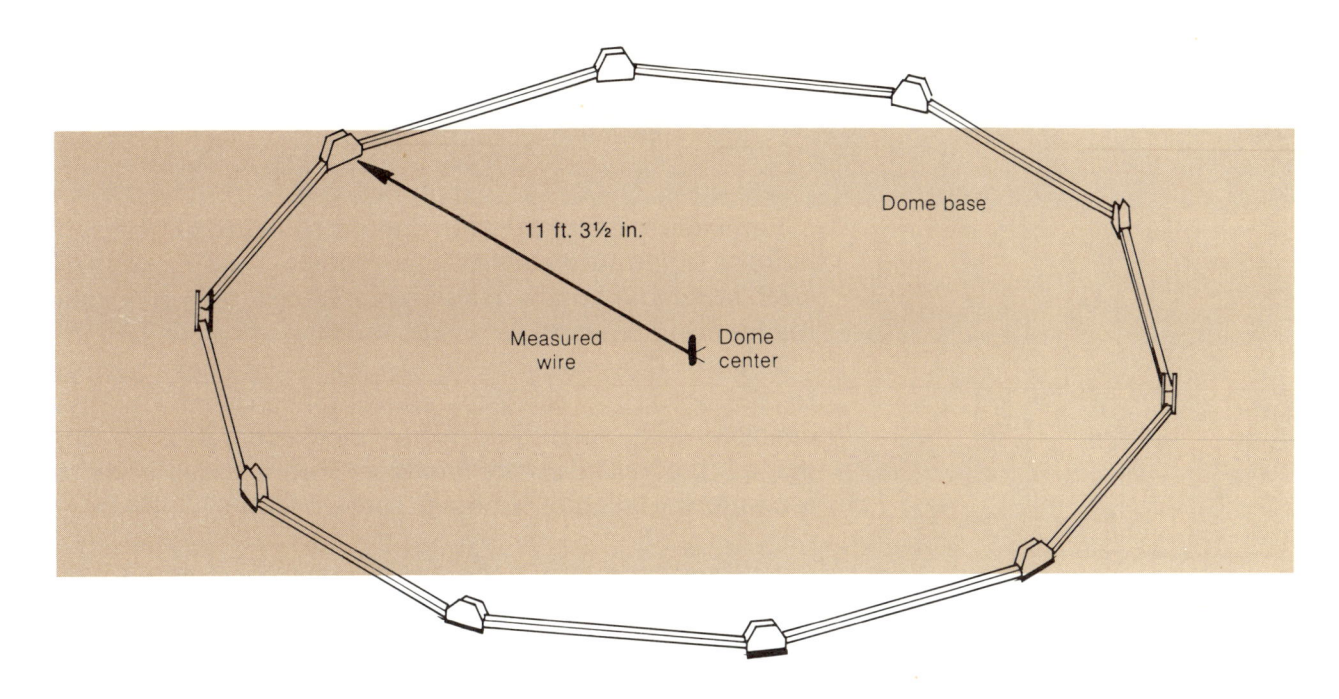

loosely secured. Using the wire as a guide ensures that you are laying out the base hubs and struts in proper geometric form.

Your first time around will probably result in a few incorrect measurements. Because it's critical that the layout be done perfectly, you must use the wire to recheck that all hubs are equidistant from the center stake — even if, at a glance, they appear to be laid properly. They may be off just a bit and a miscalculation may not be apparent.

Even a small adjustment of one base hub affects the others, so keep going around in circles to ensure that they are all the proper distance from the center stake. If you're lucky, you'll complete this task before becoming dizzy!

Figure 5-3. Double check distance from center stake to base hubs. Inner surfaces of hubs should touch an imaginary circle with a radius of 11 feet, 3½ inches.

If all hubs are exactly the correct distance from the center stake, as measured by the wire, but the circle of hubs and struts does not close, the length of the wire may be incorrect. To correct this, simply remeasure and, if necessary, adjust the wire's length. Then repeat the procedures for forming the circle.

Perhaps the hubs are equidistant from the center, the wire length is correct, but you still haven't been able to form a complete circle. You may have mistakenly used a short strut instead of a long strut; or, perhaps, one or more long struts have been cut incorrectly.

HELP! MY CIRCLE DOESN'T CLOSE

Remeasure every strut to ensure they are all the same length. If you find a short one, replace it with a properly sized strut and you're in business. Repeat the procedures for forming the circle.

A major flaw would result if wood struts have been cut to the wrong size. This shouldn't happen if you've checked and rechecked your measurements as suggested. If you find struts have been cut incorrectly, pause a moment and then consider these options:

1. Recut and redrill the struts to the correct size. (This is possible only if the struts were cut too long.)
2. Buy new 2 x 2s and cut them to the proper dimensions and drill them. (Check first to see if you can simply cut the long struts into short struts; if you can, then purchase wood only for new long struts.)
3. Read Chapter 11 on building domes of other sizes and see if this is a reasonable alternative. It's possible that the incorrectly cut struts may be suitable for a dome of different size.

You'll also encounter problems if your dome site has small hills or depressions that raise some of the base hubs and lower others. Adjustments can be made, as described in the following section on site leveling. Whether a dome is located on a flat surface or hillside, hubs and struts must be level with each other or on the same plane.

If none of these problems are yours, but your layout is still incorrect, reread the layout procedures once more. It's possible you overlooked or misunderstood instructions, which, if followed correctly, will help you build a sturdy, dome-shaped structure.

SITE LEVELING

After laying out the base hubs and struts in a circle so carefully, be sure they don't get accidentally knocked out of place. Before leveling the site, gather the plywood wedges and hammer them into the ground on the inside and outside of each hub. These will mark the position of each hub in case the base is moved.

This done, you can proceed with **relative** leveling of the site. This is not leveling to the center of the earth. (Remember, the dome may be situated on a small slope.) Rather, it is leveling the hubs to each other. As important

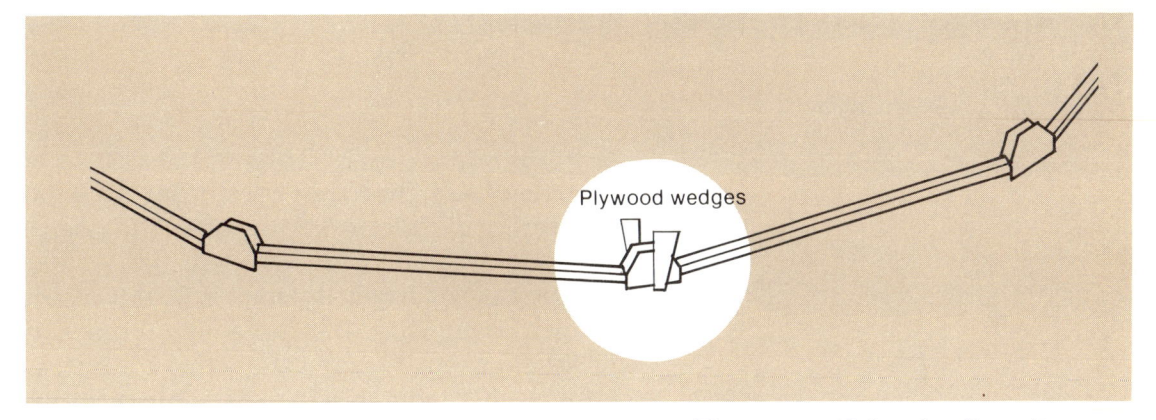

Figure 5-4. Before leveling site, use plywood wedges to hold base hubs in place and to mark their positions.

as this step is, it needn't be done perfectly, since the dome structure allows for some small height irregularities. But, for the best results, aim for as much accuracy as possible.

Look at the base hubs to see if any seem obviously higher than the rest. Using a hand shovel, dig some dirt out from under these until they appear to be level with the others. Don't attempt to pack dirt under the lower hubs; loose dirt will not provide enough structural support after settling.

Go around the base, placing a level, in turn, on the left and right sides of the long strut ends immediately outside each hub. The bubble in the level needn't be centered (this would mean hubs and struts are level with the center of the earth), but the bubble should be oriented the same way on each side of an individual hub. If the bubble is on the right side at the end of one strut, it should stay on the right when on the other strut end that enters the same hub. This shows that the hubs and struts are relatively level with each other. Since you're working in a circle, the level's indications will differ at each hub. Be

Figure 5-5. When level is placed on either side of a base hub, the bubble should be in the same position. This indicates the base is relatively level.

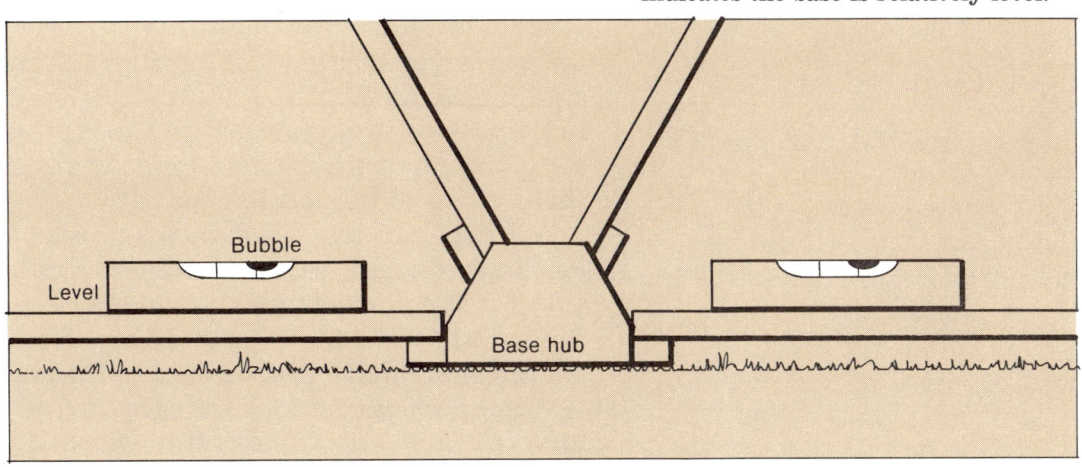

concerned only that they're similar on each side of the same hub; this alone shows that the base is relatively level.

Minor height irregularities will not affect the dome's strength or rigidity. If, after a visual inspection the hubs and struts seem to have the same height, and the level confirms this, you've completed this portion of site preparation successfully. If, however, the hubs are noticeably irregular, continue digging out dirt from under the high ones to level them. Place a brick or flat stone beneath hubs that are lower than the rest; this will help "level" them and prevent settling of the structure.

This process is likely to require that, once again, you go in circles a few times. Remember, leveling needs to be only approximate. It's best to lay out the hubs and struts in early morning; this allows time to surmount any difficulties you might encounter. Although this work can sometimes be frustrating, keep in mind the dome will provide countless hours of pleasure once completed. With luck, you may not have to deal with any of these problems anyway.

Once the base hubs and struts are laid out properly and leveled correctly, tighten all bolts and use the wire to recheck the hubs one final time to make sure they still form a perfect circle.

PREPARING THE GARDEN BED

When the dome site is still wide open is the best time to begin preparing soil for gardening. You can move a wheelbarrow, tools and equipment freely, in an environment as pleasant as the weather outside.

If you were able to recruit a few helpers, one person can prepare the soil while others dig trenches for the dome's underground insulation. (Digging the trenches and installing the underground polyethylene film is described in the following section.) If you're working alone, complete the trench digging and insulation placement first, then return to the garden bed.

Before beginning work on the garden bed, determine its shape. Chapter 9 describes three configurations suitable for the dome and explains effective, intensive agricultural methods. After reading about the different shapes, you'll have a better idea of the best one for you.

Whichever is used, take care not to puncture the underground polyethylene film when tilling the soil. To avoid this, till **no** deeper than six inches when within one foot of the frame, and plant vegetables with shallow roots in this area.

The first step in soil preparation is to use a spade to cut out squares of sod, making sure the grass and top layer of roots are removed. If this is not done properly, you may find grass growing in the garden later.

Generally, the intensive agricultural methods used in the garden require that the soil be hand-tilled to a depth of two feet. This is a sensible step toward making the soil organically rich; another is adding in top soil or other additives (see Chapter 9) as you're tilling. To make these tasks easier, use a spade or pitchfork, and remove any large rocks. The top layer of soil may be machine-tilled.

Don't be concerned by people walking on the freshly tilled soil now; it will be trampled many times before you are set up and ready for planting. Retilling at that time will be easy because the important deep work will have been accomplished. Extensive garden bed preparation is not called for until later.

To summarize, steps to be completed at this stage are: selecting a garden configuration, removing sod, tilling and enriching soil, and removing rocks.

DIGGING TRENCHES FOR UNDERGROUND INSULATION

Installing polyethylene 2½ feet deep into the soil is the most boring, tiresome work you face in building and maintaining the dome. Whatever time this task takes will probably seem twice as long. At Fordham, it took three people two full days to complete this work.

The polyethylene is inserted into two trenches dug one foot inside and one foot outside the dome's perimeter. The polyethylene stands vertically in each trench with enough height to fold toward and reach the frame, where it is secured to both the frame and its above ground covering. This forms a complete seal, protecting the dome from cold air, moisture or wetness from the soil.

To find where to dig the trenches, measure one foot inside and one foot outside any base hub, then hammer plywood wedges into the soil at these points. Repeat at every base hub and use these wedges as guides when digging the trenches in a circular fashion about the dome's perimeter.

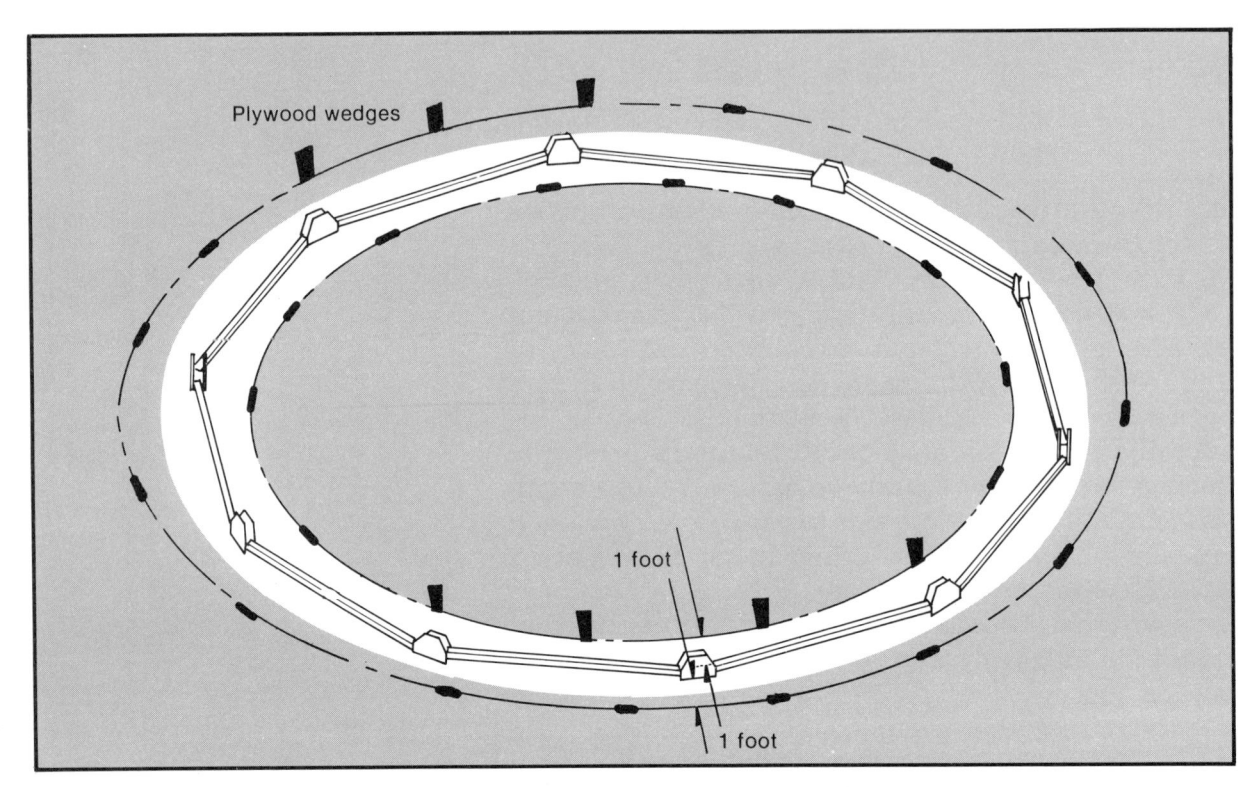

Figure 5-6. Wedges should be hammered into the ground one foot inside and one foot outside the frame. Use wedges as a guide when digging trenches.

Figure 5-7. Dig outer trench outside wedges, inner trench inside inner wedges; leave a 2-foot wide band of undisturbed soil beneath the base frame.

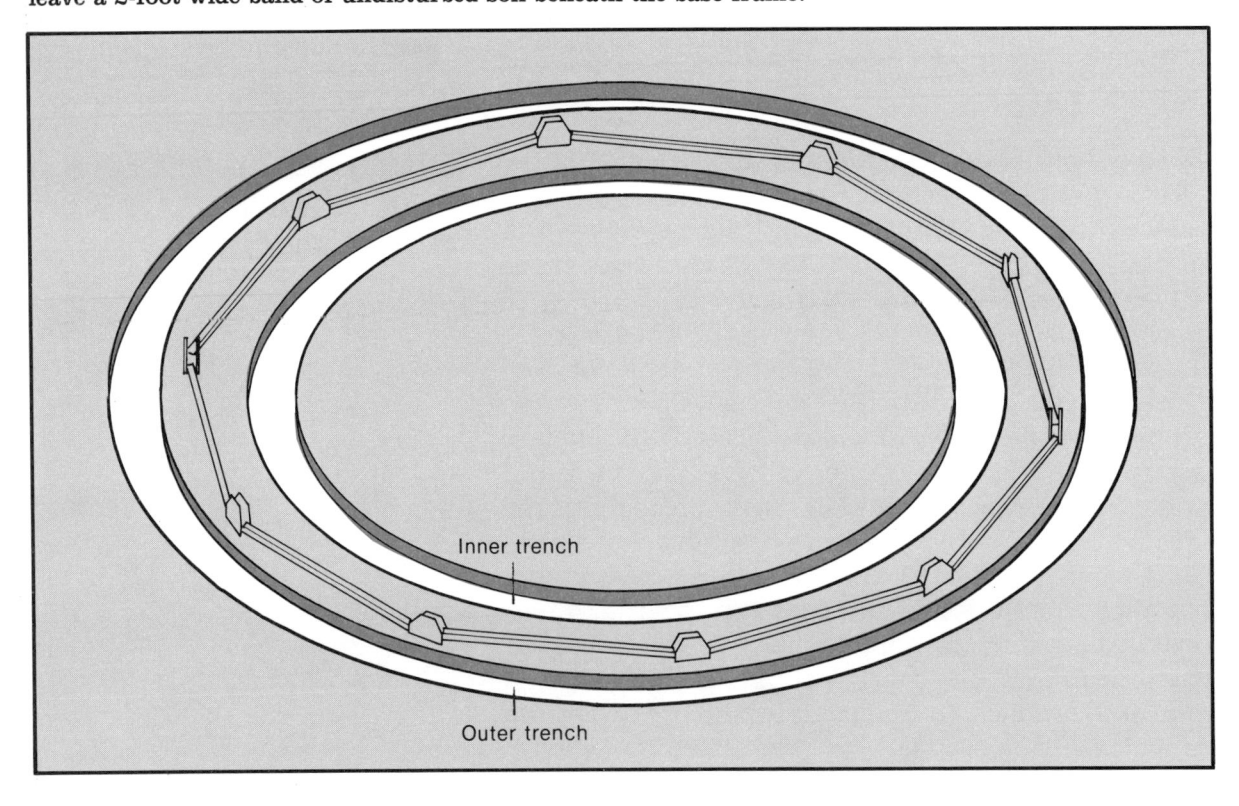

Dig the outer trench just outside the wedges; dig the inner trench just inside them, being very careful not to disturb the soil between the trenches. This two-foot wide circle of soil — which must be kept intact — serves two critically important functions: along with the underground layers of polyethylene, it helps insulate the dome from freezing temperatures and, perhaps even more importantly, it supports the entire weight of the dome. (If the soil is disturbed, the dome may settle unevenly.) Therefore, keep this soil sound and firm. The best way to do this is to work carefully on each trench while standing on the side of each trench away from the frame.

Using a power trench digger would make this task easy, but renting one is costly and borrowing one is unlikely. So, you'll probably dig all 50 yards of 2½-foot deep trenches manually. To reduce fatigue, rotate chores so no single person works for extended periods with the same tool. A long-time construction worker offered this good advice: "A slow and steady pace is what you want. Don't let people get over-exerted because that's when they may begin to get careless."

Equip everyone with narrow, pointed spades or shovels; give one person a pick axe, another a pitchfork. Be extra cautious when using these tools. The person using the pick axe starts the trenches by breaking the ground surface in the two circular patterns. (Be certain no one is standing within 10 feet of this person and that the person using the pick axe never swings it wildly. The pick axe can accidentally slip from the grasp of someone with sweaty hands.) Then the shovelers dig down about 6 to 12 inches, piling the soil on the sides of the trenches away from the frame. Large rocks should be placed in a wheelbarrow for later use.

Pick axe and shovel the soil, in turn, until both 2½-foot deep trenches are completed. The trenches should be as narrow as possible; their depth is checked easily with a yardstick.

A FEW TIPS

Everyone should wear gardening gloves to avoid blisters.

Keep your work organized. Pile the dug-up soil neatly and place all rocks in a wheelbarrow. The soil will be returned to the trenches later and the rocks will be used to hold the polyethylene vertically in place.

An outer trench, 2½ feet deep. Keep rocks in a convenient spot or wheelbarrow. Later, polyethylene will be placed vertically in trenches and then folded over and attached to frame.

If you encounter a boulder that you feel certain cannot be dislodged, don't try lifting it from the trenches. The polyethylene can be placed easily around a few obstacles like this without noticeably impairing the insulative effectiveness of the circle of soil it surrounds. (The polyethylene is not installed until after the dome securing posts are in place.)

INSTALLING THE SECURING POSTS

Having decided on the number of posts your dome will need and their lengths (Chapter 3), it's time to position them and dig their holes. Place one post on each side of the dome door, since this area of movement and stress requires extra support. The best location for the door is in the dome's insulated section because the fiberglass insulation, packed between two polyethylene layers, gives the door added rigidity and durability.

To position the door, find the base strut facing true south, then count four more struts (not including the one facing true south) in either direction and mark it. This strut will be the base of the door. The direction you select is up to you; you may want the door in view of a kitchen window, near a walkway, or away from the strongest winds.

To help you decide where to place the posts and how long they should be, review Figure 3-4 in Chapter 3. Then spend some time thinking about the amount of securing the dome needs based on its location and environment.

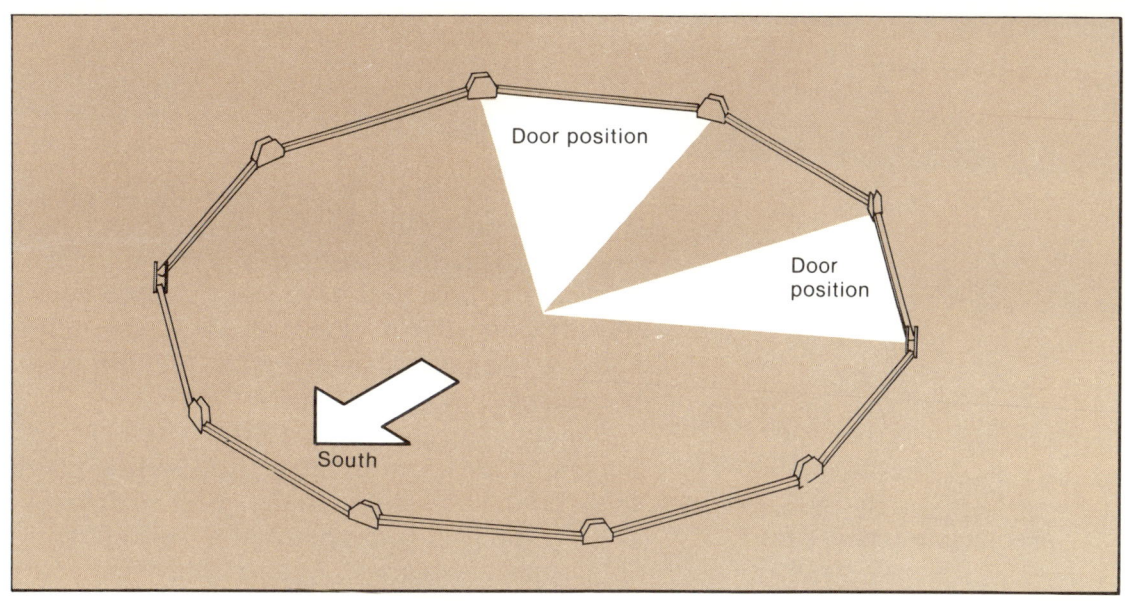

Figure 5-8. Door may be located at either position indicated, four base struts from the strut that faces true south.

The posts are placed in holes dug just inside the base hubs to which they'll eventually be connected. Use a post-hole digger to make these holes, if you can buy or rent one at a tool supply or hardware outlet. You may be able to use a small hand spade to dig the holes. In either case, keep in mind that each post must fit snugly.

Although at first it may seem difficult to dig a three- or five-foot hole with a hand tool, you can get a head start by standing in the dome's 2½-foot deep inner trench and breaking down narrow sections of its outer-facing wall where you want to locate the posts. Then dig deeper from these points until reaching the necessary depths.

Figure 5-9. To get a head start on post holes, stand in the inner trench and break down outer walls at points where posts are to be located.

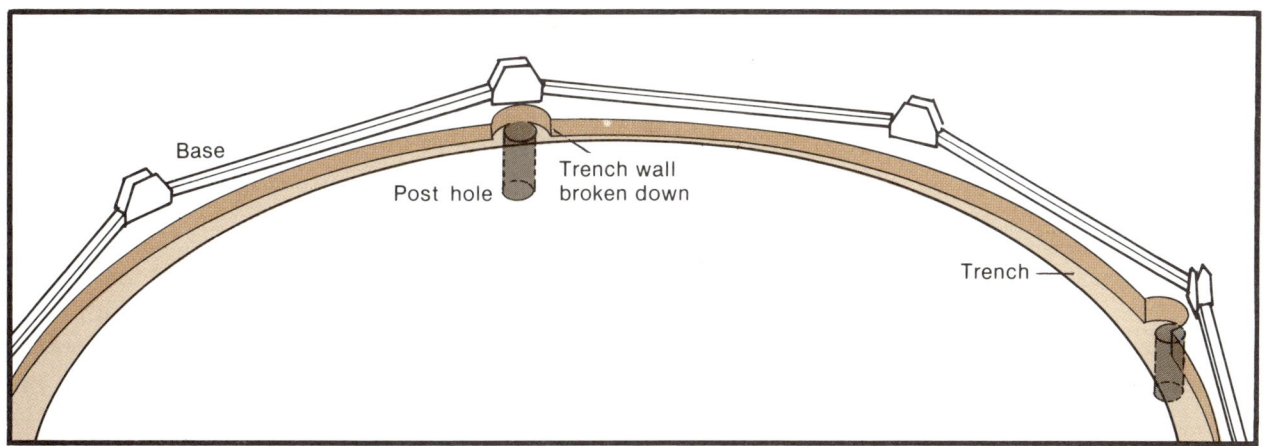

63

BEFORE INSTALLING FILM

Before installing the film underground, note some general procedures:

1. Make certain no large air gaps exist between the film and the trench wall against which it is leaning. Gaps may cause the film to rip under pressure of dirt being reshoveled into the trench. To prevent this, smooth the trench wall as best as possible and, where gaps do occur, loosen the film so it fills the gaps rather than straddles them.

2. Avoid puncturing the film with rocks or tools. Small rips are inevitable and inconsequential, but large rips should be sealed with Scotchrap 50 Tape.

3. Trenches need not be perfectly circular to be effective.

If you decided earlier to use some five-foot posts, then find you can't dig deep enough, don't be overly concerned. Instead, dig as deep as you can, place a three-foot post in the hole and save the five-foot post for another hub. If this can't be done, measure the hole's depth and shorten the post to match it. A five-foot post may not be necessary.

The top of each post should, if possible, have the same height as its "partner" base hub. When placing posts in their hole, don't waste time trying to drive them into the soil — even if they are pointed — because they're likely to be stopped by a rock. Even if they don't hit rocks, you probably won't be able to drive the posts more than 12 inches.

The closer the posts are to their partner base hubs, the better, but if they are more than a few inches apart they can be connected using one of two methods explained at the end of this chapter. Attaching posts to base hubs is the final step in site preparation.

The dome posts do not require cement footings. But, you may decide to add them if you think this added stability is desirable. Work with cement only if you are familiar with techniques for using it effectively. Simply follow routine procedures for securing any type of post. With posts in place and the cement dry (if cement is used), you are ready to install the polyethylene into the trenches. After the polyethylene is installed, soil and rocks are filled around it and the posts.

INSTALLING UNDERGROUND POLYETHYLENE

Open and spread the 8- x 100-foot roll of polyethylene flat on the ground. Using a good pair of scissors, slit it the long way into two 4- x 100-foot sections. This can be done by making an initial cut, holding the scissors firm, walking in a straight path and sliding through the film. This technique should ensure a fairly even division while taking little time.

You may notice that moisture accumulates beneath the film. That's because the solar energy trapped under the polyethylene heats the soil beneath it, causing moisture to evaporate, cool and condense on the film. Knowledge of this process has enabled downed aviators and others to obtain drinking water and survive in desert conditions.

Figure 5-10. Lay the film in the circular trenches so it overlaps about four feet.

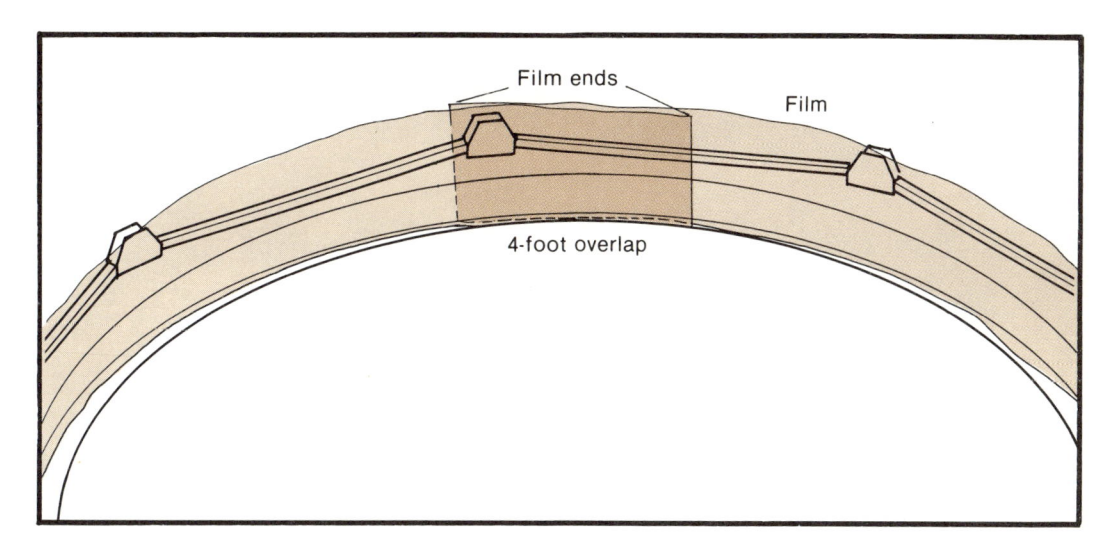

Encircling the dome are the two 2½-foot deep trenches, one about 66 feet around, the other about 78 feet. The film is 4 feet high and 100 feet around. Obviously, there's more than enough material, but don't cut off the excess yet.

Lay the film in each trench, so it stands vertically against the side of the trench facing the dome frame (outer trench: film on inside wall; inner trench: film on outside wall). When the film completely encircles the dome, inside and out, continue around in each trench another four feet so the film overlaps. Once this is accomplished, remove any excess length you want, but leave the four-foot height intact all the way around. The extra foot and a half of film protruding from the trenches will fold over to the dome frame where it will join the above-ground polyethylene to form an airtight, waterproof shell around the dome.

When laying the polyethylene into the trenches, keep it vertical by folding its protruding foot and a half toward the frame and resting rocks on top. Make sure the film just reaches the bottom of each trench. Having done this, carefully reshovel soil into the trenches.

By now, the securing posts should be standing snugly in narrow holes. To fill these, drive large rocks between the posts and the hole walls and pack the holes with soil. Avoid air gaps; the tighter the dirt, the more rigid the post. Using a short length of 2 x 2 or 2 x 4 and a hammer, compact the rocks and soil a few inches at a time until the soil is as firm as you can make it.

If you broke down sections of the inner trench walls to start post holes, refill these holes carefully. And try to avoid direct contact of rocks and polyethylene film.

DRAINAGE DITCH

If the dome is on a slight slope and subject to water run-off, you may want to divert the water by building a small drainage ditch around the dome's up-slope side.

To do this, refill the trench until the soil reaches a level about six inches below the surface. Then fill in with a four-inch layer of rocks and pebbles, followed by two inches of soil to fill the remaining space in the trench.

Rocks should not be in direct contact with the polyethylene. When finished, the trench soil should be even with the earth around it.

More effective drainage can be achieved by filling the top six inches entirely with small rocks and pebbles, and by using the remaining soil to form a mound between the trench and dome.

Once trenches are refilled, remove rocks from top 1½ feet of film, as necessary, and attach securing posts to base hubs. Top portion of film is folded toward frame and buried a few inches beneath surface.

If you're thinking of bringing in a permanent underground water or electric line, now is the time to do it. To determine whether you'll need or want these services, read the section in Chapter 8 on installing electric lines and the section in Chapter 9 on installing water lines.

SECURING BASE HUBS TO POSTS

Once the posts are standing securely near their partner base hubs, the posts and hubs can be secured to each other. Distances between posts and hubs may vary and, for this reason, there are two methods to secure them. One method is suitable only if the post is directly aligned with, and within two inches of, the hub; the other may be used even if the distance between post and hub is greater than two inches and the alignment is off.

Any post directly behind and within two inches of its partner base hub is best secured with a 1/2-inch thick threaded rod. If there is a small space between the post and hub, it should be filled with a 2 x 2 or similar block. Fit the block snugly between the post and base hub, being careful not to push the hub out of alignment.

Drill a 1/2-inch hole through the center portion of the base hub (being careful not to penetrate a hub strut) and the wood block and post. If you can't find a drill bit long enough to penetrate about 10 inches (which may require the use of a hand brace drill), you may have to drill in

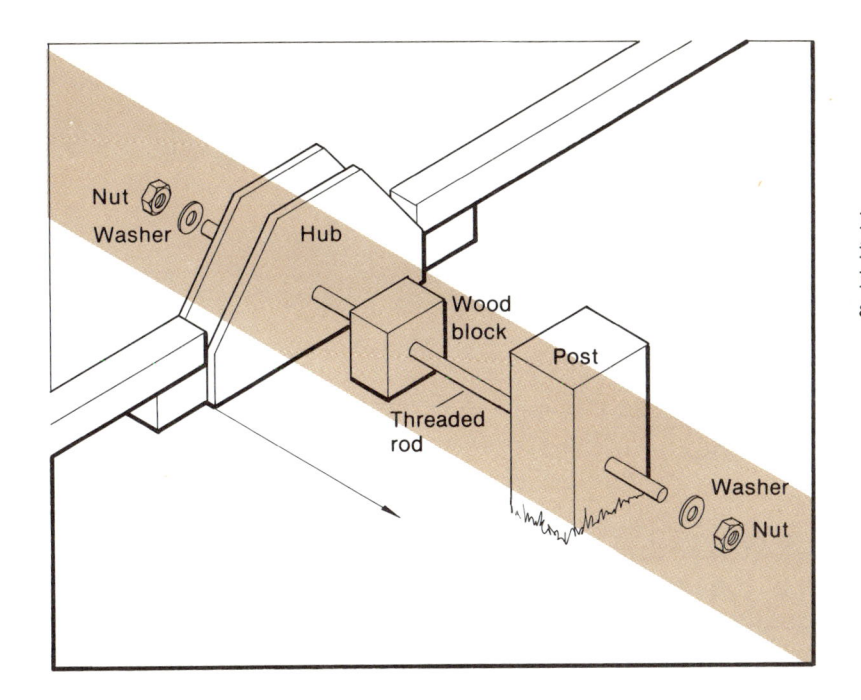

Figure 5-11. If post is within two inches of, and directly aligned with, hub, use threaded rod, nuts, washers and spacer block to secure hub to post.

from both sides, making sure the holes align to allow insertion of the rod.

The rod may be bought at most hardware stores for about 10 cents per foot. To determine the length to buy, add up the number of hub-post securings where rods are used and the length of the rod at each securing. (At some stores, rods are sold only in standard lengths.) Two nuts and two standard washers with 1/2-inch center holes are also needed for each hub-post securing.

Insert the rod through the hole from outside the base hub toward the dome's inside, leaving one inch protruding beyond the post's inner surface. Place a washer and nut on the protruding rod, but do not tighten yet. Cut off the rod extension outside the base hub so just one inch is left; place a nut and washer on this end; then tighten both sets of nuts and washers together.

When cutting the rod, use a hacksaw and be careful not to destroy the threads or the rod will have to be replaced. Throughout this entire process, do not cause any movement of the base hubs; if they are moved, reposition them immediately.

The second method for securing the posts to base hubs is used mainly when they are more than two inches from each other, or when they are not aligned. However, if you feel this method is easier, you can use it for all hub-post securings. In this method, the hubs are secured to the posts with steel brackets.

The brackets are made of 1-inch wide, 1/8-inch thick,

If post is more than two inches from hub, or not directly aligned with hub, use a steel bracket to secure hub to post.

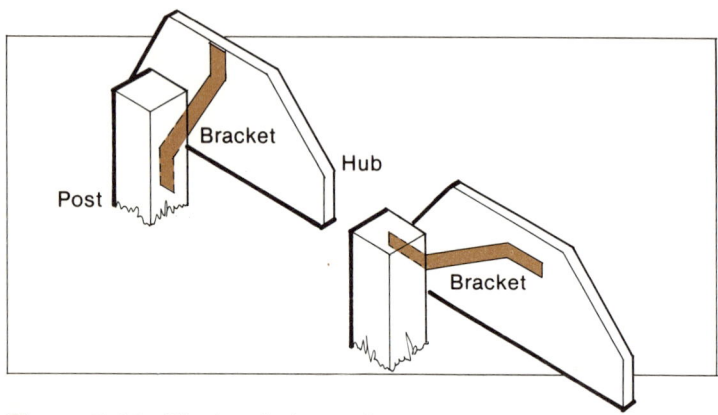

Figure 5-12. The bracket may be shaped many ways to form an appropriate securing. Shown are two possible configurations.

flat, stock steel, bent to the desired shape. The steel may be purchased at most hardware stores. The brackets are bolted to the posts with two 1/4-inch lag bolts, each two inches long, and to the base hubs with two 1/4-inch bolts, each 2½ inches long. Washers are also used.

The first step is to determine the shape of the bracket you need; Figure 5-12 shows different types that may work for you. When designing the bracket, remember the less extreme its angles, the more strength it will have.

A bend can be achieved by placing the steel bar in a vise and hammering it to the desired angle, or, if no vise is available, by hammering the bar over the edge of a curb or stone. Twists can be achieved by securing one end of the bar in a vise and turning the other end with a crescent wrench or large pliers. If no vise is available, use two of these hand tools.

Once the bracket is shaped properly, mark on it where 1/4-inch holes will be drilled for bolts. Then drill the holes as far apart on each end of the bar as possible to maximize the bar's surface contact with the post and hub it joins. This adds extra strength to the securing. If there's not enough room for two holes on each of the bar's ends, one will suffice. The bars should be painted with Rustoleum or a comparable rust inhibiter before they're bolted to posts and hubs.

ATTACHING UNDERGROUND POLYETHYLENE TO THE FRAME

The polyethylene in each trench is attached to the dome frame, over the base hubs and struts, to form a seal, insulating the dome below ground. The underground polyethylene acts as a barrier to moisture and dampness. Its top 1½ feet is folded over toward the frame from the trench and buried a few inches beneath the surface to prevent possible damage from walking.

First, clean the polyethylene's edges with a wet rag to

SITE PREPARATION

69

remove dirt that would prevent Scotchrap 50 Tape from adhering to it. Working first with the outer layer of film, clear a suitable "route" for it by removing three to six inches of soil between the filled-in trench and the frame. Dig deep near the trench, but leave the soil in place as you near the frame so the frame's support won't be disturbed. The end result should be a shallow slope from the frame to the trench.

Lay the polyethylene loosely along the ground toward the frame, leaving plenty of slack to allow for cold weather contractions. Staple it to the outer-facing sides of the base struts, one staple every two to three inches. Excess polyethylene should overlap within the dome. When reaching base hubs, continue to leave slack and staple the film to the hubs' outer-facing surfaces, allowing excess film to drape over the hubs. Continue in this manner until you've gone around the entire dome.

Then fold the film across the top of each strut and staple it there. When reaching base hubs, slit and fold the film to fashion a continuous covering over the base struts and base hubs. At the same time, base hub **struts** should be permitted to protrude through the polyethylene.

For the inner layer of film, dig down and remove up to eight inches of soil between the filled-in trench and the frame. Dig deeper near the trench and form a gradual

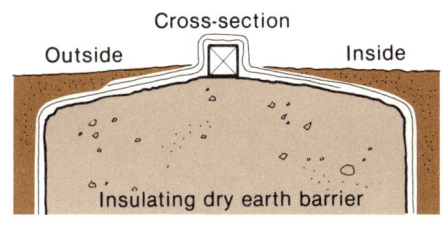

Figure 5-13. Underground polyethylene should lie on a gentle slope from frame to trench. Work with outer film first, then inner film.

Figure 5-14. Slit and fold film to fashion a continuous covering over hubs and struts. (More film may drape over the frame than amount shown.)

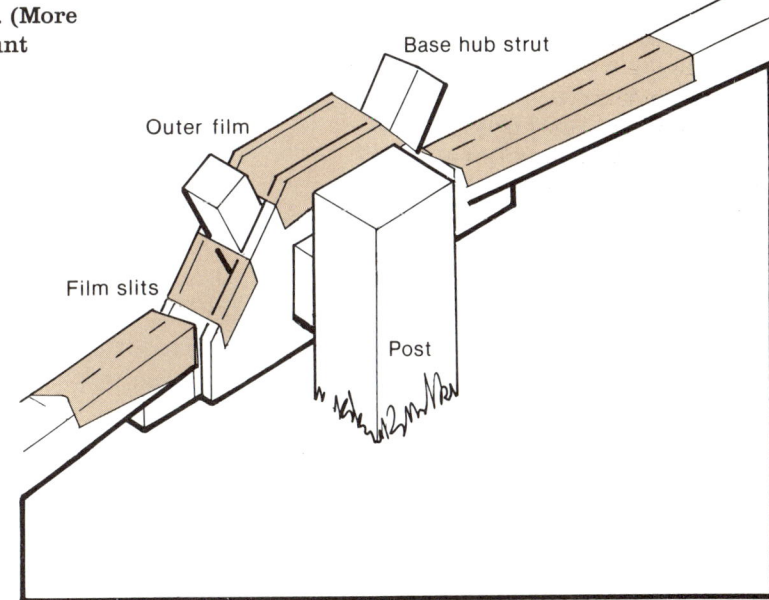

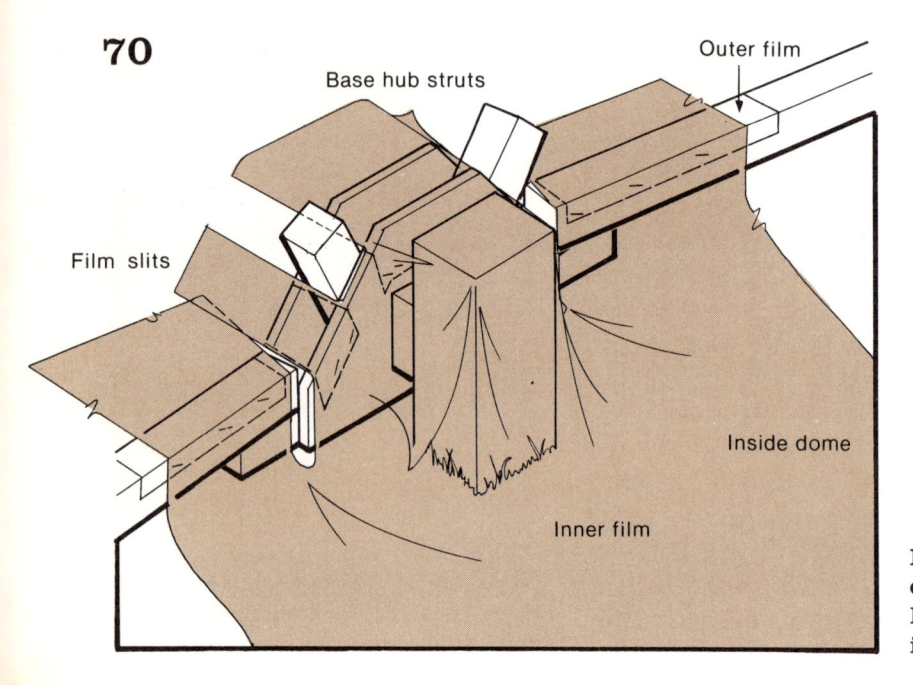

BUILDING AND USING A SOLAR-HEATED GEODESIC GREENHOUSE

Figure 5-15. Inner film layer should cover outer layer's excess, draped over hubs and struts. Staple both outer and inner layer as shown.

TROUBLE SHOOTING

If the trenches are not perfectly circular and sections of it are more than a foot from the frame, there may not be enough film to reach, or drape over, the frame. If so, cut some polyethylene from the original roll and secure it with Scotchrap 50 Tape to the short sections.

slope toward the surface as you near the frame. The deeper area near the trench allows you to use this section of soil for vegetable plants with shallow roots. The slope serves to keep the soil near the frame largely undisturbed.

Lay the film toward the frame, leaving slack and covering the **outer** layer's excess. Staple both the inner and outer layer to the inside of the base struts, using one staple every two to three inches. Following the same folding and slitting procedures as before, continue stapling the inner layer to base hubs and base struts.

By securing these two film layers to the frame's base, you've protected the insulative circle of soil from water penetration. Soil works as an insulation only if it remains dry. There may be a few spots where the two layers of polyethylene do not meet, probably at the tops of base hubs or where hub struts protrude. Secure them with Scotchrap 50 Tape.

If you decide to try fish-raising in the dome (see Chapter 9), a final site preparation task is to place the 725-gallon fish tank inside the dome. The tank will not fit through the door once the dome frame is built, so bring it in now, and leave it, face-down so it won't collect rain or dirt.

Chapter 6:
Erecting the Dome Frame

With the site preparation complete, the hardest physical labor is behind you. If you feel relief, you should feel even greater satisfaction soon after you erect the dome frame, tangible evidence of your hard work.

The most difficult part of frame assembly is supporting some sections while working on others. At least three or four friends and one or more eight- or ten-foot stepladders make this task easier.

Erecting the dome takes just a few hours, from start to finish. To prepare for this work, bring to the site all wooden frame parts, ladders, bolts, washers and tools: If your bolts have hex heads, bring a ratchet and socket set; if they have slotted heads, bring a large, heavy screwdriver. Bring a hammer, some string, and a plumb line.

These wooden frame parts belong at the dome site: 36 long struts (35 for construction, 1 extra); 31 short struts (30 for construction, 1 extra); ten hex and six pent hubs.

A FRAME WITH FOUR LEVELS

A huge pile of lumber, such as the one for this project, can be awesome or even disconcerting. So, to simplify things, think of the dome frame as a four-level structure with 40 triangles. Thirty of the triangles are small and have one long and two short struts as sides; ten are large with three long struts as sides.

   1. **First level.** This level is the dome base, made earlier during site preparation. It has ten base hubs and ten long struts, positioned on the ground in a circle and secured tightly.

71

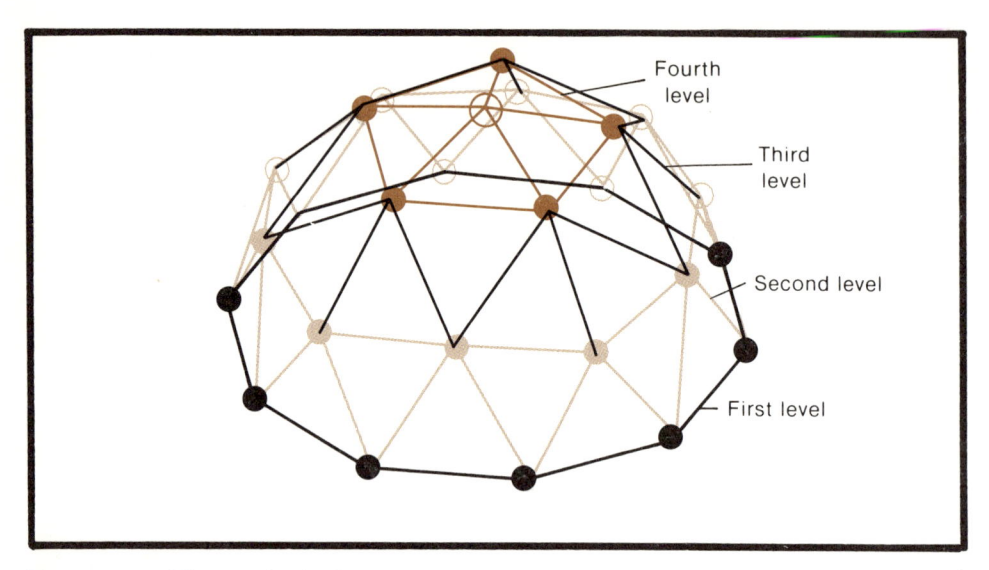

Figure 6-1. The geodesic dome has four levels, beginning with the base level made of base hubs and long struts.

2. **Second level.** This is the dome's next highest level, and it is that part of the structure from about ankle to eye level. This level is made of ten long and twenty short struts, with five hex hubs and five pent hubs. Ten long struts and ten short struts connect base hubs to the next highest row of hubs. The ten remaining short struts are used to connect the upper row of hubs. When in position, this level's struts form five large triangles and 15 small ones.

3. **Third level.** This level is the section of the frame from about five to nine feet high. It's made of ten long struts and five short struts which connect the frame's second and fourth levels. The struts form two sides of five large and ten small triangles.

4. **Fourth level.** This level, the "cap" of the dome, is made of five hex hubs, one pent hub, and five long and five short struts. These form five small triangles.

The levels are assembled in this three-step sequence:

1. Build level two on top of the base (level one).
2. Build level four on the ground in middle of the dome site.
3. Lift level four to the top of a ladder in the center of the site, and hold it in place while level three is installed to connect levels two and four.

Frame assembly is a simple, straightforward process, but holding sections in place for more than a few minutes is another matter. This is why extra hands are needed to

ERECTING THE DOME FRAME

73

help quicken and smooth over an awkward, but otherwise easy, procedure.

Since holding parts in place is important, it's best to keep needed materials and tools within easy reach. So, fill your pockets with nuts, bolts, and washers or provide everyone with nail aprons, which are often available free from lumber suppliers. Also, organize your lumber by placing one long and two short struts just outside each base hub. Alternate the hex and pent hubs in these spots, and group each hex hub with two **more** long struts and each pent hub with one **more** short strut. In the center of the site, place one pent and five hex hubs and five long and five short struts.

All lumber should now be in position, with the exception of one long and one short strut made as extras. If it

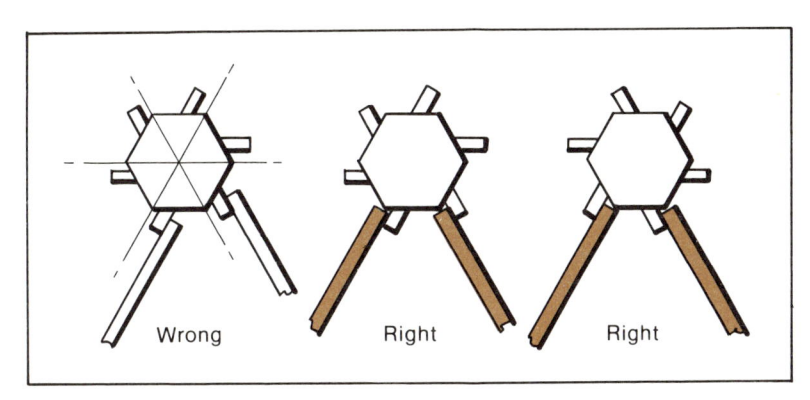

Figure 6-2.

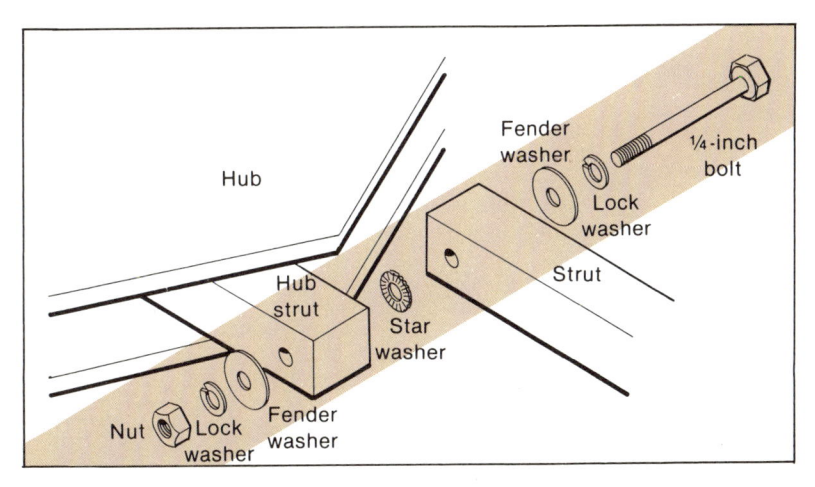

Figure 6-3.

RULES FOR STRUT-HUB ASSEMBLY

Regardless of the frame section to be assembled, one rule is constant:

Long or short struts must be bolted to the side of the hub strut that allows them to aim directly toward the center of each hub (Figure 6-2). Structurally, it makes no difference whether the long or short struts are on the left or right side of hub struts as long as they aim toward the center. But, to achieve a symmetrical appearance, you may want to position all hubs so struts enter them the same way.

Struts are connected to hub struts (Figure 6-3) with 1/4-inch bolts; lock and fender washers are placed just inside the nut and head of each bolt, and a star washer is placed between the struts. Because the frame will likely require some readjustment later, all bolts should be left slightly loose to allow slight pivoting. Struts and hub struts must be aligned perfectly so bolts may be inserted snugly, by hand, into the proper holes. If, despite proper alignment, bolts are not easily inserted, gently tap them into place with a hammer.

doesn't work out this way, recheck your placements; or, if necessary, check to ensure the correct number of struts and hubs were made.

LEVEL TWO ASSEMBLY

To start, form a large triangle above the base strut you determined to face due south. To do this, connect a long strut to the base hub at each end of this base strut, and join the two long struts on top with a hex hub. This large triangle must be erected above the due south base strut to ensure that the dome panels face correctly.

Even if you're so inclined, don't stand there all day marveling at this first triangle, no matter how nice it looks. It's time to move on and complete level two. If you're hesitant, that's understandable: You may think the triangle will fall if you don't hold it up. You're right. So move a ladder, stepladder or strut just inside the frame and lean the triangle against it. For added security, tie the triangle to the support with a string to prevent it from falling backwards.

Figure 6-4. Form a large triangle above true south base strut. Support triangle with extra strut or ladder.

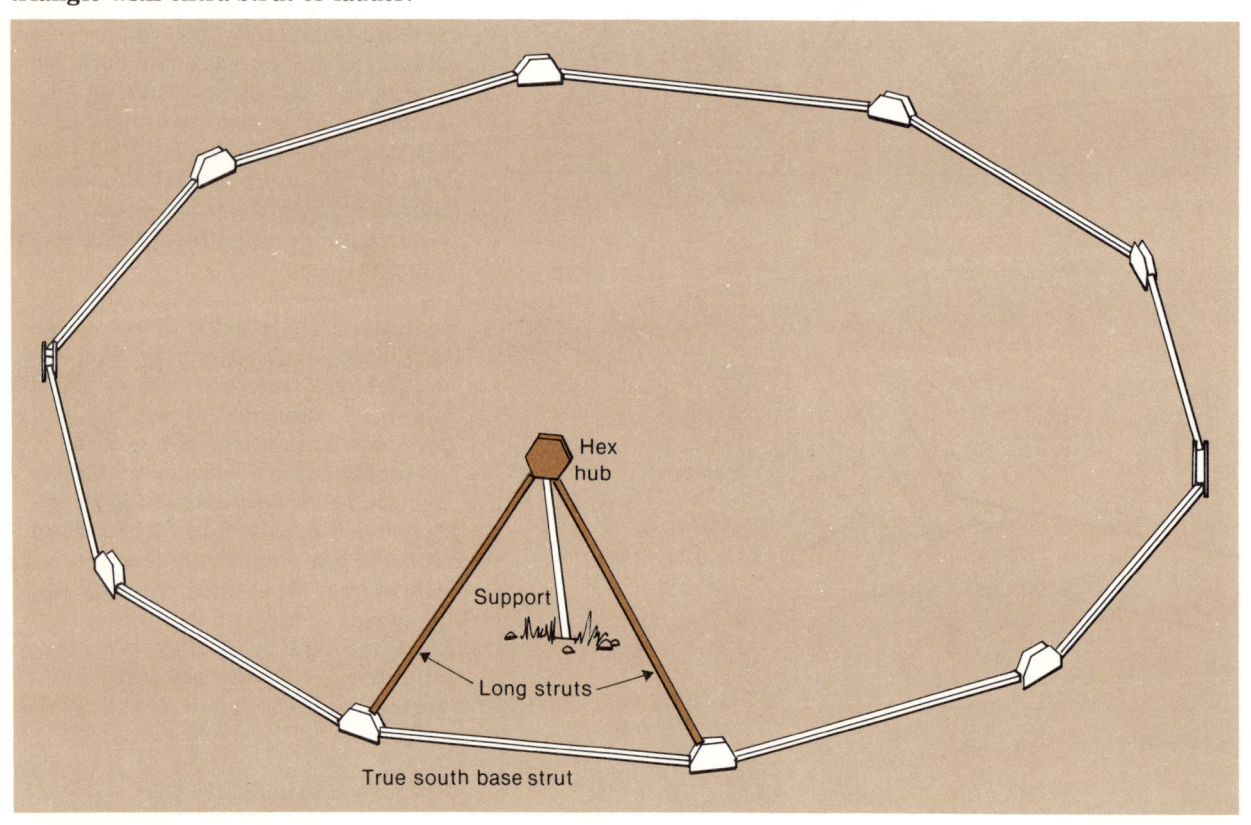

ERECTING THE DOME FRAME

Standing within the dome, move to the right of the first triangle and form a **small** triangle next to the first. To do this, connect one short strut to the same base hub used for the first triangle; connect a second short strut to the next base hub to the right; and join the struts on top with a pent hub.

Again, constructed segments must remain in their upright positions throughout frame assembly. Use another ladder or person to support the second triangle, or use remaining 2 x 2 lengths. Don't cut these 2 x 2s, or you'll be short of lengths needed later to build the door and vent.

Now, connect the hex hub of the first triangle with the pent hub of the second, using a short strut. This will form another small triangle in between the first two. You'll be able to feel the added firmness these triangles have and to envision the dome's rigidity when completed.

Moving once more to the right, form another large triangle. To do this, connect one long strut to the base hub with a short strut used in assembling the second, small triangle; connect a second long strut to the next

KEEP FRAME SEGMENTS SECURE

The more triangles formed, the more rigidity the structure has; you can feel the frame's added strength after just a few segments are assembled. But, its maximum strength isn't achieved until all parts are secured in place.

Therefore, it's important to keep partially-constructed segments of the frame in their normal, upright positions. If allowed to fall, the leverage of the long struts will cause odd conformations and possible cracking of hubs or struts. This, in turn, might require replacement of these parts, in which case you'll be glad you saved the templates and jigs.

Figure 6-5. Standing within dome, move to right of first triangle and form small triangle. Join triangle hubs at top with short strut.

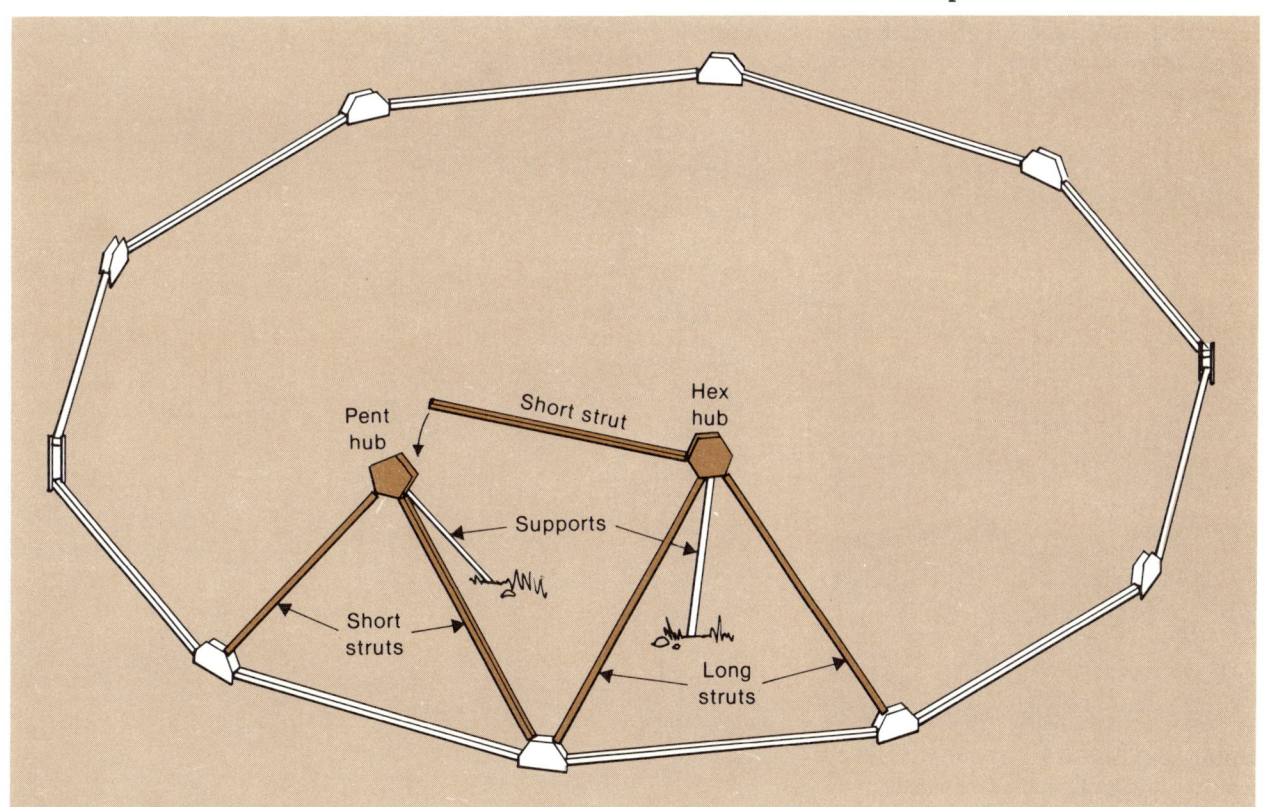

BUILDING AND USING A SOLAR-HEATED GEODESIC GREENHOUSE

76

base hub to the right; and join the two long struts on top with a hex hub. Then use a short strut to connect the pent hub of the second triangle to the hex hub of the third.

Continue in this manner until all of level two is assembled. The closer you are to completing the 10 triangles of level two, the less support is needed from ladders or helpers. You may have to support only every other triangle, rather than each one.

LEVEL FOUR ASSEMBLY

Pick up the pent hub placed in the middle of the site and connect one short strut to each of its hub struts. Connect a hex hub to the other end of each of these short struts, then connect these hex hubs to each other using five long struts. Remember, bolts connecting these should be loose enough to allow for slight pivoting.

At this point, the five long struts can't be connected with the hex hubs because the struts neither reach the hubs nor face in the correct direction. So, in order to connect the hubs, raise the center pent hub a foot or two

Figure 6-6. Level four in flat position. Note that each long strut is connected to only one hex hub.

Center pent hub of level four in raised position and long struts secured.

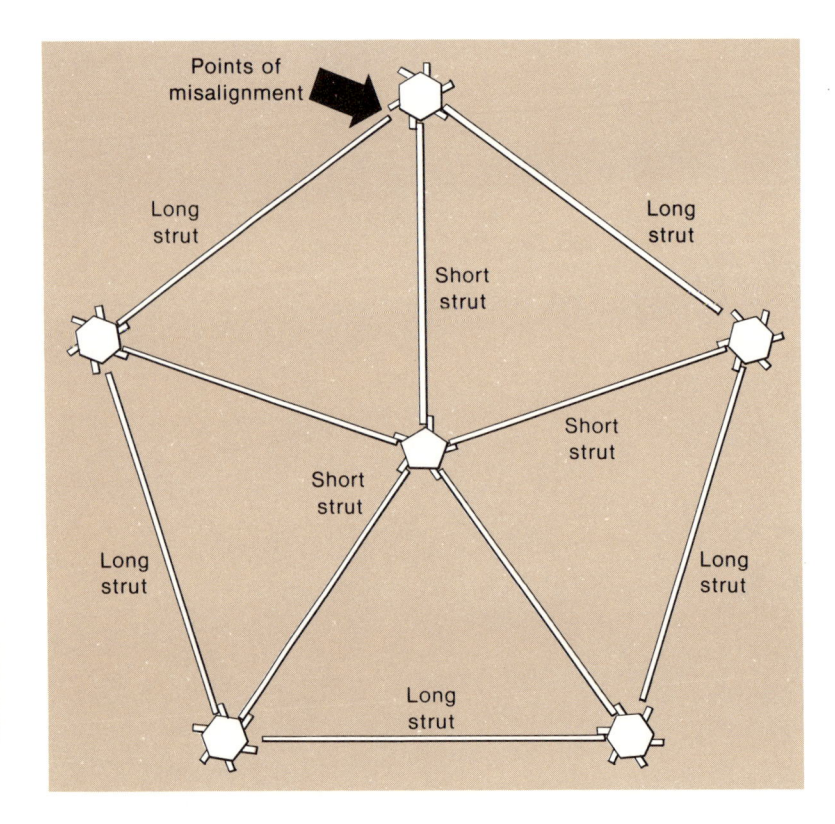

Level four completed and in position at the center of the dome frame.

off the ground; this allows level four to assume its proper shape as its struts fall into place. Keep the unit raised while you secure all connections. You can begin to see how a spherical shape can be formed from flat pieces of wood.

TOP LEVEL PLACEMENT

Before starting on level three — a series of struts joining levels two and four — the entire level four assembly must be lifted to its ultimate position; its top pent hub must be 11½ feet above the stake marking the dome's center.

Although level four is not heavy, it is difficult for anyone to hold it for the necessary length of time, or the duration of the level three assembly. So, rest level four on top supports placed on a 10-foot stepladder. A 4 x 4, cement block or scissor jack or a combination of these may be used as support that will provide the extra 1½ feet needed to achieve 11½ feet in height. Without these materials or equipment, recruit a strong person to hold level four. Hang a plumb line from the pent hub to confirm that it's centered.

Support level four with a stepladder, blocks and/or jack.

77

BUILDING AND USING A SOLAR-HEATED GEODESIC GREENHOUSE

COMPLETING THE DOME FRAME

To complete level three, use five short struts to connect the pent hubs of level two to the hex hubs of level four; use 10 long struts to connect hex hubs of level two to those of level four.

You may find it easier to connect the struts of level three to level four before raising the assembled section. Once the section is raised, it may be necessary to get a 2 x 2 and use it to push the level four hex hubs slightly upward. This provides sufficient room to comfortably connect the level three struts to the level two hubs.

In joining level three to level two, it is easiest to connect short struts before long struts. This is true whether level three struts have been attached to level four before or after raising level four into position.

Once this final stage of assembly is complete, with the bolts of hubs and struts secure, but not tight, you should be able to remove all supports and gaze at your spanking-new geodesic dome.

Figure 6-7. You may want to connect level three struts to level four before raising level four into position.

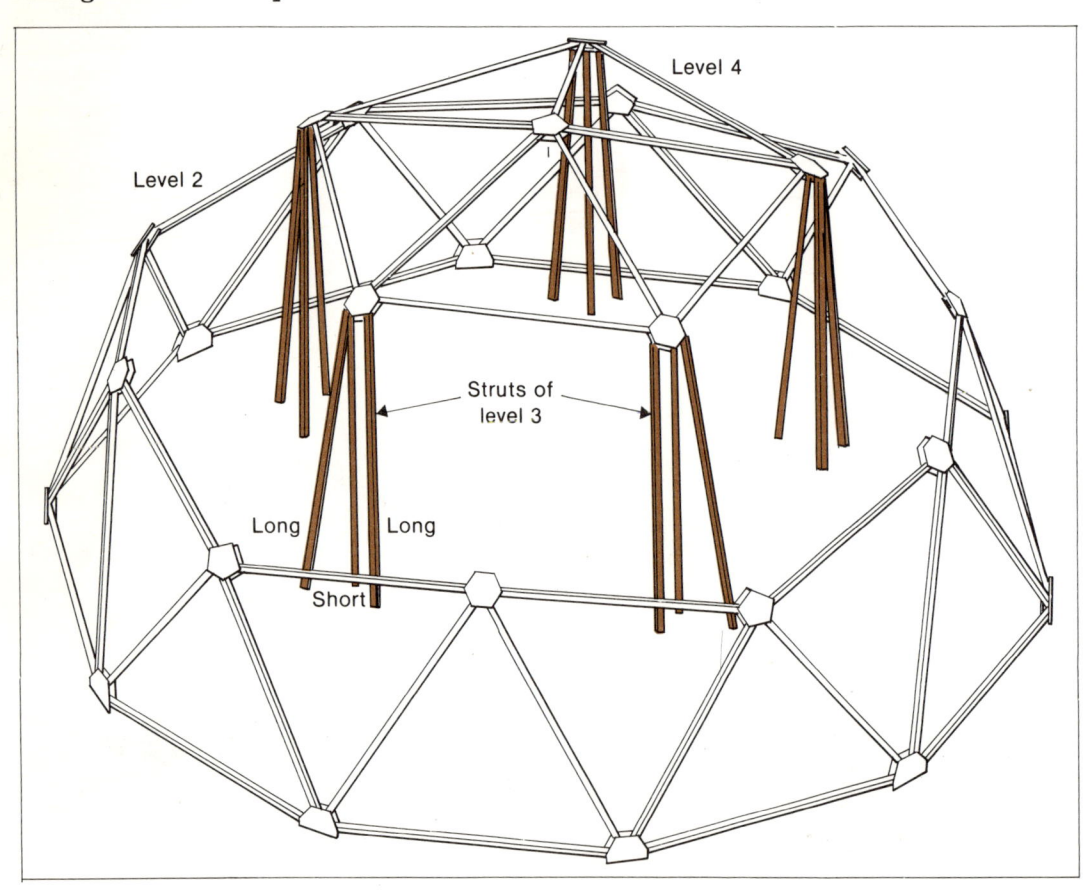

Handwritten annotations on figure:

4 × 5 = 20 DIAG LONGS
3 × 5 = 15 DIAG SHORTS
5 RADIAL SHORTS (TOP)

10 BASE LONG ⎫ HORIZ.
10 MID SHORT ⎬
5 TOP LONG ⎭

35 LONG
30 SHORT

PLATES
10 HEX
6 PENT
10 BASE

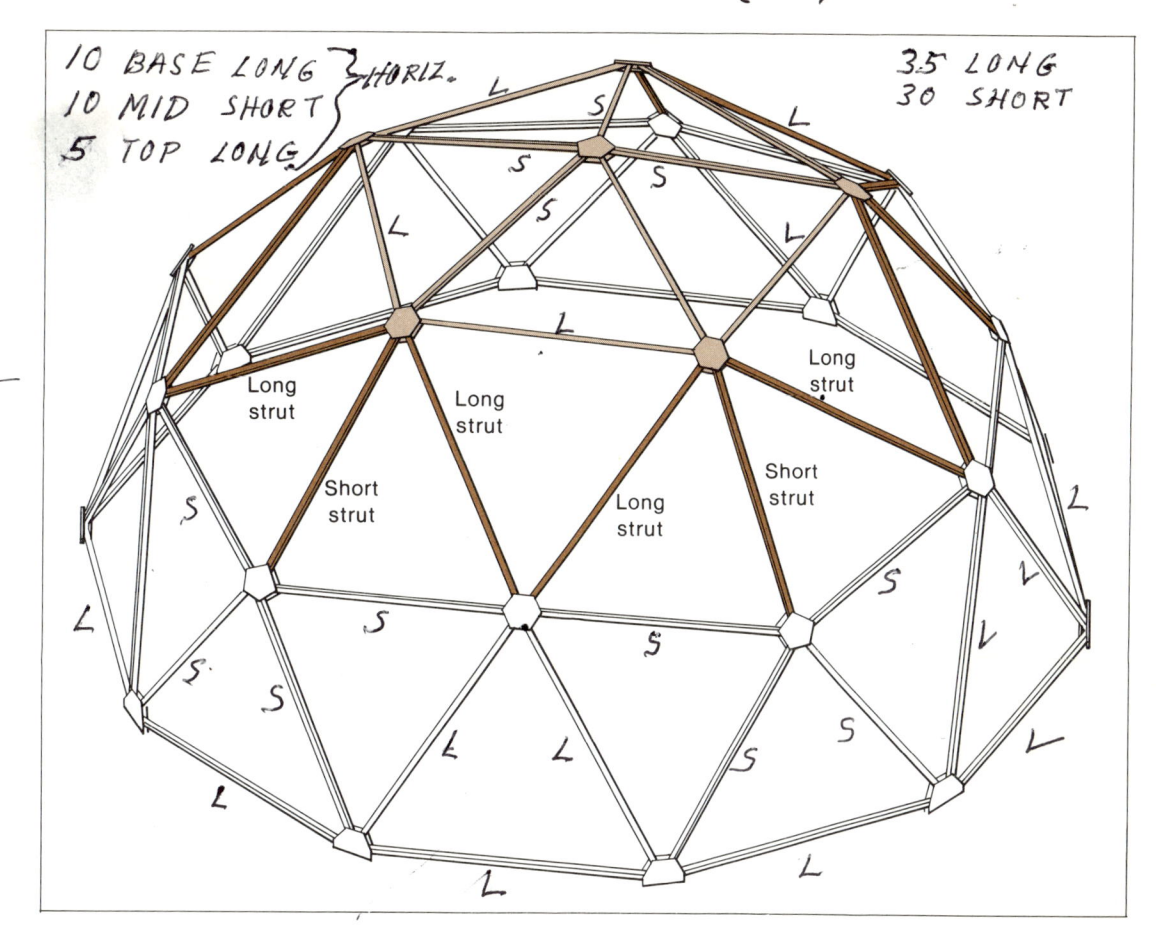

Figure 6-8. Join level three short struts to pent hubs of level two, then join long struts to hex hubs.

Focus critically on its construction: The inner flat surface of each hub must be perpendicular to an imaginary line from the center of the hub to the center of the dome, marked by the stake. Hubs that do not seem to be positioned correctly must be gently maneuvered into proper position. To do this, grasp them with one hand on each end and apply slight pressure.

When satisfied that all hubs are angled properly, tighten every bolt as much as possible without cracking the wood.

However, there's a disadvantage to this flexibility: At Fordham after two winters of use, the dome's level two pent hubs misaligned slightly, causing undue stress on the dome's outer film covering. Design changes have been made to prevent this from happening to you:

One change was using fender washers instead of standard washers because their larger surface area allows struts to be pulled much closer together. Another was placing star washers between the struts. They bite into the wood and prevent struts from turning easily.

The final change was adding extra support to the pent hub connections of level two. This was done because pent

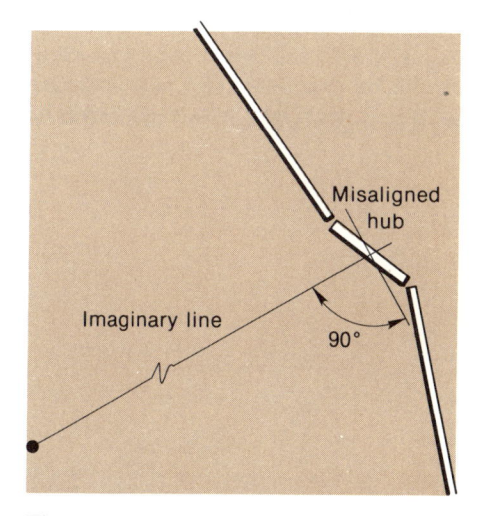

Figure 6-9. Hubs must be perpendicular to imaginary line from hub center to dome center.

79

BUILDING AND USING A SOLAR-HEATED GEODESIC GREENHOUSE

hubs are less rigid than hex hubs, which have six strut connections compared with the pent's five.

To achieve this extra support, add an extra 3/16-inch bolt (3¼—4 inches long) to three of the five connections on each of level two's pent hubs: to the joining of the level four strut, and to the two struts rising from the base. Horizontal strut connections should be left alone.

Drill a hole with a 3/16-inch drill bit through the hub strut and strut at the corner of the connection most distant from the hub. Slip the bolt through the hole and secure it with standard 3/16-inch washers inside the bolt head and nut. The bolts may have to be placed very close to the fender washers in which case the washers will overlap. This will cause no problems.

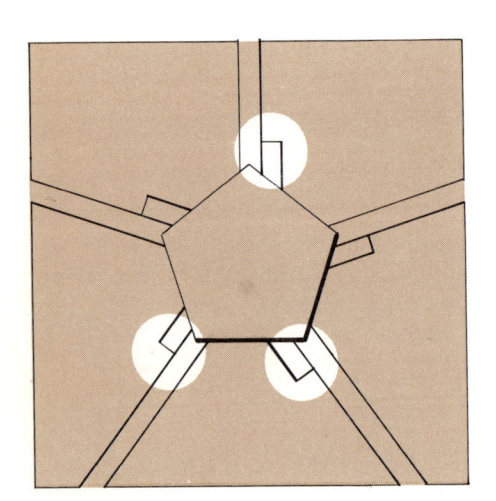

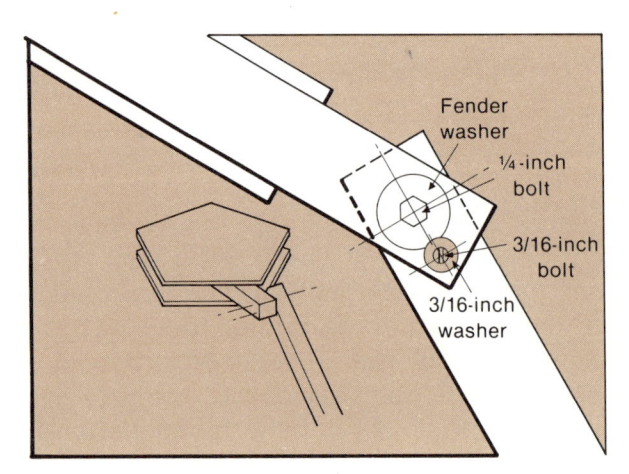

Figures 6-10 and 6-11. Add an extra 3/16-inch bolt to the three connections circled on each level two pent hub (left). The bolts are secured with standard 3/16-inch washers, which may overlap with the nearby fender washers (right).

Misaligned Base Hubs

When you are erecting the dome frame, base hubs may tend to fall outward. This is a common problem. But, sometimes, it may indicate a serious construction error and, therefore, it should be corrected:

Go to each misaligned base hub, move it two to three inches outward, straighten it vertically and then allow it to tilt just slightly inward. If, after you readjust hubs this way, they still fall outward, there are five possible reasons:

ERECTING THE DOME FRAME

81

1. The dome's circular shape may not be as round as it should be, causing hubs to be unequal distances from the center. To correct this, readjust base struts as shown in Chapter 5. This can be done without reducing the structure's rigidity even though its entire frame is assembled and in place.

2. The radius (from the center stake to base hubs) may not be the required distance, 11 feet, 3½ inches. To correct this, readjust base hubs.

3. The dome site may not be leveled adequately. If so, work the soil as explained in Chapter 5.

4. Struts may be cut to the wrong size. This is unlikely, though, because incorrectly cut struts should have been noticed earlier. But, check the sizes anyway, and recut if necessary.

5. Struts may be placed incorrectly, meaning a short strut was placed where a long one belonged, or vice versa. Look carefully at the entire frame to find any misplaced struts. If you find any, take heart, misplacing struts is a

Once you complete it, inspect the frame carefully. Shown is a frame built for an exhibition near the Washington Monument by the Fordham Urban Solar EcoSystem (FUSES) team.

mistake many dome builders make. Simply replace them correctly.

If, after checking, you can not determine what is causing the problem with the base hubs, simply force the hubs into an upright position and secure them with stakes.

Misplaced Struts

If, during assembly, you find struts do not fit where they should, it is usually because other struts were placed where they do not belong. One out-of-place strut will fit, though awkwardly, and because of this may be hard to find when you learn of the error later.

During final alignment of the dome, you may see a hub in an assymetrical location — too high or low, too far in or out. This is caused by a misplaced strut, which must be found and repositioned correctly. The FUSES team made this mistake and realized it only after seeing two short struts remaining after the frame was fully assembled; one long and one short strut should have been left. The dome was examined until something amiss was spotted: one of level four's hex hubs protruded slightly more than the others; a long strut had been placed where a short one belonged. The struts were switched and the protrusion disappeared.

After the frame is assembled, it's possible that some hubs (particularly the pent hubs of level two) might be pushed in and out easily, although their bolts are tight. Again, a misplaced strut connected to these hubs is the cause, and it must be replaced.

FRAMING THE DOOR AND VENT

Now that you've erected the dome frame, you're in the home stretch. Only a few more major tasks need completion before you can tend to your year-round garden. One of the remaining tasks is to build the dome door and vent.

The door frame is formed by the struts of one large, level two triangle, selected and marked according to instructions in Chapter 5. Three tiny struts of varying lengths are fitted into the corners of the triangle to complete the frame.

The small 2 x 2 struts are added to the frame to prevent drafts at hard-to-seal corners of the triangular door,

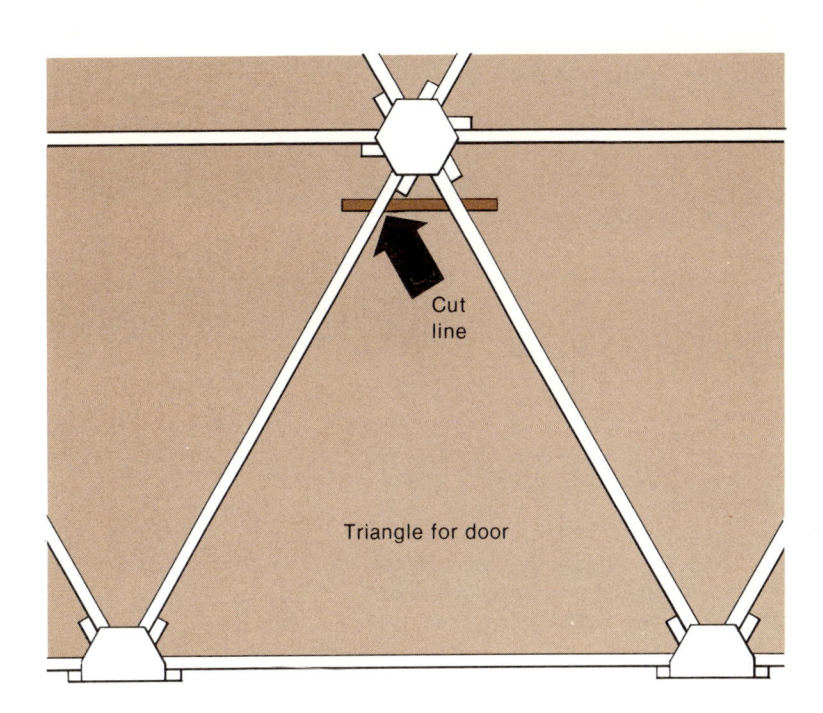

Figure 6-12. Position 2 x 2 strut, then mark cut lines, using frame as a guide; repeat process for other triangle corners.

such as the angles close to hubs or angles created at points where struts join hubs. The hubs, themselves, are slightly tilted and difficult to seal.

Position the three tiny 2 x 2 struts as shown in Figure 6-12, flush against the triangular door frame where hubs join the triangle's struts. Using the frame as a guide, draw lines on the small 2 x 2s, indicating the angles at which they'll be cut to fit where needed.

Cut the 2 x 2s to size, position them and, using a 1/8-inch bit, drill two starter holes for screws. The starter

Figure 6-13. After cutting struts to fit in corners, stain them and then screw them in place.

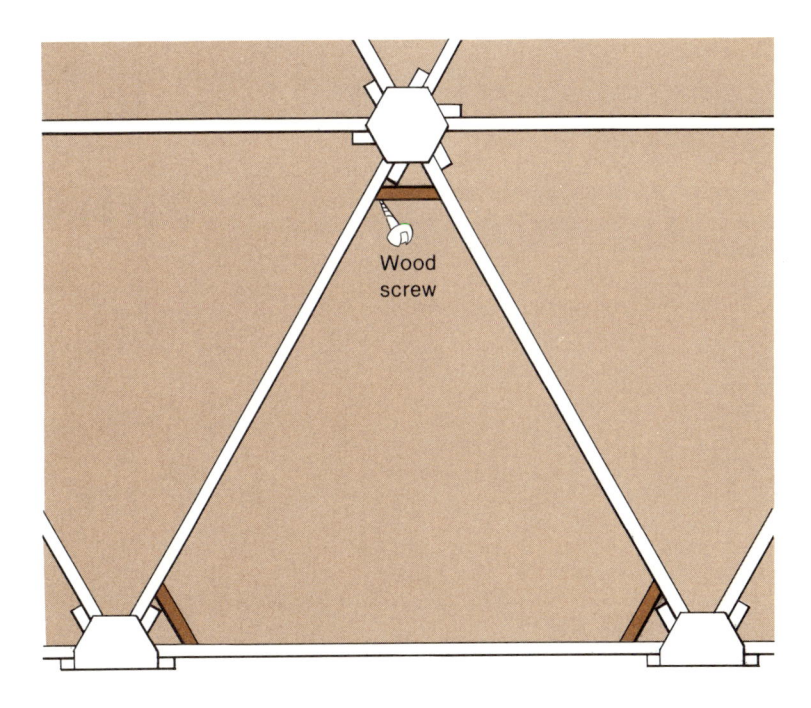

83

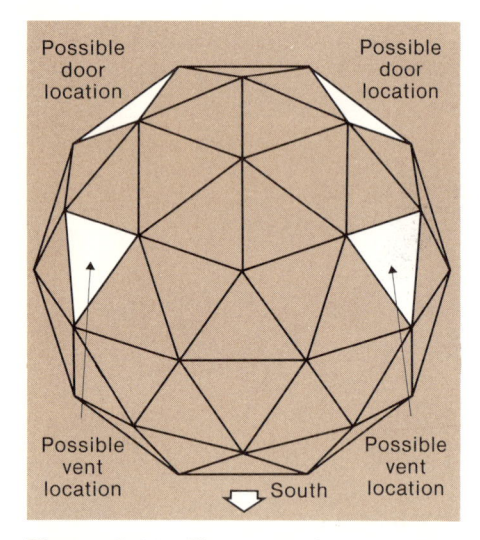

Figure 6-14. Shown are two possible vent locations. Vent and door should *not* be on same side.

holes should be drilled from the longest side of the 2 x 2 diagonally into the frame. Coat each 2 x 2 twice with redwood stain, let dry, then secure to the frame with two 1½-inch No. 8 wood screws.

The frame for the dome vent is made the same way, but first you must find its position. To locate the vent, stand in front of the true south base strut, count two base struts over, in the opposite direction from the door; in level three, directly above this base strut, is a large triangle which is adjacent to, and just south of, the small triangle that forms the vent (see Figure 6-14).

BUILDING THE DOOR AND VENT

The door and vent, although different sizes, are built exactly the same way: they are triangles, formed of three 2 x 2s joined at corners by three plywood plates which resemble base hub plates. Because the door and vent are built alike, instructions in this chapter referring to the door apply to both.

To start building them, cut six plywood plates to sizes shown in Figure 6-15. These will be used to bracket the 2 x 2s that form the triangular door and vent.

From within the dome, position a 2 x 2 as shown in Figure 6-16, flush against one of the door frame's struts. Using the door frame dimensions as a guide, draw lines, indicating the size and angle at which this 2 x 2 will have to be cut to fit snugly. Cut along the inside of these lines,

Figure 6-15. Cut six plywood securing plates, using dimensions shown.

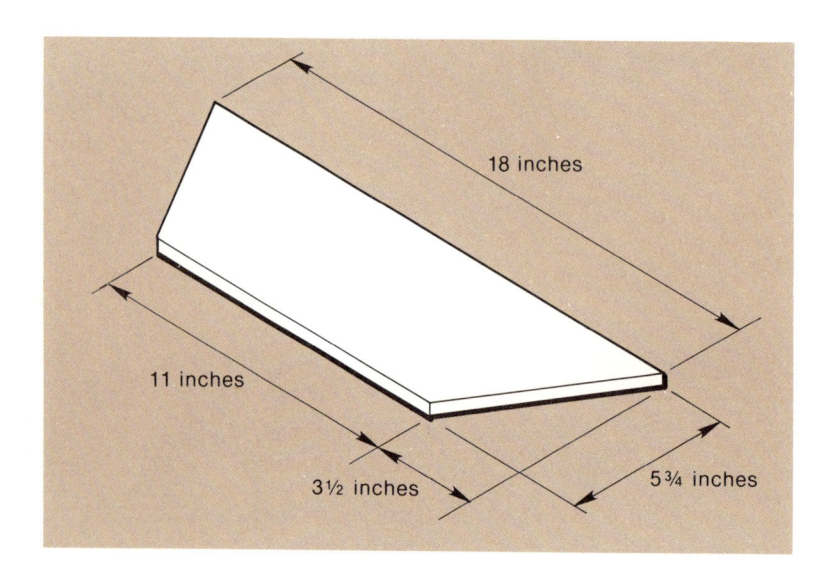

84

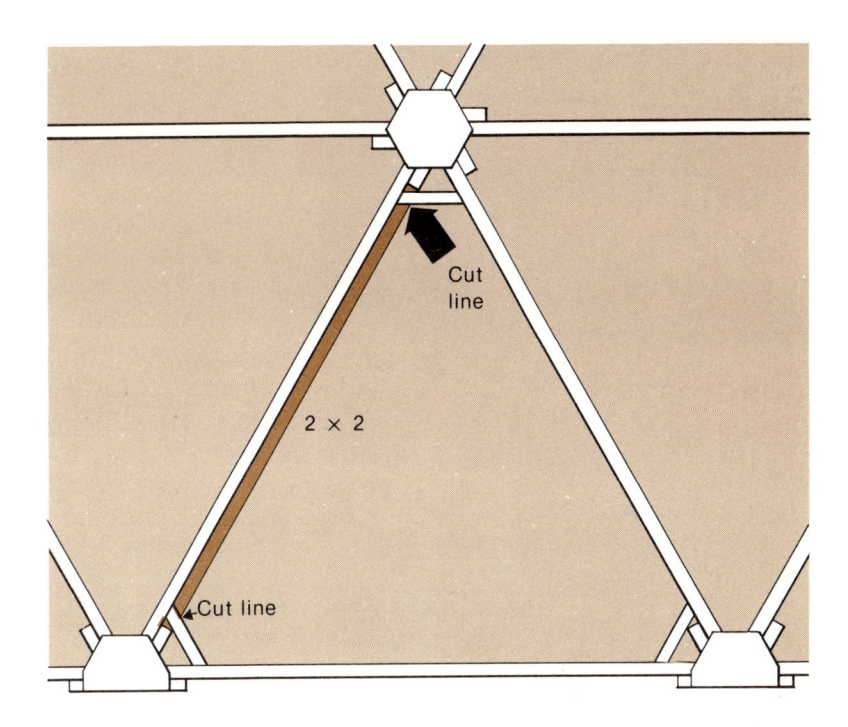

Figure 6-16. From within dome, position 2 x 2, then draw cut lines, using frame as a guide.

making sure that the 2 x 2's angles are correct, and that its length is a saw kerf width or ¼ of an inch less than the dimension indicated by the lines. Repeat this procedure for the remaining 2 x 2s of the door and vent.

Coat each 2 x 2 and plywood plate twice with redwood stain and let dry. Then hold the 2 x 2s in position flush against their partner struts in the dome frame. Insert heavy cardboard, at least 1/8 inch thick, between the 2 x 2s and struts, spaced intermittently down their full lengths. These temporary cardboard pieces provide

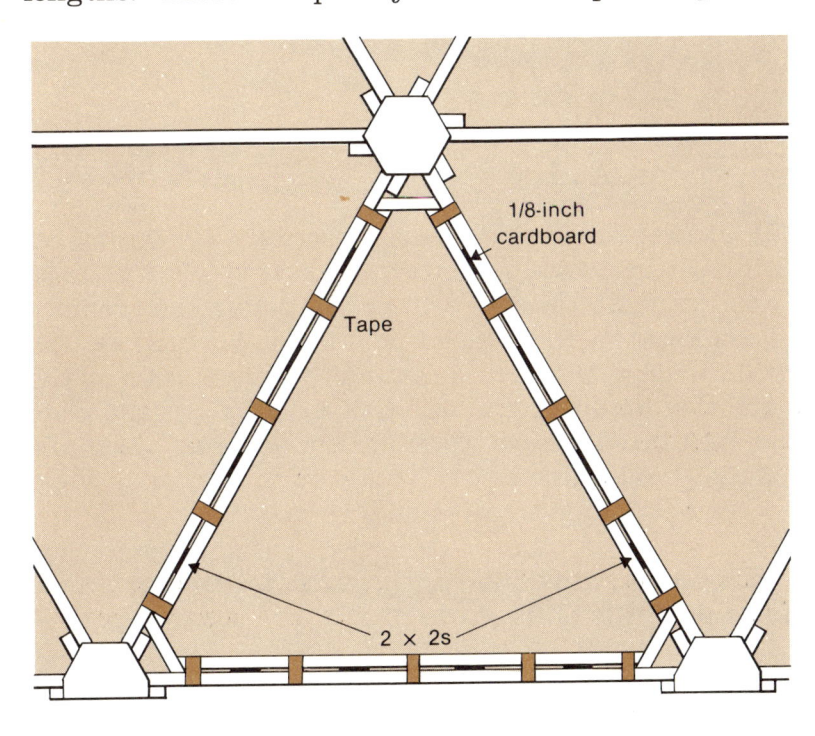

Figure 6-17. Hold 2 x 2s in place, insert cardboard spacers and then tape 2 x 2s to frame.

85

enough space between the door and frame (and vent and frame) to allow for the layers of film and tape to be affixed later. After inserting the cardboard, tape the 2 x 2s to the frame to hold them in position temporarily.

Each plywood plate connects to the outer sides of two 2 x 2s and holds them in place. The plates are larger than needed so they'll extend two inches beyond the sides and tops of the 2 x 2s. When the door and vent are closed, the plates overlap the struts and small corner 2 x 2s of the frame.

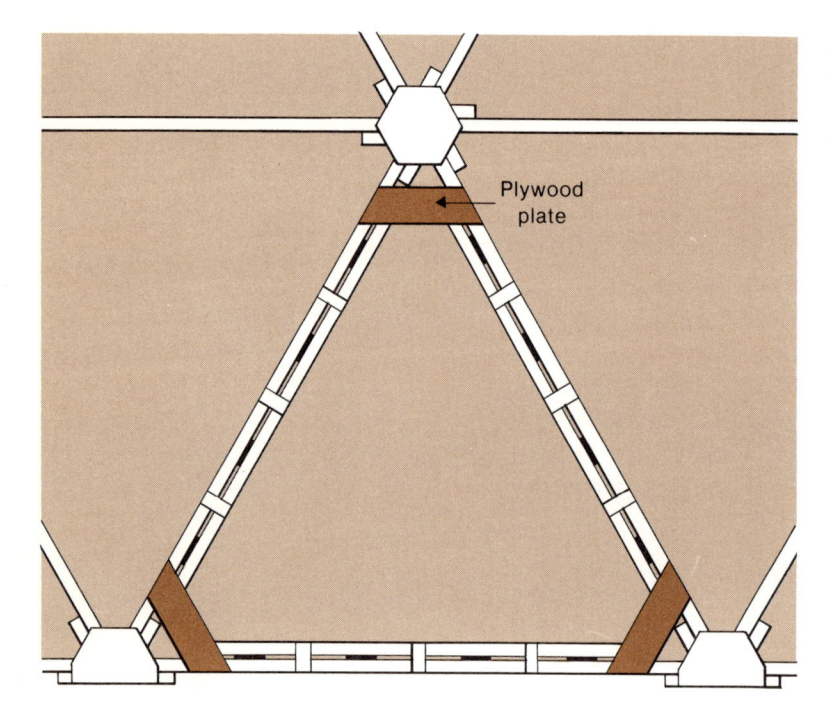

Figure 6-18. Place plywood plates on outside and outline on inner surfaces the two 2 x 2s to be attached to each plate.

Hold one plate in place just as described, and outline on its inner surface the door's two 2 x 2s to be attached to it. Do the same for the door's other two plates, then remove all 2 x 2s from their taped positions. Working on the ground, align one 2 x 2 at a time with its outline on the plate, then hammer one nail halfway through the plate and into the 2 x 2, as a temporary securing. Don't be concerned if the struts pivot easily on this one nail; when the entire triangle is formed, there won't be much movement.

Pick up the entire door and position it within its frame. If the door fits snugly, the 2 x 2s are secured permanently to plates. If too loose, too tight, or if not even a close fit, remove the bad plate — 2 x 2 attachment and resecure it. Generally, it's better to have the door a bit loose than tight because the door and frame (and vent and frame) can be sealed with weather stripping. If it's too tight, it simply cannot close. Also, keep in mind that there must be enough space for hinges.

To secure 2 x 2s to the plates permanently, drill starter holes (using a 1/8-inch bit) through the plates, partly into the 2 x 2s. Two holes per 2 x 2 connection are needed.

Figure 6-19. This is a view from the inside of the dome of the door in place.

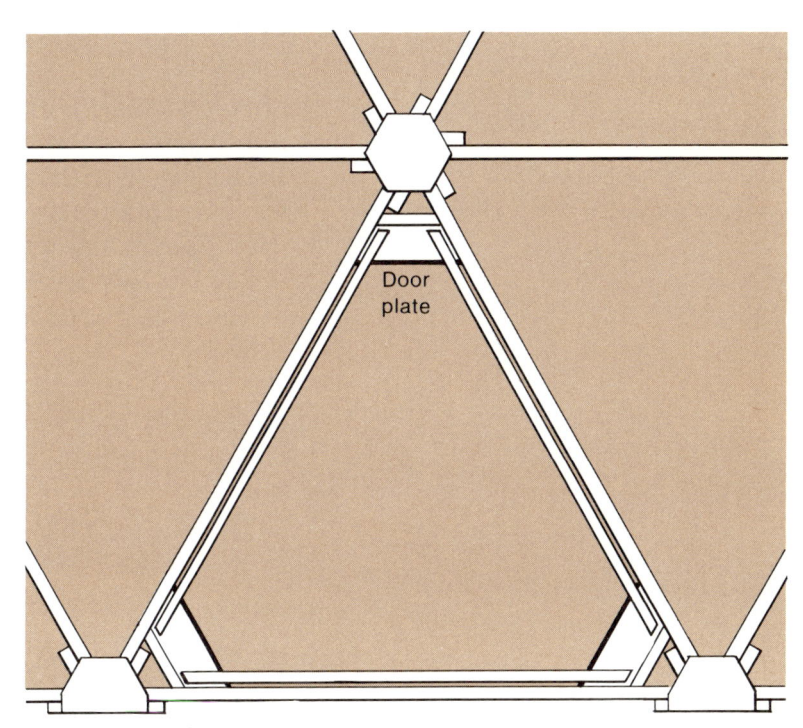

Secure plates to 2 x 2s with 1½-inch wood screws through each hole.

Now, you'll have to determine which way the door and vent will open, keeping in mind one rule: To reduce breezes that rush into the dome when door or vent is opened, and to prevent wind from blowing them out of your hand when they are opened, let them swing toward the north.

So, depending on the side of the dome the door and vent are located, the 2 x 2 to be hinged to the dome frame can be on either the left or right side.

When the door and vent are hung, they are impossible

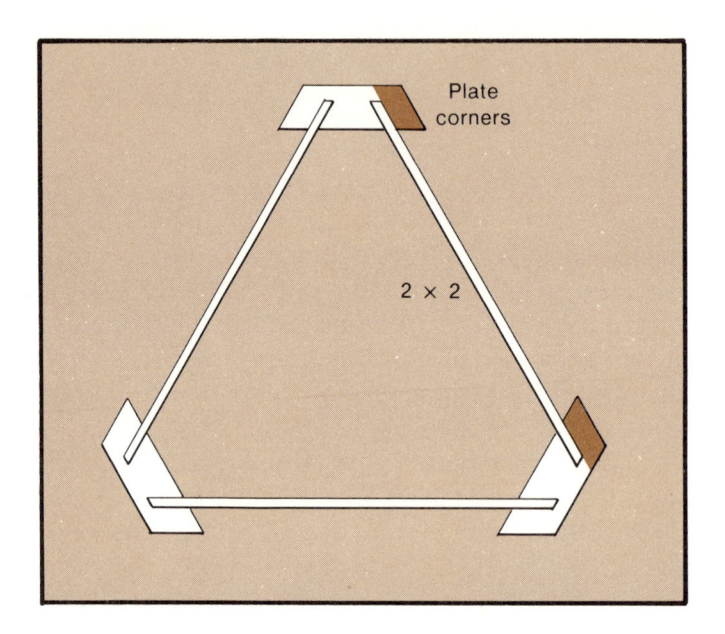

Figure 6-20. After considering winds, decide which way you want door and vent to open, then trim plate corners so plates are flush with 2 x 2.

to open if the two-inch overlap of each plywood plate extends beyond the 2 x 2 that is hinged to the frame. So, with a saw, trim the plates along this edge of the 2 x 2 so they'll be flush with the 2 x 2.

Having constructed the door and vent, there is nothing to do with them at this stage of the dome's construction. Put them aside while you cover and insulate the dome frame.

Chapter 7: Covering the Dome

You've come a long way, having turned a once vacant site into something resembling a jungle gym. After installing the polyethylene covering, the structure will look like a dome-shaped greenhouse.

The dome is covered with two layers of Monsanto "602," a resilient polyethylene film attached to the frame with staples and tape. It would seem simple and convenient to cover the dome with a single piece of film, but that's not possible without producing large creases and folds.

There are better ways to cover the frame. And all steps described in this chapter — installing the inner and outer film layers, packing parts of the dome with fiberglass insulation, and covering and hanging the door — should require no more than 15 hours for two people to complete.

For the exterior layer, you'll need the following three sizes of Monsanto "602" with a thickness of 6 mils:

- One 14- x 14-foot square to cover level four
- Ten rectangles, measuring 6 feet, 10 inches x 14 feet, to cover all of level three and most of level two. Each rectangle covers three triangles (a triad) of the dome
- Five 6½ x 6½ x 7-foot triangles, to cover the dome's five small triangles directly under the pent hubs of level two

For the interior layer, the same sections are cut from Monsanto "602" with a 4 mil thickness. All sections will be cut from sheets measuring 14 x 100 feet, folded in half to fit on a seven-foot wide roll. As you'll soon see, this fold can be a helpful reference point when cutting the film.

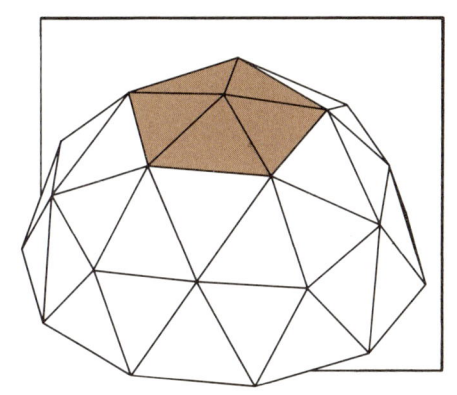

Figure 7-1. A 14 x 14-foot polyethylene square is used for level four.

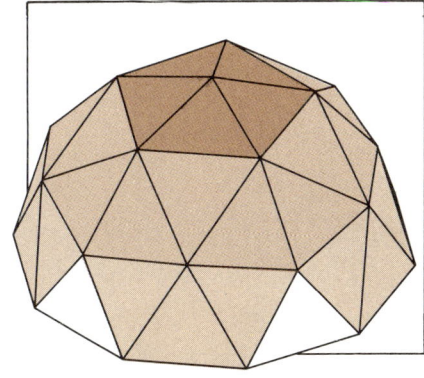

Figure 7-2. Ten rectangles cover level three and most of level two.

89

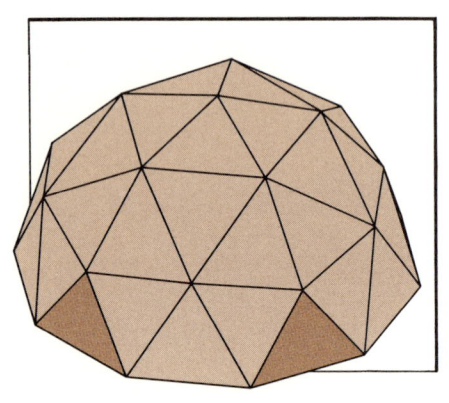

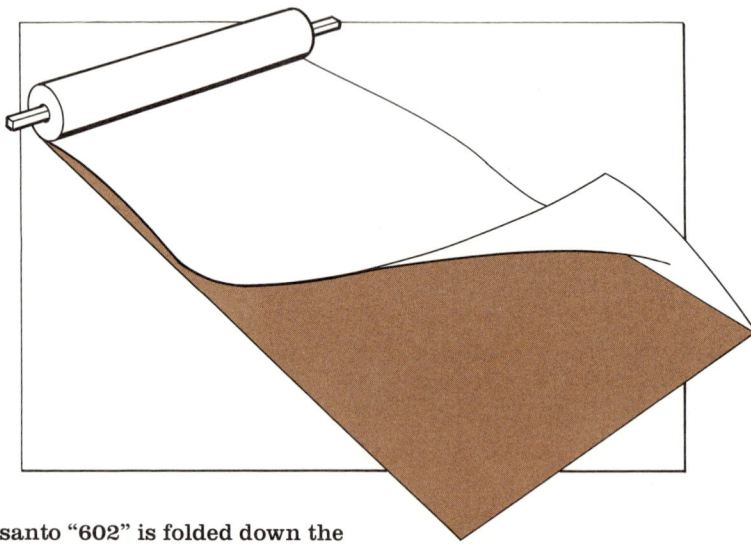

Figure 7-3. Polyethylene triangles cover small, level-two triangles.

Figure 7-4. The 14-foot wide sheet of Monsanto "602" is folded down the middle to form a manageable 7-foot wide roll.

COVERING PROCEDURES

Generally, the best time to build the dome is in early fall, when summer gardens are ending and it's advantageous to have a greenhouse. Temperatures usually have declined from their summer highs. And, installing the dome covering on a day 60°F. or cooler is ideal.

The film should be cut as you need it — not all sections in advance — to help keep it clean and avoid confusion. Spread the roll on a relatively clean surface, such as asphalt or grass. Then, using a good pair of scissors, slit the film into sections along predrawn lines. After making an initial cut, hold the scissors firmly in a slightly open position, walk in a straight path and slide through the film. This gives a smooth edge and takes little time.

Scotchrap 50 tape is used to seal and waterproof all seams, and to strengthen the film at points where excess wear and abrasion occur. These points include everywhere the film is stapled, meaning tape is needed at every permanent attachment. Also, tape is needed where hub struts and hubs connect because they meet at angles and have sharp protruding corners; here the outer layer of film must be covered on **both** sides with small squares of tape to prevent puncture.

In addition to taping, there's another way to help preserve film — leave slack at all sharp corners, even though the film is flexible and will compensate for most contraction. If ample slack is not left, the film will stretch unnaturally, become brittle and perhaps tear during cold winter weather.

Slack must be left in the centers of triangles and at points where hubs and struts meet. At these corners —

90

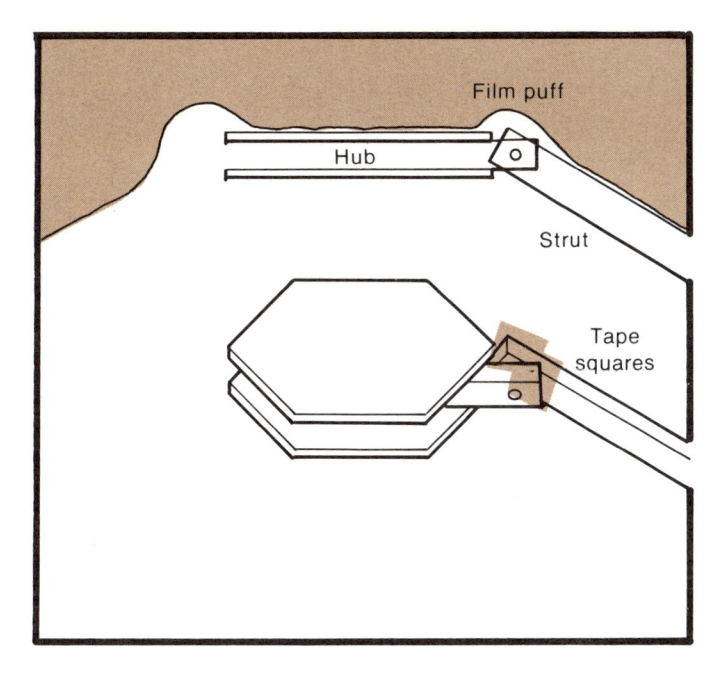

Figure 7-5. Leave slack "puffs" at points where hubs and struts meet (top); and use tape squares at sharp edges.

and nowhere else — the film should bellow out slightly like a puffed sleeve. When securing film to struts and top plates of hubs, lay it flush (but not taut) against the wood so seams can be taped easily to make waterproof seals.

It's best to leave ¾ to 1 inch of slack in each of the dome's triangles even if you're installing on a 60°F. day. If temperatures are higher, increase slack proportionately up to about 1¾ to 2 inches at 90°F. or more.

The film is extremely pliable — even if it is taut, you can push it in one inch. But this is not the way to gauge slack. To measure slack, gently press a finger against the center of each triangle until you begin to feel the slightest resistance; the distance you're able to press with virtually no pressure indicates the amount of slack.

Make sure film and tape are dry and clean before application; dirt, moisture and air bubbles impair the ability of the tape to adhere properly.

Never stretch the tape; if you do, cold weather contractions will cause it to pull away from the film as it tries to resume its natural shape.

ATTACHMENTS

A temporary attachment is used to hold film in place while it is positioned correctly and adjusted for slack, before the film is attached to the frame permanently. Make temporary attachments by stapling through the film into the center of a strut's outer-facing side; use an additional staple at each hub.

BUILDING AND USING A SOLAR-HEATED GEODESIC GREENHOUSE

The wrap-around attachment is permanent and is used only on a strut that has no other film from the same layer already attached to it. (Film attached to a strut from one side prevents film from the other side from wrapping around the strut.) To make a wrap-around, first attach the film temporarily in position and slacken it properly. Then trim the film's edges, leaving a 2-inch excess to wrap flush over the strut's outer-facing surface and down its side. Apply squares of tape to the film edge every four inches, then staple through tape and film into the strut's side twice through each square. Where hub struts enter hubs, the film must be slit to allow film on top of the hub to be secured directly to the hub plate.

Figure 7-6. Wrap-around attachment with tape squares stapled in place.

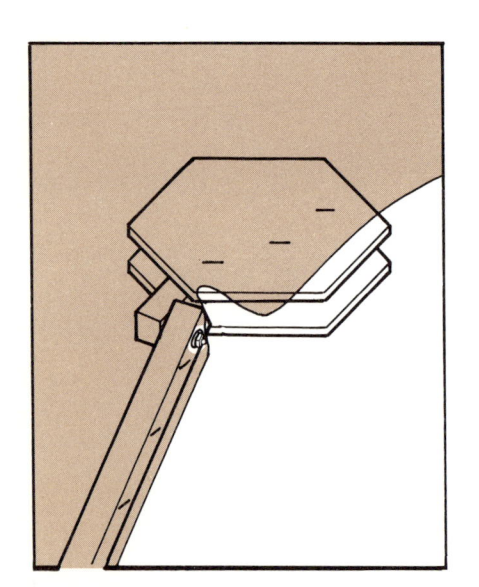

Figure 7-7. Where hub strut enters hub, slit film so it lays flat, directly on top of hub plate. Bolt should push through hole in film.

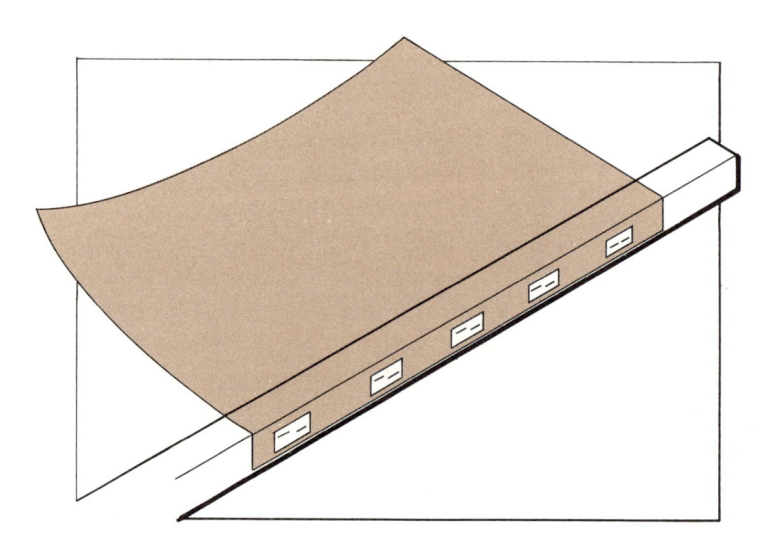

When film is wrapped around, then stapled, to a strut, pressure on the film is distributed along a large surface area of the strut. This type of attachment is ideal because it adds strength to the dome covering. The wrap-around attachment would be still stronger if it were continued around the bottom of the strut, but this is not done because it would create pockets for water to accumulate and rot the wood.

Although the wrap-around attachment is used wherever possible, it is not practical for all parts of the dome. Therefore, there is another way of attaching film to the frame.

A seam attachment is used only on a strut that has film from the same layer wrapped around it already from the opposite side. This attachment serves to secure film to the strut and creates a waterproof seam between the two sheets of film.

Make a seam attachment by first attaching film temporarily in position and slacken it properly. Then trim the film's edge so it covers just three-quarters of the strut's outer-facing surface.

Apply a tape strip to the film so that half the tape covers this new sheet's edge and its other half covers the first sheet of film attached to the strut. This tape strip must run the entire length of the strut, and three-quarters across the hub above it and the hub below it. After taping, follow the path of the tape from the higher end to the lower, and staple twice every three inches through the tape, both sheets of film and into the wood.

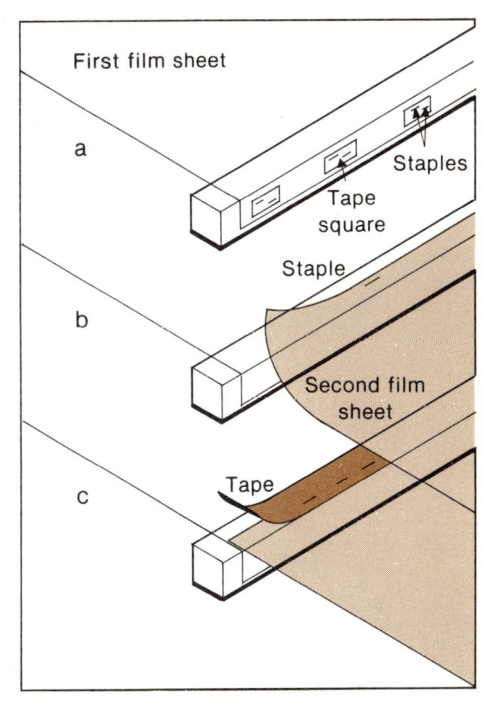

Figure 7-8. (a) Strut with film attached, (b) second piece attached temporarily, and (c) tape and staples applied to both pieces.

COVERING LEVEL FOUR

The outer layer of level four is covered with the 14-foot square sheet of film. Take your roll of 6-mil Monsanto "602" and unroll 14 feet without unfolding the film. Use a tape measure to check this length along each edge and, at 14 feet, draw markings with a felt-tipped pen. Draw a line connecting these marks, using a smooth length of 2 x 2 as a straight edge. This line, parallel with the end of the film, forms the 14-foot square. Cut along the line using procedures described earlier in this chapter.

Having done this, mark the center of this 14-foot square and use this mark to position the film properly over level four. The center is along the film's fold, seven feet in from either end. Find the center spot and cover it with a square of tape that should bend over the fold.

Looking up through the dome frame, you can see how important ladder positioning is to successful covering; the task requires work at specific points in a sequence that calls for a lot of moving around. Covering the frame is much easier if two people work together from both sides of the dome, so round up a couple of friends and two ten-foot stepladders. Eight-foot stepladders can also be used, but smaller sizes make the job difficult.

If you have just one stepladder, you will have to move it

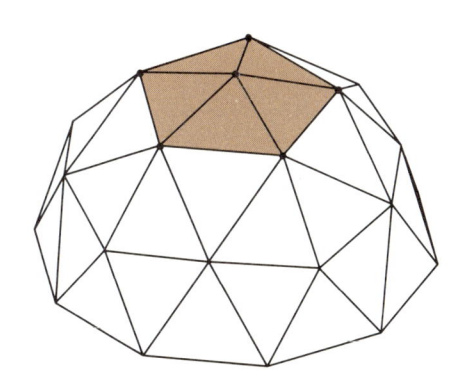

Figure 7-9. Level four.

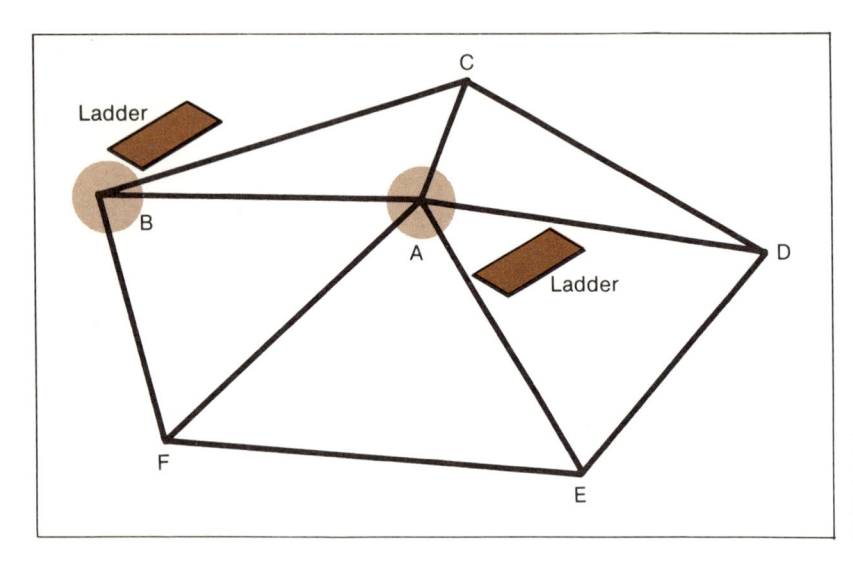

Figure 7-10. To start, place stepladders near hubs A and B. Hub B should be the northernmost hub in level four. The strut leading to hub B points nearly due north.

back and forth to positions about the frame. But, if you have two stepladders and two friends, one person should be on a stepladder opposite you; the other friend should remain on the ground, calling out the positions for sections of the film covering and handing up materials as needed.

Position the stepladders as indicated in Figure 7-10 so you and a friend are as close as possible to hubs A and B, respectively. You both should have hammers and loaded staple guns with you. The film, still folded so it's easily managed, is handed up to you. Unfold the film and drape it over the five small triangles of level four. Place the film center, marked with tape, directly over hub A, the top center hub. Face what was the inside of the folded film

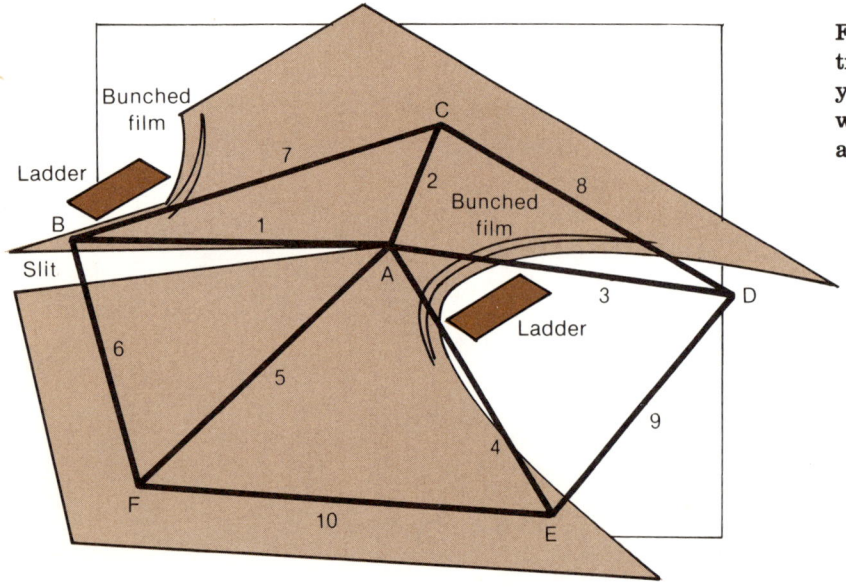

Figure 7-11. Bunch film so triangle 3-4-9 is uncovered while you work on level four. Slit is made when film is cut for strut 1 wrap-around attachment.

94

down, toward the dome, because it's cleaner than the outside. You won't be able to cover the triangle through which you are working, so bunch the film in front of you, and leave triangle 3-4-9 uncovered for now.

Using three staples, secure the taped center of the film to the center of hub A. If your staple gun is not heavy duty, it may not be able to drive staples fully into the plywood; in this case, shoot the staples partially into the wood, then gently hammer them the rest of the way. Throughout the dome covering, staples must always be driven fully into the wood.

Proceed to secure the film to strut 1: lay the film atop triangle 1-2-7; it should be wrinkle free, but **not taut**; leave slack as described earlier. Attach the film temporarily to struts 1, 2 and 7; then trim the film edge and make a wrap-around attachment to strut 1.

Make a cut only far enough over so the film comes over the top and down the side of strut 1. When you reach the end of this strut that is nearest hub A, cut inward or closer to the strut so there's only about 1/2-inch overhang. If your cut is too far outward, leaving too much excess, you might find that when you make the final seam attachment of level four, the film will not align.

Strut 2's attachment is different, and it's used on only a few struts in the entire dome (struts 2,3,4 and 5). First, move the second ladder near hub C, then apply a strip of tape to the film resting on strut 2 and hubs A and C. Here's how to do this:

At hub A, unroll about three feet of tape; hold onto the end of the tape and pass the roll to the person at hub C, who should extend the tape until there is enough to cover three-quarters of hub C, the entire strut 2 and three-quarters of hub A. Don't cut tape from the roll yet; instead, apply the tape to the top of hub A, then reach across to strut 2 and gently pat the tape in place while your friend keeps it aligned. Continue down the strut as far as you can; your friend on the second stepladder finishes the remaining portion of strut 2 and hub C, then cuts the tape from the roll. Remember to apply the tape properly; **never** stretch it and deliberately leave slack (puffs) in the film near the meeting points of hubs and hub struts.

Once the tape is applied, staple through it, the film and into the wood every four inches. To complete attaching of the outer layer of film to this first triangle, make a wrap-around attachment to strut 7.

TAPE PROBLEMS

When taping the film, a few things you didn't plan on may occur:

1. Tape may be misaligned, if applied either to the wrong side of a strut or off-line. To correct this, gently pull the tape off the film and reposition it.

2. Air bubbles may develop between the tape and film. If noticed during application, lift the tape and reapply it; if noticed after entire strip is applied, puncture the bubble or staple through it and smooth the tape.

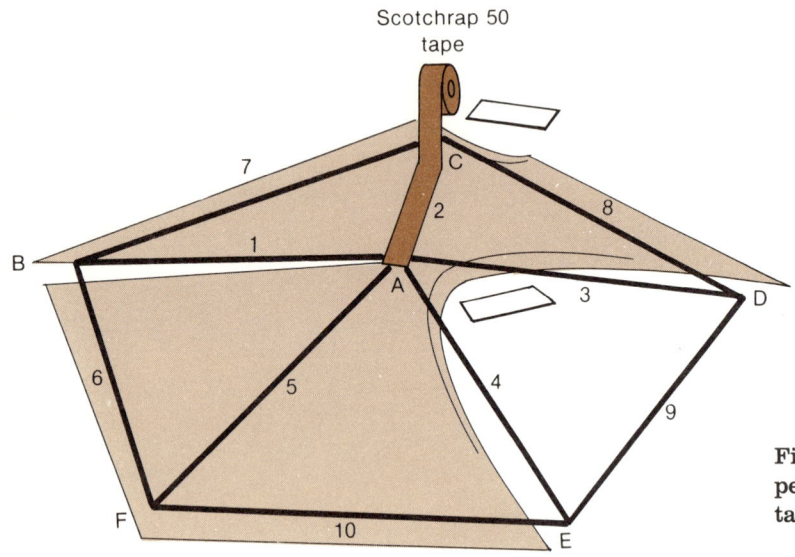

Figure 7-12. At hub A, pass roll to person at hub C, who can help apply tape to hub C and strut 2.

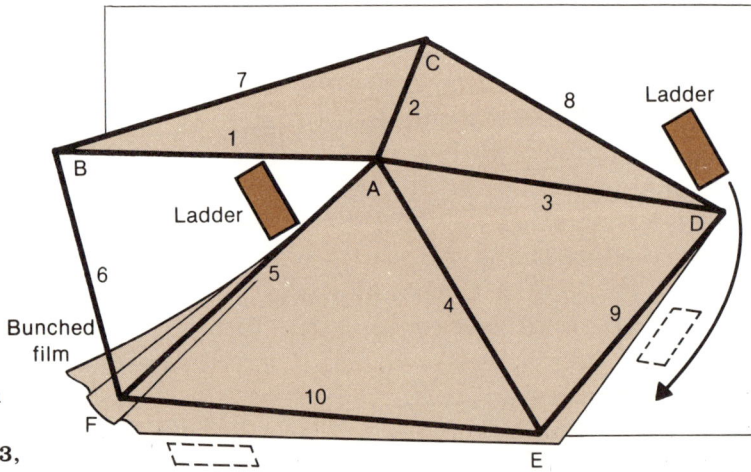

Figure 7-13. One stepladder is in triangle 1-5-6; move the other as indicated to secure film to struts 3, 8, 4, 9, 5 and 10.

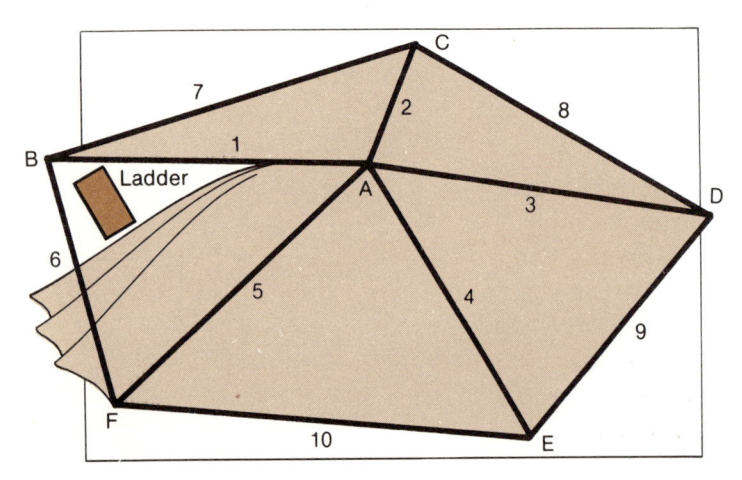

Figure 7-14. To start strut 1 seam, place stepladder just near enough to reach hub A, then align film along top half of strut.

96

COVERING THE DOME

Continue around level four. Position stepladders as shown in Figure 7-13, and follow procedures described earlier to secure film to struts 3, 8, 4, 9, 5 and 10. After attaching film to strut 10, return once more to strut 1, which already has film wrapped around it. Here, the first seam in the dome covering is made, enclosing level four. This is a complicated task because the ladder in triangle 1-5-6 must be moved from place to place.

To make the seam, position a stepladder as shown in Figure 7-14, just near enough hub A for you to reach it and staple into its top surface. With some of the film bunched in front of you, align as much of the film along the top half of strut 1 as you can, and attach it here temporarily. Don't make a permanent attachment yet because your position in the middle of the triangle makes it impossible for you to judge whether you've left enough slack and aligned the film correctly.

Climb off the stepladder and, from the other stepladder outside hub B, align the bottom half of the film edge so level four is fully covered (Figure 7-15). Check to see if the top half is still well aligned. If it's not, climb up and try again. If it is, climb up to attach the top half permanently:

Working with polyethylene is made easy with friends, positioned so they can help align film as necessary.

Figure 7-15. From hub B, align bottom half of film so level four is covered. Once film is aligned and upper half is taped and stapled, complete seam attachment, also from hub B.

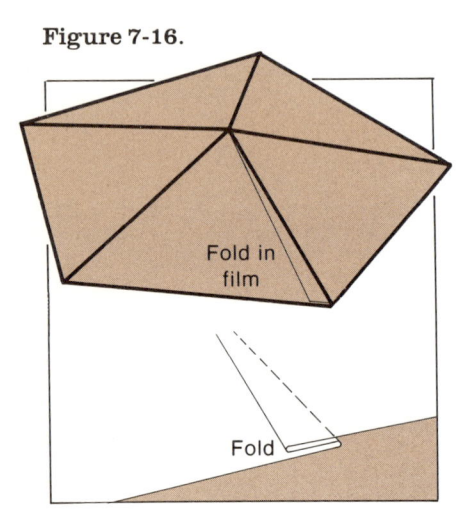

Figure 7-16.

BUNCHING FILM

When covering horizontal struts, the film may bunch inadvertently. This is caused by film that was misaligned when connected to the two vertical struts of a particular triangle. To correct this problem, fold the film over so it lies flat and staple it to the strut. It's not pretty, but if the film is folded down (Figure 7-16) so rain and snow won't be caught in it, the dome covering will still be effective.

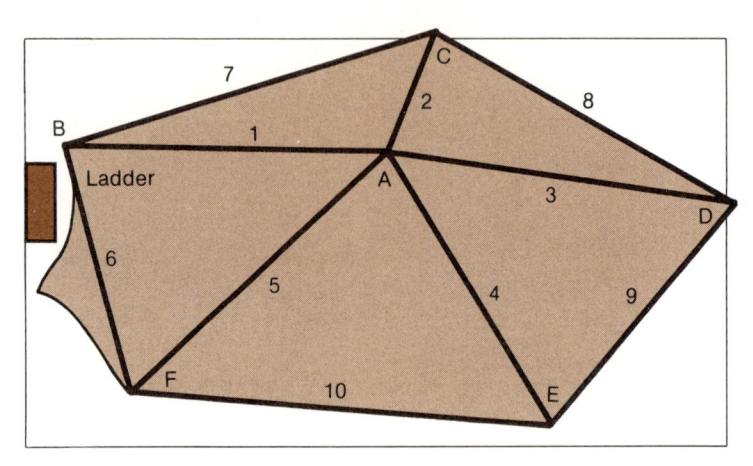

Trim the film (down to the temporary staple farthest down the strut) so, when the film is attached, this cut edge runs down the center of the strut, overlapping the first film covering by about one inch. It must be cut this way so when tape is applied to film atop the strut, half the tape will adhere to the first covering and half to the overlap, creating a waterproof seam.

Apply tape from three-quarters across hub A down to the temporary staple farthest down the strut, and staple every three inches through the tape and both film coverings into the frame.

From back on the second stepladder just outside hub B, you or your friend should next attach the film temporarily to hub B and the bottom half of strut 1, then trim the film's edge and continue taping and stapling down as before, completing the seam.

The last film attachment made on level four is the wrap-around attachment on strut 6. When this is done, trim excess film along the bottom edges of all horizontal struts (6, 7, 8, 9 and 10) and along the outer facing surfaces of hubs, leaving film over the upper three-quarters of each plywood hub plate.

COVERING LEVEL THREE

Having completed the most difficult dome covering maneuvers, you can now begin work at a more reasonable height, on the outer layer of level three, then level two. The same techniques are used as before, meaning the tasks should be familiar and easier to accomplish.

Level three has 15 triangles, covered by five rectangular film sheets, each measuring 6 feet, 10 inches by 14 feet. Every sheet covers a triad (three triangles), and each triad has two small triangles flanking a large triangle; this pattern appears five times in level three.

98

COVERING THE DOME

99

Cutting Film

As an extra precaution, measure a triad to make sure a 6-foot, 10-inch sheet of film will cover it adequately. If you made some design changes, you may want to adjust the size of the film sheets used to cover level three triads.

To determine the size film sheet you need, extend a tape measure from the center of strut 10's top edge to the bottom edge of hub G's plywood plate and add two inches for slack. The distance should be about 6 feet, 10 inches. If so, cut a section this size from the film roll, giving you a sheet that measures 6 feet, 10 inches by 14 feet. Remember to measure down both edges of the roll. Draw the cut line using a 2 x 2 as a straight edge to assure a parallel cut.

Triangles formed by the dome struts are convenient references in descriptions of how to cover the dome. Level three triangles include not only the vertical struts connecting levels two and four, but also the horizontal struts of these levels.

For example, in the first triad (a three-triangle section) of level three, strut 10 is one of these horizontal struts; on it is a wrap-around attachment from level four. Because of this, the new film from level three is secured to strut 10 with a seam attachment. But, film is secured to four other struts in this triad — 13, 14, 15 and 16 — with wraparound attachments. Struts 11 and 12 require no attachments.

To secure the film to the frame, first position stepladders as shown in Figure 7-19, as near hubs E and F as possible. Find and mark the midpoint of strut 10, then open the new film sheet, facing its inner-folded side toward the dome. Cover the triad with it, so the crease remaining from the fold extends from the midpoint of strut 10 down to the center of hub G.

Make temporary attachments to struts 10, 13, 14, 15 and 16, positioning the film so its top edge extends one inch above strut 10, and so all three triangles have the correct amount of slack.

Then climb off the ladder and examine the sheet to see that it's laid out smoothly and aligned properly. If it's not, readjust it. If it is, trim the film's top edge so it lies flush with — and is three-quarters of the way up — strut 10. Then tape and staple the film to the strut, using a seam attachment.

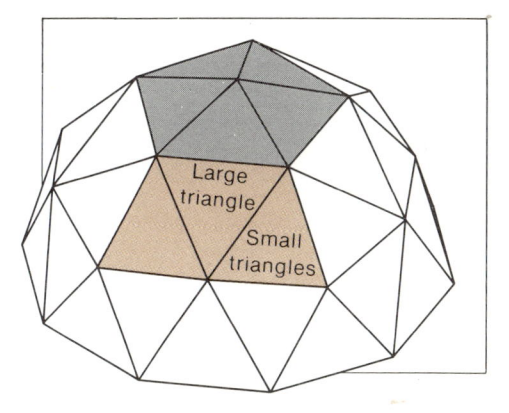

Figure 7-17. Each rectangular film sheet covers two small triangles and one large triangle (a triad).

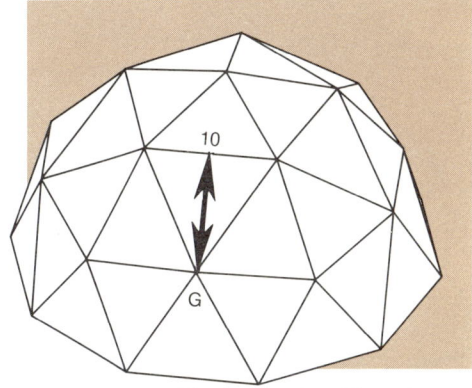

Figure 7-18. To determine film sheet size, measure from strut 10 midpoint to bottom of hub G and add two inches for slack.

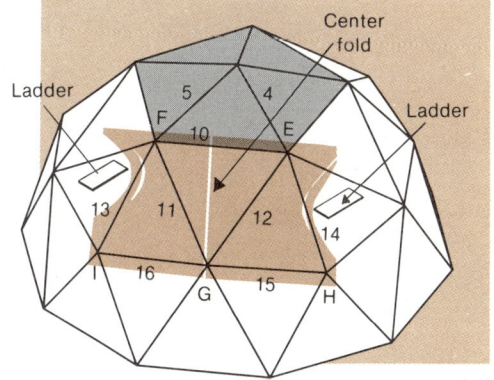

Figure 7-19. Cover triad so film center fold or crease extends from strut 10 midpoint to center of hub G.

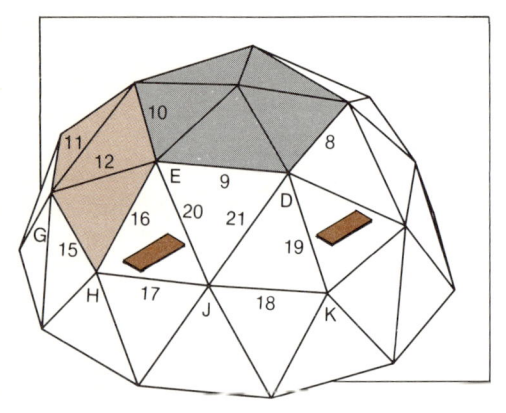

BUILDING AND USING A SOLAR-HEATED GEODESIC GREENHOUSE

100

Figure 7-20. To cover next level-three triad, place stepladders near hubs D and H.

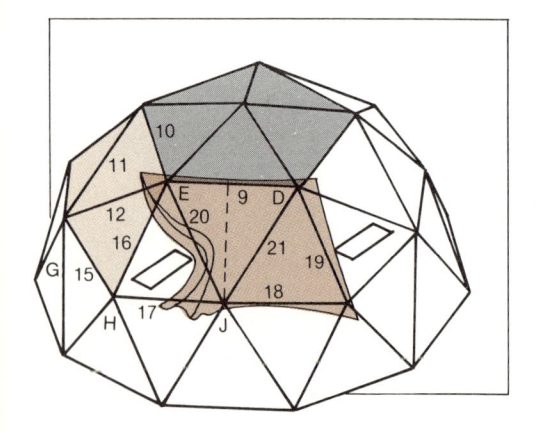

Figure 7-21. The person inside triangle 16-17-20 should bunch film to leave part of triangle uncovered.

Continue around the triad, making wrap-around attachments on struts 13, 14, 15 and 16. (Remember to apply protective squares of tape near wood points.) Then complete securing the film sheet by applying a strip of tape first to the film where it rests directly atop hub F, then down strut 11 to hub G; and, from hub E, down strut 12 to hub G. The tape strips enhance the film's strength and add to the dome's uniform appearance.

The four remaining triads of level three are covered similarly, the only difference being the next three each have three wrap-arounds and two seam attachments, and the last has two wrap-arounds and three seams. As more and more of the frame is covered, the need for more seam attachments increases.

The more triads that are covered, the more difficult it is to install film because access to parts of the frame becomes increasingly limited: stepladders can not be placed inside the dome within areas that are covered due to the lack of height clearance, and stepladders placed outside the dome near these covered areas are too far away to allow a person with short arms to reach certain hubs and struts. The dome's spherical shape is the culprit here, but the problem can be minimized by positioning stepladders as shown in the illustrations.

For example, to cover the next triad, position the stepladders as shown in Figure 7-20, as near hubs D and H as possible. Measure and cut a film sheet to cover this portion of the dome, then make temporary attachments to struts 9, 18 and 19. The person inside triangle 16-17-20 (you or a friend) should bunch the film in front of himself, to leave part of the triangle uncovered. Then, he should climb off the stepladder, move it aside, position the film to cover all of the triangle 16-17-20 and check to see if the film is laid out properly. Once satisfied the film is positioned as it should be, move the stepladder back inside triangle 16-17-20, climb up it, and, with the help of a friend on the other stepladder, form a seam attachment along strut 9. Also, start a seam as far down strut 16 as you can.

To complete the seam on the lower half of strut 16, you will have to reposition the ladder outside hub H as shown in Figure 7-22. Once you complete this seam, however, you won't be able to reach hub E easily; so, before you do this, make wrap-around attachments on struts 18 and

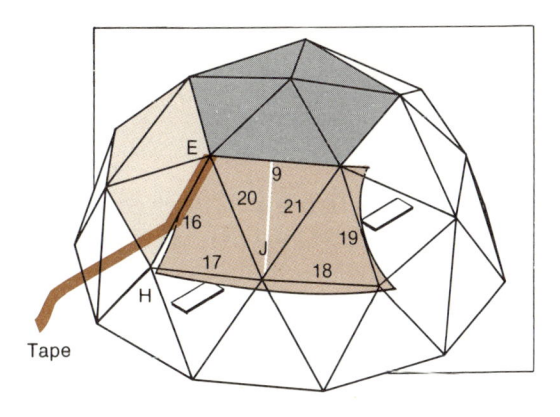

Figure 7-22. Place stepladder outside hub H to complete seam on lower half of strut 16.

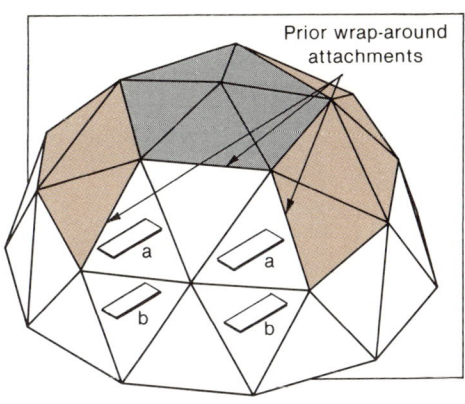

Figure 7-23. To complete last level-three triad, first place stepladders inside dome (a), then outside (b).

19, and apply a strip of tape to the film down the full length of strut 20, as was done earlier on struts 11 and 12. Then apply tape on strut 21 in the same manner, and, finally, secure the outer hub plate to hub E.

Now, you can move the stepladder near hub H outside triangle 16-17-20 to complete the seam on strut 16 and form a wrap-around attachment on strut 17. Trim film where necessary.

These same procedures should be followed for covering the next two triads of level three. The last one, as mentioned earlier, requires two wrap-around and three seam attachments, and calls for the stepladder movements shown in Figure 7-23. The seam on each side of this last triad is made the same way the seam was made for strut 16. Be sure to secure outer hub plates as you go around the dome installing film; you won't be able to reach all hubs easily later.

OUTER HUB PLATES

To attach outer plates to the hubs, first find the plates and hubs that correspond with each other. Remember you numbered them earlier; just match up the numbers.

Puncture the film on top of each hub at the center point where a ¼-inch hole was drilled and through each of the three points where starter holes were drilled for screws. Align the holes of the outer plate and hub, and secure them with a ¼-inch bolt through the center and three 1-inch No. 8 wood screws through the other holes.

If bolts or screws do not fit through the holes easily, simply widen the holes by redrilling.

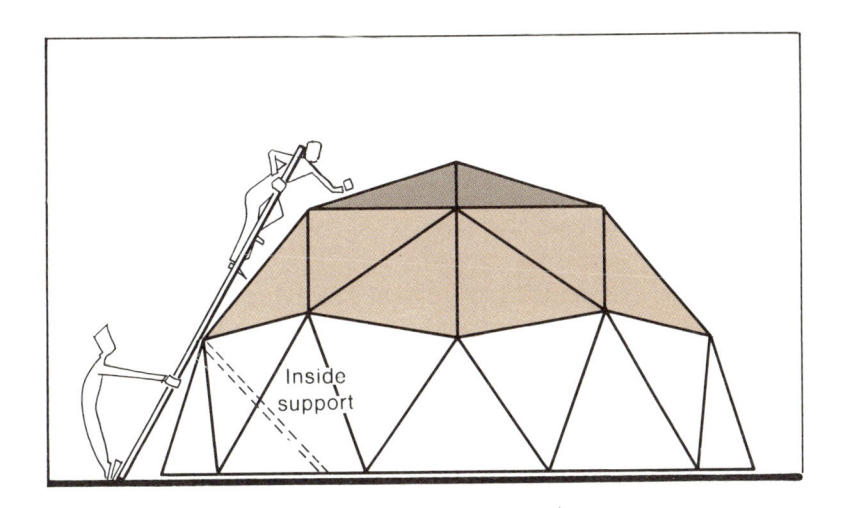

Figure 7-24. For hard-to-reach spots, ask a friend to hold a ladder, leaning against a hub, preferably a hex hub. Protect dome by placing a rag between ladder and film; buttress supporting hub from inside with a stepladder or 2x4, or ask friend to push hub. Never lean a ladder against a strut.

With levels three and four covered, you may see flying insects gathered near the dome top. They were living at the dome site and, when disturbed, flew straight up. Don't worry about them; if they don't leave, the ladybugs you bring to the dome later will have a feast.

COVERING LEVEL TWO

With exactly half of the dome's outer layer in place, you can put your stepladders aside and forget about acrobatics for now. Covering level two is easier because it's more accessible. Level two is made of five triads, separated by five small triangles. Although inverted, the level two triads are the same size as those for level three.

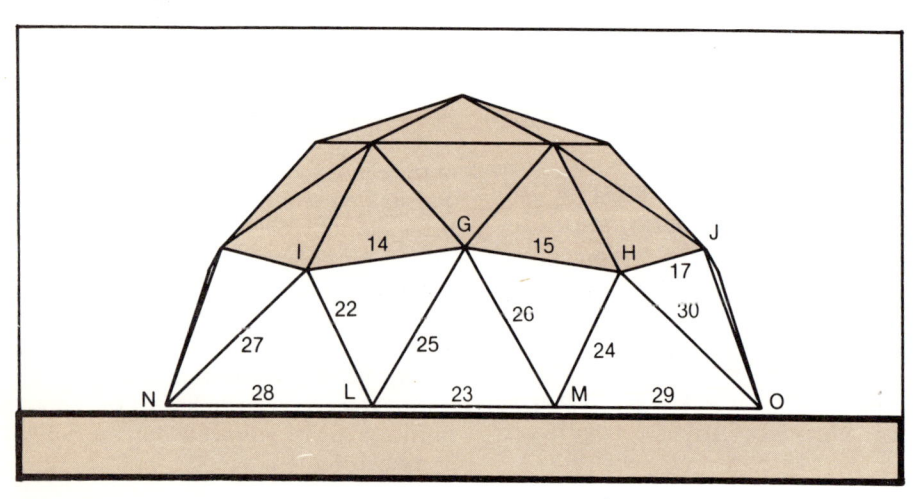

Figure 7-25. The first level-two triad to be covered is bordered by struts 14, 15, 22, 23 and 24.

To cover level two, start with the triad bordered by struts 14, 15, 22, 23 and 24. Cut a piece of film for it using the same measurements as level three (6 feet 10 inches x 14 feet). Then attach the film temporarily as before. Check to see that it's aligned properly with enough slack, then start securing the film to struts and hubs permanently.

Struts 14, 15 and 23 receive seam attachments; struts 22 and 24 have wrap-arounds; struts 25 and 26 have tape strips running down their full length of film covering. And the four other triads are covered the same way. Strut 23 and all other base struts are covered with seam attachments because the underground polyethylene is secured to them already.

COVERING THE DOME

103

Having completely covered all level two triads, you must use seam attachments on all struts of the remaining five smaller triangles. When covering these triangles, the most difficult step is cutting the film to the correct size. The desired dimensions are:

From the top of hub I's outer plate to the center of base strut 28 should be 5½ feet; from hub I to the bottom of hub L should be 6½ feet; from hub I to the bottom of hub N should also be 6½ feet. From the far edge of hub L to the far edge of hub N should be 7 feet.

Before cutting the film, be sure these dimensions coincide with those for each of the five remaining triangles of your dome. If not, cut the film, as necessary, to achieve the needed dimensions. If the frame dimensions are the same as those stated above, follow these steps:

Unroll 5½ feet of film and unfold it to make a 5½ x 14-foot section. Outline with a felt tip pen three sections on the film, as shown in Figure 7-26. Cut the film along these lines to make three sections, each large enough to cover a small triangle.

Figure 7-26. Using the dimensions shown, outline three sections on the film. Once cut, the sections are placed on small triangles, then trimmed.

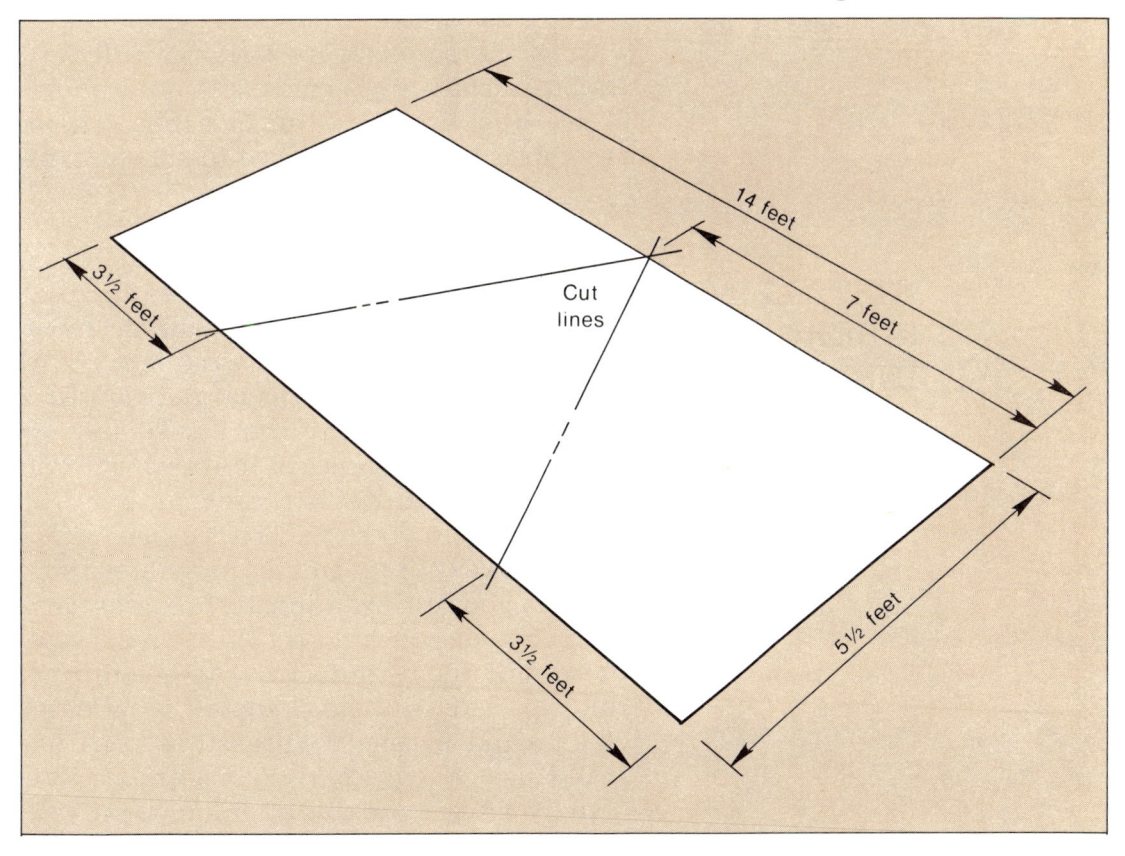

TROUBLESHOOTING

If instructions are followed carefully, there's not much that can go wrong when covering the dome. Probably the worst error is to cut film from the roll incorrectly. If film intended for level four or a triad of level three or two has been cut incorrectly, it's possible these large pieces can be recut into the proper size for small level two triangles. If no film remains to cover these small triangles, particularly the last northern triangle, buy an extra small roll of film or gather scraps of film and tape them together on both sides with Scotchrap 50. Patched film may be used on northern triangles because light transmission is not a factor on this side of the dome.

With one of these film sheets, cover one of the dome's small triangles; make temporary attachments, then check to see if the film is aligned properly with enough slack. When satisfied with the alignment, trim the film and make seam attachments on all three struts to enclose the triangle completely.

Cover three more triangles this way. Leave one triangle open on the northern side for air circulation. If the dome is fully enclosed and temperatures increase sufficiently, the air inside expands and a seam might pop. If it's a warm day, don't be surprised if temperatures exceed 100°F. inside the dome.

Cut a slit for the door (the large triangle of level two with securing posts on each side) so air can circulate throughout the dome while you install film on the small triangle that still remains open. If you made few errors when cutting the film, you'll have enough left to finish the dome's outer covering. Also slit the vent covering to help keep inside temperatures down. Both slits should extend from four inches below the highest 2 x 2 used to frame out each triangle to within six inches of the strut directly below it.

Once the outer layer of film is fully attached to the frame, install any remaining outer hub plates, then check the entire dome to ensure that all necessary protective tapes have been applied to sharp corners.

INSTALLING FIBERGLASS INSULATION

Twenty-one of the dome's triangles are to be packed with 3½-inch thick fiberglass insulation. To identify them, stand at the due south base strut and go two base struts over in both directions; the large triangles above each of these base struts in levels two and three are the northernmost triangles of the dome left **un**insulated. All triangles to the north of these four **are** insulated, including the two northernmost triangles of level four. The door and vent are insulated separately later.

When you first examine the fiberglass insulation on its 15-inch wide roll, it looks thin. That's because it's compressed by the manufacturer to one third of its 3½-inch thickness for shipping. Install it as described in this chapter and, in time, it will assume its natural thickness.

Because you install the fiberglass while inside the dome, it's best to do this after sundown; try it during the

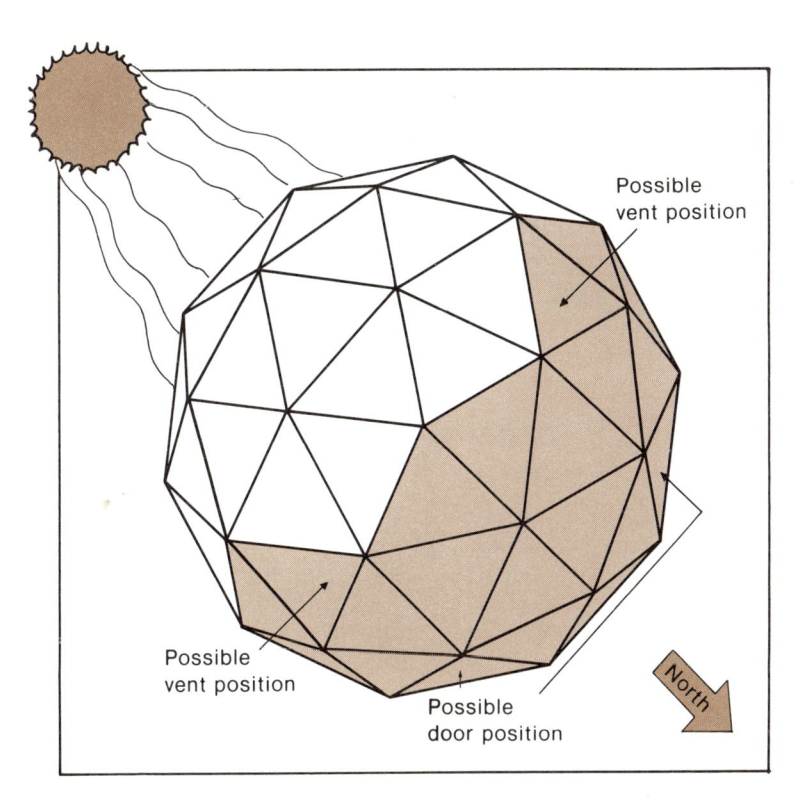

Figure 7-27. The dome's 21 insulated triangles are indicated in color. Possible door and vent positions are also identified as reference points.

day and hot temperatures will change your mind quickly. At night, illumination is needed, preferably a large fluorescent light; a fan to circulate air is also helpful.

The dome should be dry during fiberglass installation to reduce condensation on the inside surface of film. To dry the dome, open the door and vent slits and circulate air with a fan a few hours before you begin installing fiberglass and the inner film layer. Keep the fan on while working.

Place all six fiberglass rolls just outside the dome, but don't leave them there overnight if the installation takes more than one evening. Instead, store them in a dry place, but not in the dome because you don't want glass fibers in your garden.

Each of the 21 triangles to be insulated is packed, one at a time, with 15-inch wide strips of insulation, with the foil vapor barrier facing in toward the garden. It is not important to pack the triangles in any particular order; and the techniques used for one triangle apply to all others.

Select any triangle to be insulated, measure the distance along a strut from the bottom edge of a top hub to the top edge of a bottom hub, and add six inches to arrive at the length of fiberglass you need. Then cut it from the roll, using a utility knife or large pair of scissors to cut through the fiberglass and the foil vapor barrier at the

INSTALLING FIBERGLASS

One word of caution: Be careful when installing fiberglass insulation. Many people are allergic to fiberglass and experience itching, skin rash, and discomfort from direct contact with fiberglass. Wear gloves, suitable clothing, safety goggles and a face mask to prevent inhalation of fibers. Use these precautions and you should have no problems or discomfort. When finished, wash with cold water to keep your skin pores closed while you remove any fibers.

105

Hold the first 15-inch wide fiberglass strip as shown, then staple cardboard lip to strut.

Place the next fiberglass strip flush against the first, with cardboard edges overlapping.

same time. Make sure all cutting is done outside the dome to keep fibers out.

There are two 1-inch wide, folded cardboard strips on both edges of the foil vapor barrier. Unfold them and bring the entire 15-inch wide strip into the dome. Hold it along the strut just measured, allowing the lip of the cardboard strip to overlap the strut. Staple through the lip into the strut, first in the middle, then once every three inches, working toward both ends. Finally, trim the edges of the fiberglass strip so it fits snugly within the triangle.

Fiberglass trimmings should be separated from the paper backing and stuffed between the hubs' plywood plates; the greatest R-value is achieved when the entire space between film layers is packed with insulation. Also, make sure all fiberglass edges in all triangles are flush against strut edges and flush against each other.

The next fiberglass strip in the triangle is placed next to the first and secured to struts at its top and bottom. To do this correctly, first measure along the unattached edge of the first strip, add six inches to arrive at the length you need for the second strip, cut the fiberglass and bring it into the dome. Position it flush against the first strip, unfold its cardboard edges to overlap the first, then trim the fiberglass as necessary and staple it to the

Examine completed triangle insulation carefully to ensure that there are no clear spaces between strips and struts.

struts at its top and bottom. Continue this way until the triangle is fully packed.

Walk outside the dome and look at the insulation. If clear spaces can be seen between any strips or struts, the fiberglass is not packed tightly enough. Reposition the strips closer together and fill any remaining gaps with trimmings. Fully packed triangles retard heat loss the best.

Continue insulating the 21 northern triangles in this same manner, except in level four; because fiberglass is suspended horizontally here, the strips flop down unless they are supported during installation. To keep the strips in place, cradle them with a series of strings spaced intermittently the full length of the triangles' struts. These strings are secured to the struts with staples.

INSTALLING THE INNER COVERING

The inner covering is a layer of 4-mil Monsanto "602." This polyethylene is installed in nearly the same way as the outer layer, but the task is easier because attachments on the inside of the frame are not as prone to stress as the outer ones. So, inner attachments needn't be perfect, as long as the seams are tight. Second, all the struts

BUILDING AND USING A SOLAR-HEATED GEODESIC GREENHOUSE

108

INSUFFICIENT FILM

If you miscut a lot of film and don't have enough for the inner covering, be sure to use full, correctly cut sheets on the southern side where light transmission is important. Light transmission is not a factor on the northern side, so you can try to salvage some miscut film by installing it there. Small pieces may be used after taping them together on both sides with Scotchrap 50. Or, you can use standard polyethylene that may be left over from the underground insulating. Of course, you can always buy an extra roll of 4-mil Monsanto "602" to complete the inner covering.

COVERING THE DOOR AND VENT

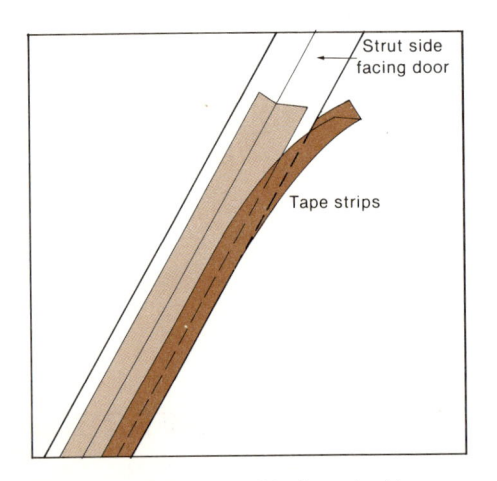

Figure 7-28. For added protection, apply two strips of tape on door frame struts and 2 x 2s.

and hubs are easily reached from the inside so ladder movements are less frequent and less complicated.

A few different techniques are used inside. For example, because insulation is attached to the struts on the northern side of the dome, the inner film layer can't be wrapped around struts. In all parts of the dome, simply secure the film to the inner-facing sides of struts, using seam attachments. Using wrap-arounds would create pockets for water to accumulate.

Due to gravity, the inner film layer must be attached to every strut or it will bow downward. This is unlike the outer layer of film, which drapes over some struts. When the inner layer is not secured with a seam attachment, attach it to the frame by stapling twice through tape squares, spaced every six inches along the film, and into the struts.

After applying the inner layer of film to the frame, slit the door and vent triangles as before so you won't trap yourself inside your brand-new geodesic dome. After slitting, trim the film's edges so wrap-around attachments can be made to the upright struts of the door frame and vent, and to their six tiny frame-out 2 x 2s. To make this securing easier, first slit both film layers at the points where struts connect to the small 2 x 2s. Tape must be used to seal these slits. On the door frame, this means applying six 6-inch long tape strips, each extending from the inner to the outer side of each strut, and covering the side of the frame that faces toward the door.

To protect the film further against abrasion caused by opening and closing the door, apply tape on all three door frame struts and the three small 2 x 2s. Apply two strips of tape down the full length of each of these struts so the strips align in the middle of the side facing the door and cover this side completely. Each strip also should fold over to cover part of the struts' inner and outer edges.

With the film and frame fully protected, you can begin covering the door. If possible, use a large, miscut section of film that would otherwise be wasted. Or you can use new film from the roll, but try to conserve as much as possible because film is needed for the vent, which is covered the same way the door is covered.

Lay the door, with its outer side down, on top of a 6-mil

COVERING THE DOME

109

thick film sheet. Using the door as a guide, cut the film into a triangle large enough to cover the door and make wrap-around attachments. Enough extra film should be left around the plywood plates to allow the film to be draped easily over each entire plate, including the ends of 2 x 2 lengths secured to them. Don't staple the outer layer to the door yet.

Next, place the door atop a 4-mil film sheet, and cut it to the same size as the outer layer. Then pack the door with fiberglass insulation (with its foil vapor barrier facing inside) and, having done this, wrap the 4-mil layer around the door's struts and plates. Secure the film to the door's struts with wrap-around attachments, making sure the film remains flush against all wood surfaces. Film bunching keeps the door from fitting snugly, so staple the film all around the door so it conforms to all the door's corners and bends.

Once the inner layer is attached, the outer layer should be installed, using wrap-around attachments. The outer layer also must lie flush against all wood surfaces. In order to protect this film from abrasion, the 2 x 2s of the door should be taped the same way the door frame was taped.

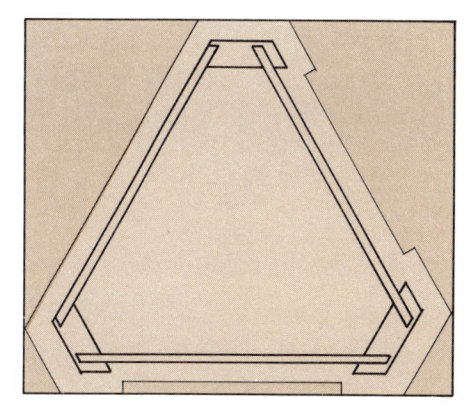

Figure 7-29. Lay the door on a film sheet, then cut film as indicated, leaving enough excess for wrap-around attachments.

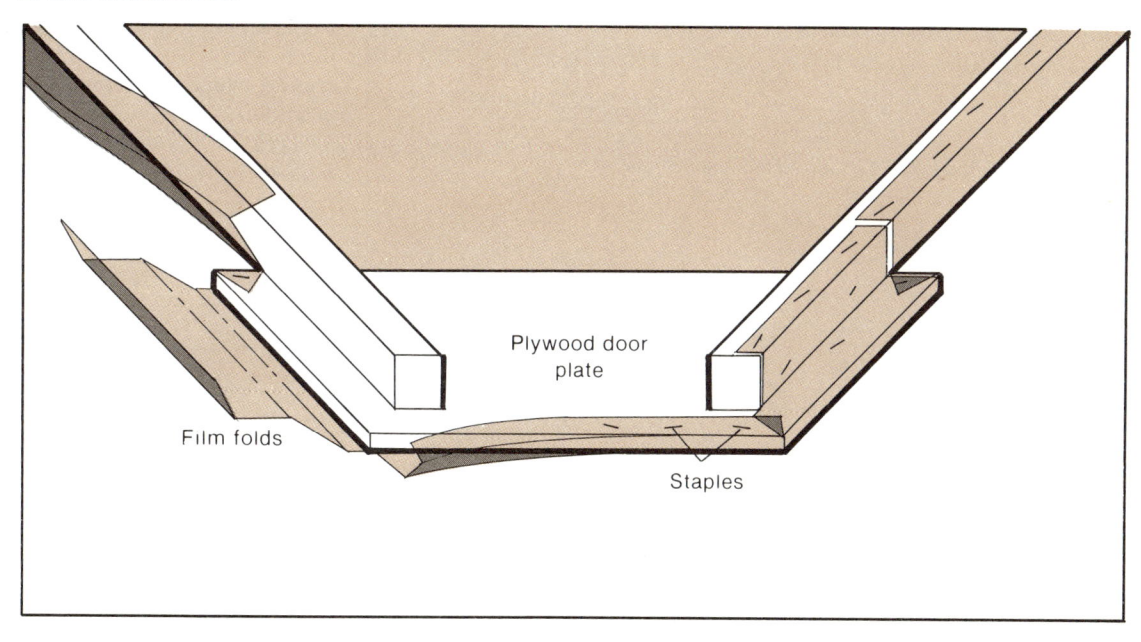

Figure 7-30. Secure the outer film layer to door, using wrap-around attachments. Film must be flush against all surfaces of 2 x 2s and plywood plate in order for door to close. Note that, for clarity, inner film layer and insulation are not shown in this illustration.

HANGING THE DOOR AND VENT

A MISFIT DOOR

There are two problems you may encounter when covering and hanging the door and vent. First, they may no longer fit into their frames once insulated and covered with film. The only remedy is to readjust the size of the door (that's right, start again), which is why you should keep alert and mindful of correct dimensions when building dome parts.

Second, the door may not open, or may open with difficulty. Probably the hinges need realignment to correct this.

With the door lying on the ground, outside up, position two 3-inch door hinges a foot and a half from each end of the door's 2 x 2 to which they'll be attached. The hinge plates should be secured to the 2 x 2's outer side, with the hinge pivot pin as nearly parallel to the door edge as possible.

Before hanging the door, secure furring strips to the frame's inner surface with 1-inch wood screws every four inches, in a way that allows the strips to overhang the frame as much as possible. The furring strips, coated twice with redwood stain before they are used, serve two purposes: They are a doorstop and a mounting surface for heavy weather stripping (applied later). Therefore, the furring strips should be cut into six pieces to conform with the outline of the door frame. Having done this, position the door in its frame, secure the hinges and swing it back and forth to see how nicely it works.

The vent should be covered and hung the exact same way as the door.

To keep the dome door closed, use a hasp on the door's outer side that can be secured to the frame with a lock. To keep it closed when inside, use a hook on the door's inside that can be held to the frame with an eye. If you want to keep the door open sometimes, secure an eye bolt to one of the dome's outer hub plates, one located near the door's

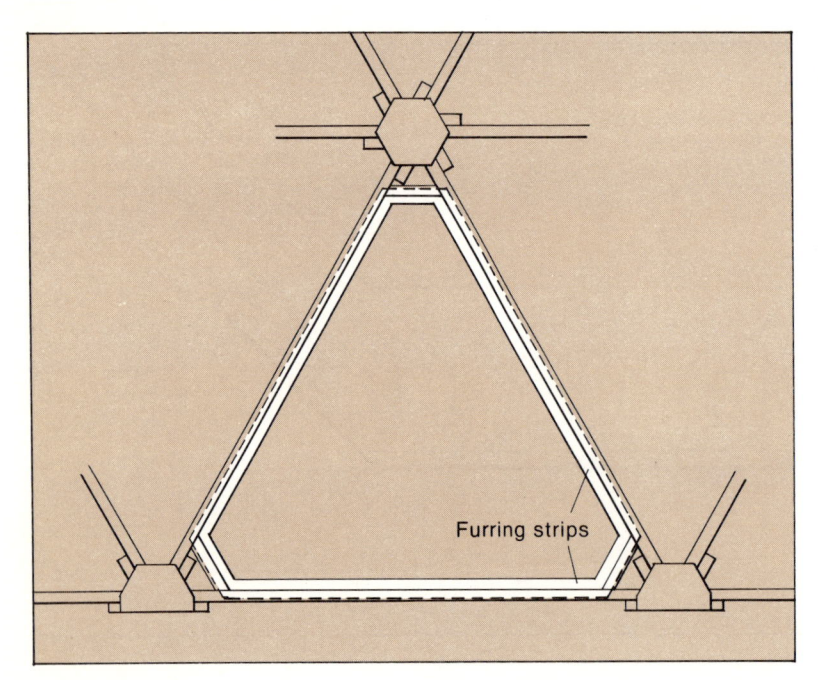

Figure 7-31. Secure furring strips to inner surface of door frame. Strips should overhang frame as much as possible.

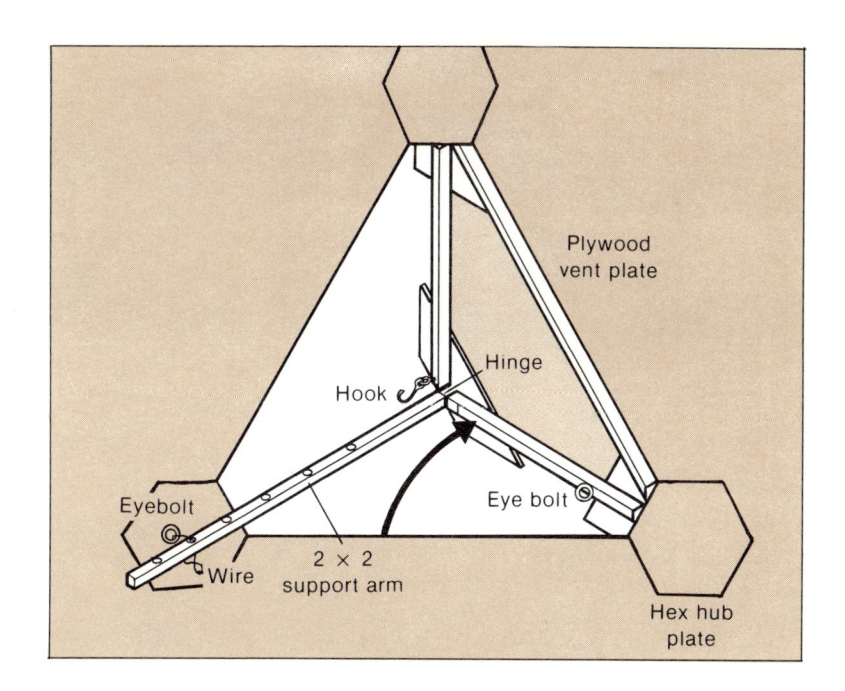

Figure 7-32. Use a 2 x 2 support arm to prop vent. A hook and two or three eye bolts may be used to secure vent and support arm.

edge when it's swung open. Then tie a short wire between the eye bolt and the door hasp. Cabinet handles may be added to either side of the door to make it easier to open or close.

The simplest way to keep the vent open is to prop it up with a length of 2 x 2, much the way the top of a grand piano is held up. The 2 x 2 may be designed to hold the vent at various levels. To make this prop, proceed as follows:

Attach a 2-inch hinge to one end of a 57-inch length of 2 x 2, and drill nine ¼-inch holes, spaced every six inches along its entire length. Cover the 2 x 2 with two coats of redwood stain. After it dries, attach its hinged end to the southernmost corner of the vent (not the vent frame). The 2 x 2 should be able to rest horizontally on the dome frame, flush against the inner side of the vent. The prop also swings open to stand against the southern corner of the vent frame.

Now install an eye bolt into the inner plywood plate of the hex hub in the southern corner of the frame. By securing a heavy wire to this eye bolt, and through one of the many holes in the 2 x 2, you can adjust the vent opening to different positions.

Another eye bolt may be added in the northern corner of the vent so the 2 x 2 can be tied up into its horizontal position, out of the way, when the vent is closed.

And a third eye bolt, or a hook, can be screwed into the vent's southern corner and secured to the eye bolt in the hex hub to secure the vent in its closed position. This prevents the vent from flying open accidentally.

Completed dome-shaped, geodesic greenhouse at Fordham University. You can expect the film to contract during cold periods and to remain slack during warm weather.

After completing the dome covering and accessories, turn your attention to the underground polyethylene that is probably still exposed in certain areas. You can protect the polyethylene, and make the dome more attractive, by covering it with soil left over from the trenches. It's most effective if you create mounds of soil, about six inches high, flush against the dome's frame — inside and outside — except, of course, near the door.

Chapter 8: Maintaining and Operating Your Dome

Depending on the season, different methods are required to maintain proper dome temperatures. During winter, maximum heat retention is desirable so the dome garden can thrive despite freezing temperatures outside. In summer, ventilation is necessary to remove excess heat. And, during fall and spring, when weather varies, flexible procedures are needed to maintain an environment that encourages food production.

The garden will be most productive if you grow the right crops at the right time of the year; in other words, select vegetables that are suited for temperatures attainable in the dome during various seasons. To help make these selections, check the planting schedules in Chapter 9. But, it's important that you understand now how to keep temperatures in the dome just right for your garden.

This means you'll have to be able to observe the range of temperatures within your dome at different times. To do this, you should get three thermometers — one that gives maximum and minimum readings and two common

PART ONE: TEMPERATURE MAINTENANCE

Figure 8-1. To get accurate temperature readings in the dome, arrange thermometers so they're shielded from sun.

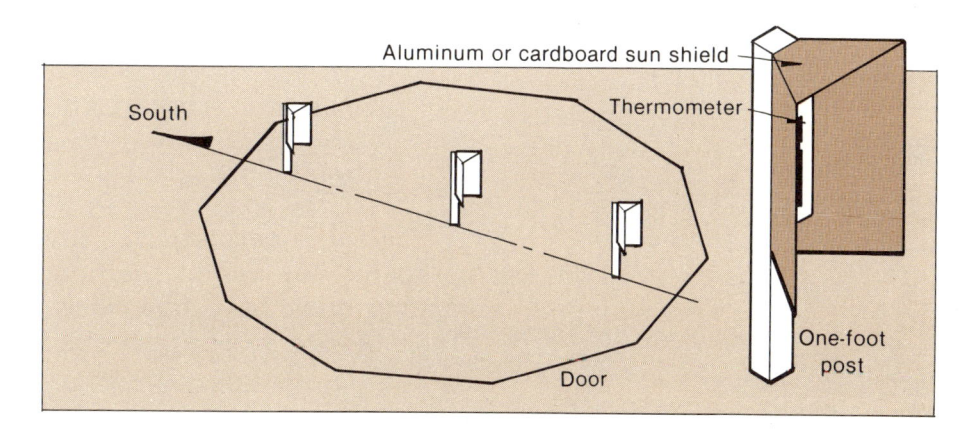

household thermometers. Place the max-min, which registers the lowest and highest temperatures since its last periodic check, in the center of the dome, about a foot above the soil. Place the second thermometer on the dome's southern side, the third on the northern side near water storage containers; place each on a stake one-foot above the ground. To achieve reliable readings, shade each thermometer with aluminum foil or cardboard.

WINTER HEATING

Using water storage correctly inside the dome is the most important step you can take to keep the dome warm enough to grow vegetables during cold winter months. The volume of water storage needed is based on the climate in which you live, as shown in Figure 3-7. Amounts stated in this figure are suggested first-year minimums. After observing your dome's performance during its first winter of operation, you'll be able to adjust this amount, as necessary, by adding or removing containers.

Of course, local climatic variations within regions are not accounted for in Figure 3-7, and your water storage needs may differ slightly from those suggested. But, as a start, follow the guidelines as closely as possible because they should be an accurate indication of water storage needed for your dome.

SETTING UP WATER STORAGE

By now, you should have decided which water storage containers you'll use. At least three different combinations are possible:

— Using only 30- or 55-gallon drums

— Using 30- or 55-gallon drums plus many one-gallon containers — a slightly more effective combination

— Using 30- or 55-gallon drums and a 725-gallon tank — a combination recommended only for those who want to raise fish

The containers selected must first be assembled and prepared for use in the dome. The 30- and 55-gallon drums must have lids. They may not be open barrels because each will be placed in the dome, filled with water and sealed shut to prevent evaporation. Before painting and placing the drums in the dome, inspect them for leaks for two reasons: You don't want to waste time painting unusable drums. And second, if you wait until after the drums are placed in the dome before finding a leak, there will be problems. You'll have to siphon water from the drum, using a hose extended outside the dome. And, when doing this, you can't prevent at least some leakage of water and drum remnants into the garden soil.

So, drums that look suspect should be filled with water near a sewer or drain to check for leaks; if one is found, discard the drum. If no leaks are found, drain the water from the drum and prepare it for use in the dome.

Before bringing these drums into the dome, wire brush them lightly to remove rust; make sure the exteriors are clean and dry; then paint them using two thin coats of Martin's flat black latex paint or a comparable substitute. Even though only the drum side facing the sun needs to be painted, paint the entire exterior because the exact positions of the drums won't be known until they're placed inside the dome.

The one-gallon plastic containers are not painted, but they are filled three-quarters full with water. The water is then dyed by adding Martin's flat black latex paint. Add the paint to the water in small doses at first; then continue adding until the water is just dark enough so that when each jug is held up to the sun, no sunlight penetrates.

The 725-gallon tank is used as is, and requires no preparation.

Using 30- and 55-Gallon Drums

Locate the drums one at a time near the dome's northern wall, and look at each drum as you place it; if it's not standing straight, move it aside while you level the ground under it. The drums should stand straight in a semi-circular line conforming with the dome's shape. They should be about 1½-2 feet from the wall to allow height clearance for the second row of drums that will be placed on top of them. Space must also be left for the door.

Once the lower drums are positioned, with a ½-inch space between each of them, they should be filled with

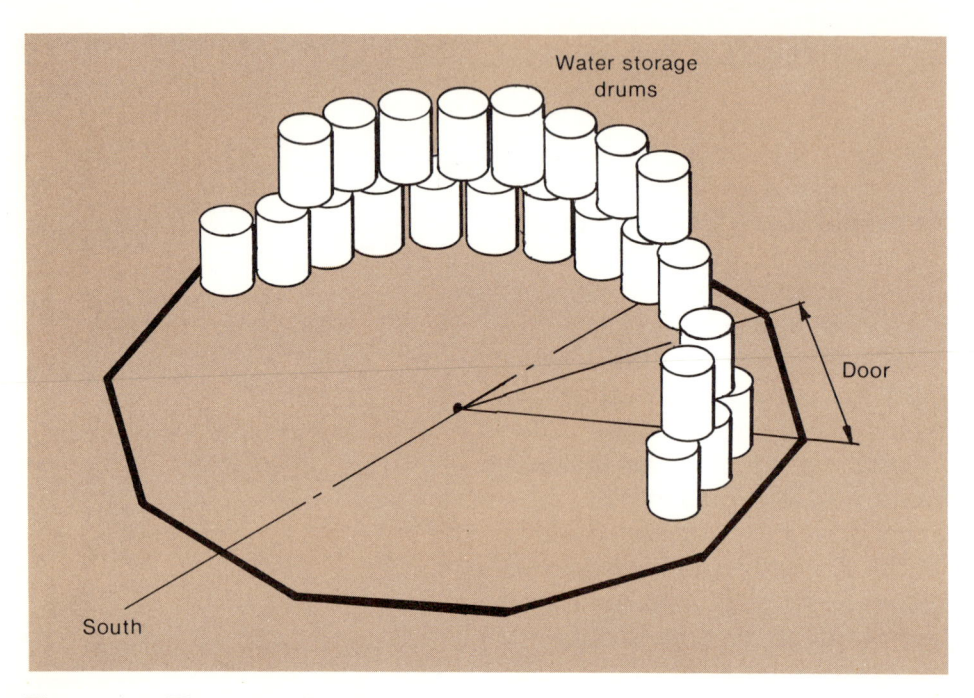

Figure 8-2. Place 55-gallon drums near the dome's northern walls, but leave space in front of the door free for exit and entry.

water, and allowed to warm before they are sealed. When full, each will weigh several hundred pounds.

After completing the bottom row, place the next on top in pyramid-like form, so each drum rests on top of two others, and then fill them the same way. Be sure to leave all spouts of bottom drums uncovered for access later. If you have difficulty steadying the upper row you may want to place small plywood blocks atop the center of the drums in the bottom level, then rest the upper drums on these.

For maximum stability, and to conserve gardening space, always place one more drum on the lower level than on the upper. Also, leave one lower level drum with nothing on top of it. A plastic garbage pail will be placed on this drum to hold water for use in the garden; this is explained in Chapter 9. Because the arrangement requires an odd number of drums, if your water storage needs (indicated in Fig. 3-7) add up to an even number, add an extra drum.

If you are mixing 30- and 55-gallon drums, use common sense and never rest a large drum on top of a smaller one. Otherwise, follow the procedure above, as if you used only one size.

Using Drums and One-Gallon Containers

If you decide to add one-gallon jugs to your water storage supply — the most effective water storage method described in this book — use the drums to provide the

Figure 8-3. Using a combination of 30- or 55-gallon drums and one-gallon jugs is an effective way to store heat for the dome.

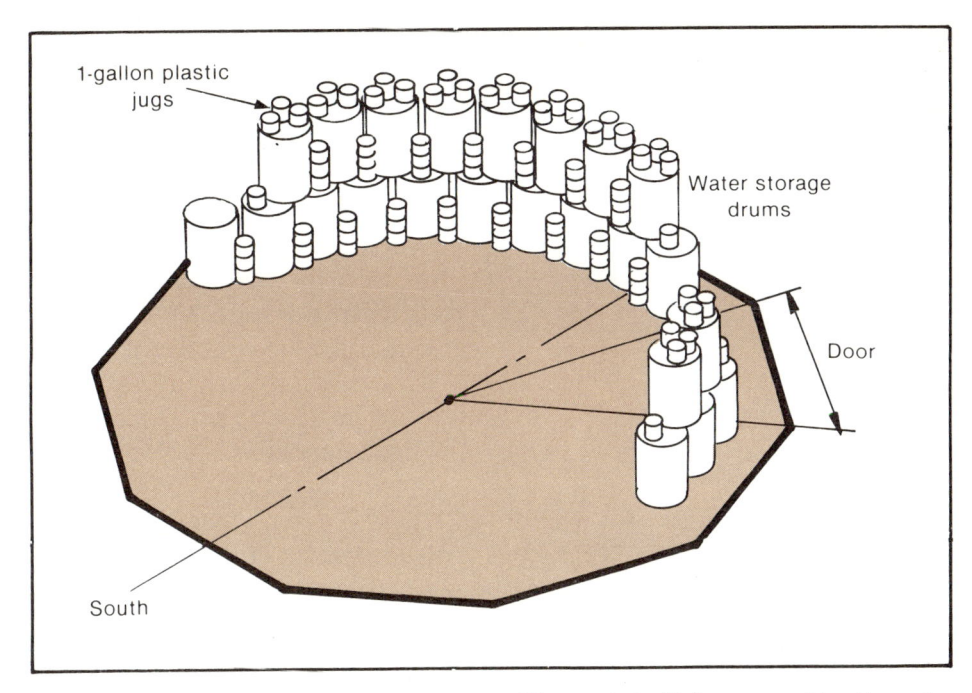

minimum heat storage needs and use the jugs for supplemental storage. The drums should be positioned the same way as before, except three inches apart instead of ½ inch, so jugs can be leaned into the grooves between the drums without shading them excessively. Place the jugs between drums on both levels, and on top of the drums of the upper level, using as many jugs as are available to you.

Should you decide to use the jugs as an afterthought, having already placed the drums ½-inch from each other, place them first on top of drums, then lean them into the grooves. Shading from the jugs will reduce slightly the effectiveness of the water storage, but the net result of adding the jugs is favorable.

Using Drums and a 725-Gallon Tank

The large tank should be used only if you plan to raise fish because it uses a lot of space and, although it holds a great volume of water, its surface area equals little more than three 55-gallon drums. Therefore, the 725-gallon tank's heat storage contribution is equivalent to only about 200 gallons.

The tank should be inside the dome already; if not, remove film and a strut from near the door so it can fit through. Before placing the tank near the dome's due north base strut, level the ground and place it on a 1-inch thick styrofoam sheet large enough for the tank to settle into uniformly. If you don't want to buy a five-foot square of styrofoam, use a layer of small styrofoam pieces from packaging.

Center the tank on the styrofoam, and fill it with water to within an inch of its brim. Making the water dark enough for heat absorption is explained in Chapter 9.

Drums comprising the rest of heat storage capacity should be placed on both sides of the tank, using either method described earlier.

REDUCING INFILTRATION

Infiltration is the movement of air in and out of the dome through cracks in its covering. If seams are taped properly, the dome probably loses less heat through infiltration than any other greenhouse design; this is because of its uninterrupted double-layer cover that continues 2½-feet underground.

To reduce infiltration at the dome's vulnerable spots — around the door and vent — apply weather stripping liberally. Mount thick foam weather stripping on the wooden strips attached to the inside of the door and vent frames, and to the inner side of the two-inch overlap of their plywood plates. Apply a thinner weather stripping along the outer edges of the door and vent 2 x 2s.

A good way to determine how effectively your weather

Figure 8-4. Add weather stripping along furring strips attached to door and vent frames and to plywood plates.

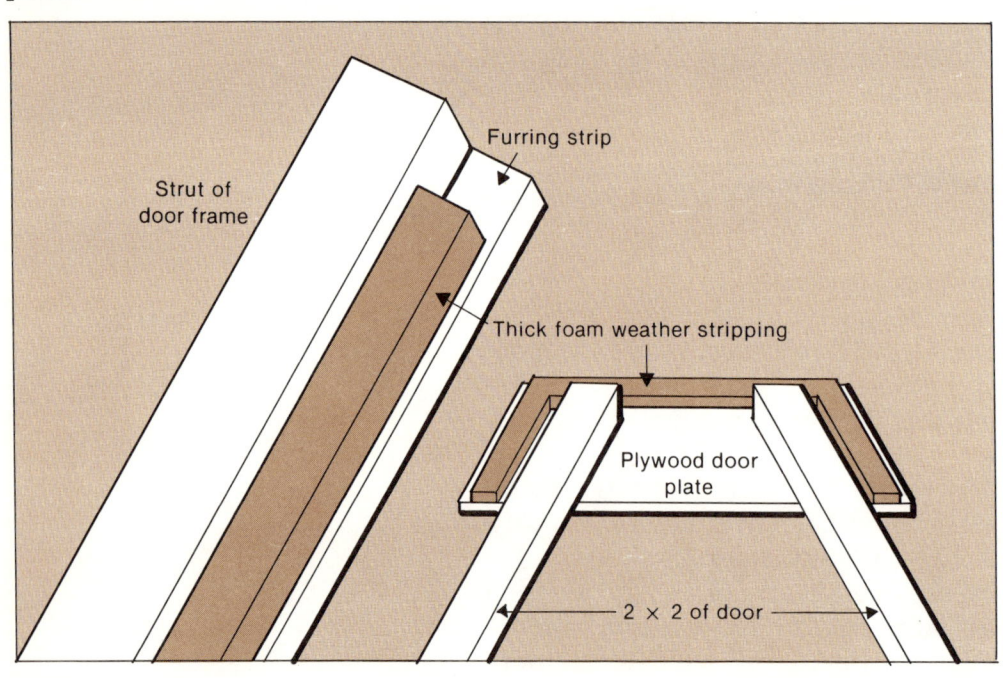

stripping reduces infiltration is by moving a lighted candle slowly around the weather-stripped cracks of the door and vent. If the flame flickers, air is entering.

In addition, when cold weather sets in during late fall, and the vent is not needed, you can tape it closed from the outside, insuring a tight seal. Ventilation needed in the dome during late fall, winter and early spring can be achieved by leaving the door partially open.

If you live in an extremely cold climate, or you cannot weatherstrip your door properly, you may want to add a second closure inside the dome to help reduce infiltration. To make this, buy an 8 x 7-foot vinyl sheet for about $15 from an upholstery store. The sheet should have a zipper down its middle, and if possible, the zipper should have prongs or small handles, on both sides.

Attach this sheet, leaving plenty of slack, first to the base strut, then around the rest of the door, using Scotchrap 50. The sheet can be taped directly to the inner layer of film that surrounds the door; it need not be secured to the door frame itself. When fully attached, you'll have an effective second barrier against infiltration. (This should not be confused with an air lock, which would create an alcove, preventing cold air from rushing into the dome when someone enters or exits.)

Figure 8-5. Tape and staple the vinyl sheet to the door base strut and tape it to the inside film layer.

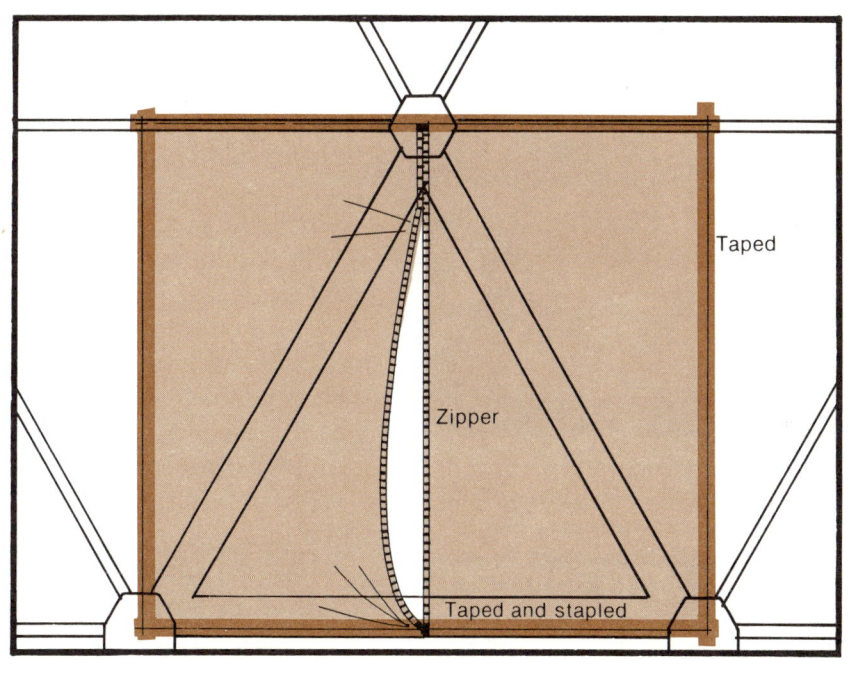

To enter the dome with this second barrier in place, you have to open the door and unzip the vinyl, then walk through the vinyl, close the door and rezip. Although the door and vinyl are open at the same time for a few seconds when you enter, this is the only time air can move freely in and out of the dome. The rest of the time the vinyl reduces infiltration effectively.

TEMPERATURE REQUIREMENTS

The temperatures to maintain in your dome depend on how you use it, and the dome's uses can be many. People have asked how to set up a dome for growing everything from ornamental trees and flowers to large numbers of tomatoes for sale. It can be used to grow seedlings for sale, or it can be hooked up to provide solar energy to your home. Other uses are described in Chapter 10.

But most of you will use the dome to house a year-round vegetable garden. And what you grow will determine the temperatures you need to be successful. During the two or three coldest months of winter, it's advisable to grow vegetables that enjoy colder weather, such as lettuce, spinach, peas, radishes, carrots, cabbage and many others listed in Appendix 5.

The temperature requirements of these plants, expressed as air temperatures, are sometimes overstated. A more critical requirement for plant growth is adequate soil temperatures. As long as the roots of these cool-weather vegetables are about 50°F., growth will continue with little slowdown. Soil temperatures below 50°F. are tolerable, but will retard vegetable growth. If a 50°F. soil temperature can be maintained, cool-weather crops can withstand occasional sub-freezing air temperatures.

Try to maintain **average** nighttime air temperatures in the dome of about 40°F. The mercury may dip below freezing on a few cold winter nights. Cool-weather crops can tolerate these temperatures if they are the exception rather than the rule, partly because the lower nighttime readings are offset by warm daytime temperatures in the dome. Dome temperatures often exceed 70°F. even on cold sunny winter days, keeping soil temperature above 50°F.

However, if you have a special application for the dome, such as raising roses, or if you want to grow "summer" vegetables throughout the winter, warmer temperatures may be required.

Though the wind was blowing and snow covered the rest of New York when this photo was made, the thermometer tells the story in the Fordham dome. Left-hand reading shows air temperature a comfortable 78°F., right-hand reading shows soil at 58°F.

TEMPERATURE EXPECTATIONS

The temperatures you'll be able to maintain inside your dome depend on many factors. Climate is one; the amount of sunlight your geographic region receives and, specifically, the shading your dome receives, are others. Altitude, wind, smog and other atmospheric conditions also affect temperature.

Generally, if you live in a moderate to cold climate, you should have no problem supporting a thriving garden throughout the winter. But, if you are in a harsh or very cold climate, or some of the above factors prevent you from maintaining adequate temperatures in the dome at night, there are things you can do to improve the situation.

First, observe the garden and see how its growth is affected by the lower temperatures. If the effect is slight, there is no need for concern. But if you do want to raise the dome's temperatures, increasing the amount of water storage is the first and most effective step you can take.

If your dome is set up for a special purpose that requires warmer temperatures, or you are in a region that has extremely cold winters, you may want to add auxiliary electric heating. In most very cold regions, auxiliary heating will be needed for just a few hours on certain nights of the few coldest weeks of winter. Because of the heater's limited use, and the effective way the dome retains heat, its operating costs are kept to a minimum.

We suggest you use a submersible 800- to 1,000-watt heater, submerged in one of the 55-gallon drums, in the middle of the lower level. Heat will be transmitted first to water inside the drum, then to the air inside the dome, and continue to radiate for awhile after the heater is turned off. Heat transmitted to the dome in small amounts over a long period of time is more effective than heat transmitted quickly from a space heater.

Two types of submersible heaters are available. One is a heating coil generally used in electric hot water heaters; the other is a coil designed to be buried in soil. If a submersible heater is used, it, and the drum housing it, must be grounded to an electrical box (if you have one inside your dome) or to the third ground wire of an extension cord.

If you can't locate a submersible heater, or choose not to use one, a 1,000-watt electric air heater is another alternative. It should be placed on the ground facing the water storage drums.

Whichever type of heater is used, it can be turned on

and off with a thermostat set at 35° to 40°F. or higher if necessary, or with a timer preset for a desired number of hours.

ELECTRICITY

Obviously, electricity is needed for the dome heater, and for lights or power tools you may use. If you haven't done electrical wiring, it would probably be wise to forego the convenience of an electric outlet inside the dome. It would be simpler to use a heavy-duty outdoor extension cord, plugged into another source, for the few times each year electric power might be needed. The cord must be rated for outdoor use and have an adequate load capacity. Capacities are usually stated on cord packages.

Outdoor cords are readily available in lengths up to 100 feet, and less likely to be available in longer lengths. But, remember, the required thickness of the cord depends on the distance the electricity is being carried; for example, don't use two 50-foot extension cords rated for 1,000 watts to carry this load 100 feet. Instead, use a 100-foot cord rated for this capacity.

Extend the cord into the dome, through its door, to the heater, which must be grounded. Plug the cord's other end into an outlet that has no major appliances on the same fuse. The cord's third prong also must be grounded.

If you have electrical experience, or know someone who does, and you'd like to install a permanent underground electric line to the dome, here's a brief explanation of what must be done:

The thickness of the wire must conform to federal and local regulations, so ask a local supplier about this first. Run the wire through aluminum conduit and then place it one foot underground, from source to dome.

At the source, which may be your house, the wire can surface along the foundation and enter through a basement window frame. Once inside the basement, it should be connected directly to its own fuse or circuit breaker.

An easier way to do this is to connect the wire's end to a male plug which is inserted into an outlet that has no major appliances anywhere on its line. Check local electrical codes to make sure this is permissible.

At the dome, the electrical line should surface within six to twelve inches of the frame and enter the dome through a base hub. Once inside, the line should be connected to a standard **outdoor** electrical box because of the dome's high humidity. The box can be secured to the inner side of the base hub.

OTHER WAYS TO MAINTAIN TEMPERATURES

Solar greenhouse designers commonly use other methods to maintain temperatures inside their structures. Many of these were reviewed by the FUSES team and rejected for the dome due to their high costs or impracticality. Some were described briefly in Chapter 3, but one used quite often deserves mention here.

This is the **night blanket,** a curtain or insulating blanket draped over, or just inside, the clear surfaces of a greenhouse at night to help reduce heat loss.

It is not used in the dome because it's difficult to drape a curtain or blanket over the dome's spherical surface and, more importantly, it's expensive and inconvenient. The blanket must be draped late afternoon every day during cold weather and drawn early each morning. Mechanisms to do this automatically are prohibitively complex and expensive, so it's usually done manually. Having to be at the dome at specified times each day costs time, and, in our opinion, this loss is not offset by reduced heat loss with the blanket.

Because the Fordham dome has worked so well in New York City, certain additions that might enhance its ability to retain heat have not been used. However, if you want to raise your dome's average temperatures, or if you need an auxiliary electric heater during the winter but want to reduce your dependence on it, you may want to incorporate some of these options:

A **ceiling** of 4-mil Monsanto "602," **seam-attached** to the horizontal struts of level four and draped parallel to the floor, creates a small dome attic. It helps insulate the structure by creating another dead air space, and prevents warm air from rising to the dome top where it dissipates quickly.

The ceiling probably won't reduce light transmission into the dome during winter, because sunlight this time of year enters the dome from a low angle. However, the ceiling should be removed near the beginning of March, when the sun's path is higher.

Probably the best way to judge the ceiling's effectiveness would be to record the dome's minimum daytime

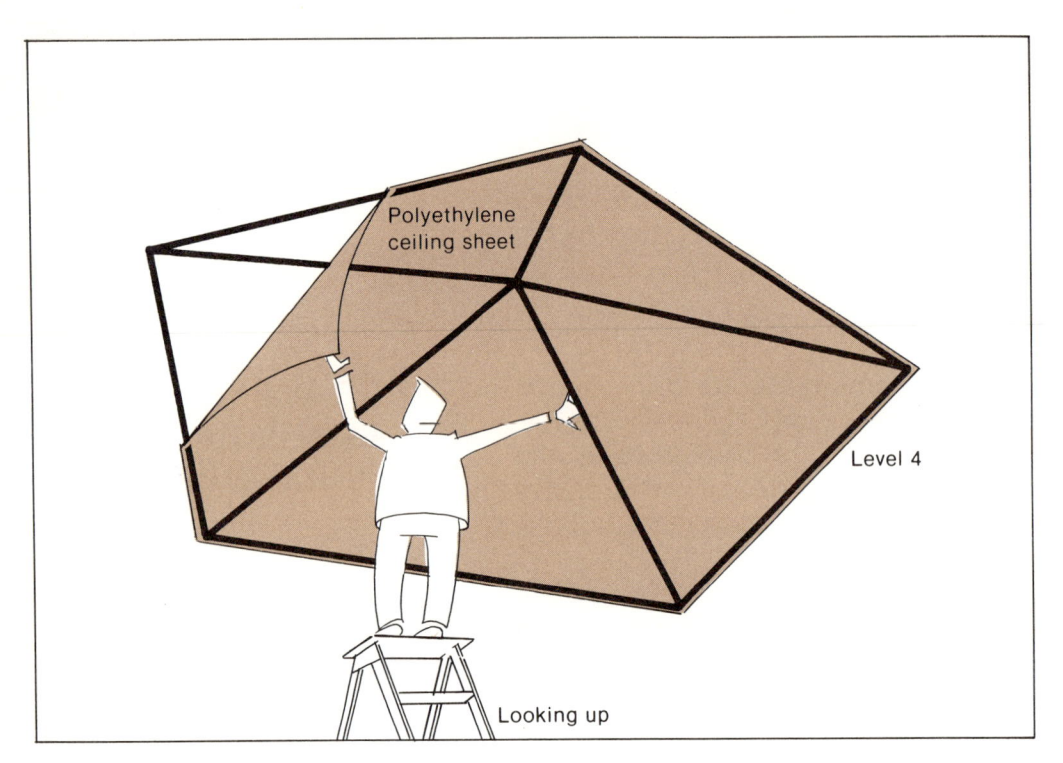

Figure 8-6. Use seam attachments to secure a ceiling sheet to the horizontal struts of level four.

Figure 8-7. A tent-like air lock may be fashioned to help reduce heat loss when the door is opened.

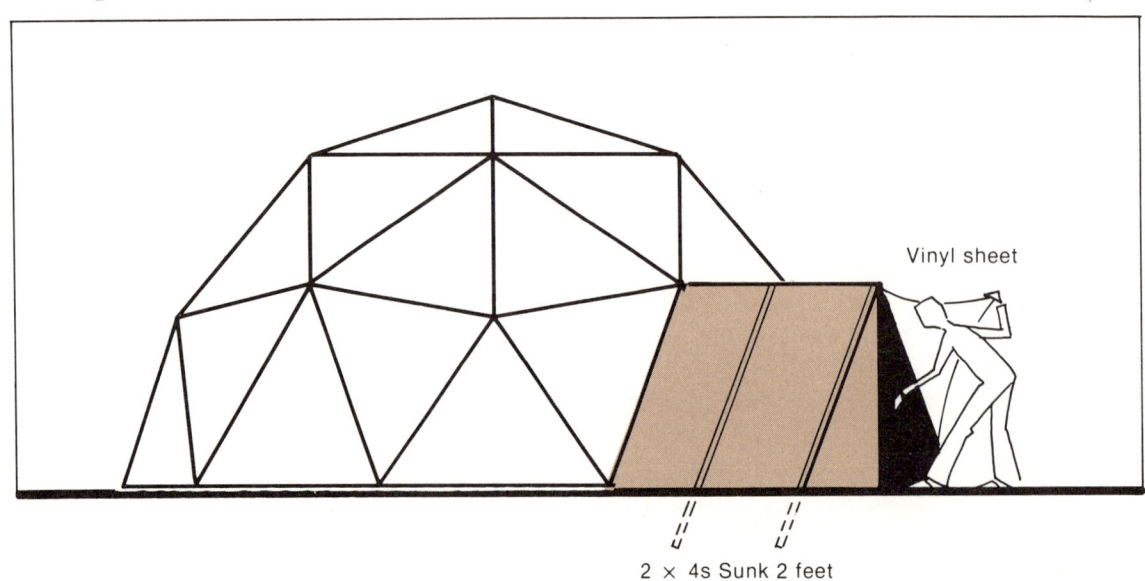

and evening temperatures for a period before and after its installation.

If you think the dome loses heat through frequent, or even infrequent, opening and closing of the door, you may want to add an **air lock.** An air lock will prevent cold air from rushing into the dome when the door is open.

Briefly, to build one, first rehinge the door so it opens inward. Once this is done, there's clearance to locate the air lock's triangular frame outside the door. The frame is made of a pair of 2 x 4s embedded two-feet into the soil two-and-a-half feet from the door, and another pair of 2 x 4s five feet from the door. Connecting the top of each triangle to the door frame is a single 2 x 4 length.

Cover the frame with a layer of 6-mil Monsanto "602," which should be secured and taped to the dome, and extended into the soil to prevent wind from lifting it. The front of the air lock through which you walk can be closed with a zippered vinyl sheet, as described in the section, "Reducing Infiltration."

SUMMER COOLING

During hot weather, the problem of maintaining suitable temperatures inside the dome reverses. You may want to shade your dome in summer to reduce high temperature build-up. A special shading cloth sold by greenhouse distributors is fine for this. It should be draped over the outside of the dome and tied in place.

Opaquing compounds are not suggested because they're not easily removed from polyethylene for the colder seasons.

Without ventilation the dome may become too hot to support a thriving garden. To help, grow only vegetables that can stand the heat, or they may never get into the kitchen. It helps if the dome is located where its door can be left open without concern for vandalism. Leaving the door and vent open permits cross-ventilation.

If this isn't enough ventilation, or if you can't keep the door open all the time, there are other options: You could build a second small vent, half a triangle in size, on level two's northern side. This vent needn't be capable of opening or closing, it can simply be an opening cut into both layers of film and covered with a screen. The vent should be sealed when the cooler weather approaches by taping pieces of film over the openings in both layers.

Place a fan at the vent to draw outside air into the dome and circulate it. Turn the fan on when needed, off when not, or plug it into a timer for preset hours of operation. More complex greenhouse venting methods, requiring thermostats to turn fans on and off and ducts to circulate air, are not needed.

Another possibility is to build a screen door. This would have to be built so it could swing into the dome and wouldn't interfere with the film-covered door. The covered door could be left open while the screen door prevented the entry of undesirable insects, animals or people.

A screen door and a screen over the vent may also be desirable to prevent the escape of beneficial insect predators placed in your dome (their use will be described in the next chapter). The vent screen can be stapled directly to the frame on the inside. It must have a small opening in the southern corner. The vent support arm passes through this opening and into the dome when the vent is shut.

If unwanted entry is not a problem, the screening on the door can simply be stapled onto the frame and left unattached on one side, allowing entry, and then, when necessary, hooked closed onto the protruding ends of finishing nails.

A less time-consuming, no-cost method of venting the dome is removing the film from one or more small, level-two triangles. Again, you may want to cover these triangles with screening. And, of course, the film should be replaced in the fall in the same way it was originally installed.

If all this is still not enough hot-weather protection for your garden, or if you think these measures are too bothersome, you might forego gardening in the dome in the summer. Then you could rest the dome's garden beds and replenish them with compost. And you could tend your outdoor garden which should be flourishing if it was started earlier than usual with seedlings raised inside the dome.

SPRING AND FALL

These two seasons affect the dome in identical ways. They each have periods of intensely sunny days and very cold nights, which means care is needed to maintain a fairly consistent environment within the dome. During the hottest periods of these seasons — the end of spring and beginning of fall — open the vent as much as possible. In early spring or late fall, leave the vent open only a small amount or close it, depending on the weather. When winter approaches, the vent should remain closed and be sealed with tape.

Although this sounds as if the dome requires constant attention, it's not so. Most often the vent can be left partially open day and night, requiring only an adjustment every few days or when extreme weather is encountered. If, after a season or two, you find you don't care for tending the vent, you might want to install an automatic vent opener that will open and close the vent as needed. A controlling mechanism is operated by gas pressure which changes as temperatures fluctuate. The opener can be bought from most greenhouse suppliers for about $20.

PART TWO: GENERAL UPKEEP

The dome requires a minimum amount of attention to keep it running well. And there's not much that can go wrong with the structure — certainly nothing that is not easily corrected. However, it's a good idea to check the dome periodically so anything that has gone wrong can be corrected promptly.

Probably the first irregularity you'll discover is moisture between the double layer of film. No matter how well you seal the inner layer, moisture builds up because dampness permeates everything. Although this moisture reduces slightly the amount of light entering the dome, it is no cause for action unless it starts collecting in pockets. If this happens, slit the inner layer to let the water drain away, then tape the film closed.

Vandalism or accidental puncturing of film also may be a problem. Film can be repaired by taping it with Scotchrap 50. (For aesthetic reasons, you may want to use a clear weatherproof mylar tape for minor dome repairs despite its higher cost.) However, if a rip is large, or there is more than one damaged spot in a triangle, you may want to use new film to re-cover this part of the dome.

Whether you are replacing film on a small triangle or one triangle of a triad, the same procedure is followed: Trim film on the frame to within two inches of the triangle's struts, and make wrap-around attachments with these edges. The new film is then secured to these struts with seam attachments.

A third problem you may encounter is a slight misalignment of level two pent hubs. This shouldn't happen if you've correctly followed the preventive measures outlined earlier. But if it does, simply realign the hubs and tighten them in place; you also may want to secure them in position with mending bars or corner brackets.

Another, perhaps simpler, way to realign the hub permanently is to press it and then hold it in place with a length of 2 x 2 sunk nearly a foot into the ground inside the dome. The hub and 2 x 2 may be attached with an angle iron.

CLEANING THE GLAZING

Since dirt reduces light transmission, it is a good practice to clean the glazing, both inside and out, at least twice a year. September and February are good times for these cleanings. The glazing is easily cleaned with only water and a rag or sponge. Try to reach as much of the dome as possible; areas that can't be reached should be hosed down well. If you have problems with sap or other dirt that doesn't come off with just water, a mild detergent can be used on the outer layer but is not suggested for the inner layer.

REPLACING FILM

The dome covering must be changed periodically because the sun's ultraviolet rays and abuse from weather cause deterioration. However, Monsanto "602" is specially treated for long life. At Fordham, the dome's southern outer layer, which is exposed to the most intense sunlight of any film on the dome, has lasted two years. Yours may last longer, if you don't live in the south and don't receive intense summer sunlight.

After using this film for about a year, you'll notice a faint yellowing. Since this barely reduces light transmission into the dome, don't change the film yet. Tests have shown a two-year-old double layer of "602" still transmits 97 percent of its original level. The film should be changed only when it becomes brittle or shows signs of tearing where it is stapled to struts and can't be repaired with tape.

The dome's northern outer layer receives no direct sunlight and, because it is insulated, light transmission is not a concern. Therefore, its useful life is longer, perhaps as long as six to eight years. Change the film when it shows signs of tearing where it is stapled to struts.

The southern inner layer receives no abuse from weather, and considerably less exposure to ultraviolet rays than the outer layer protecting it. Naturally, it lasts longer because of this, probably as long as six to eight years.

The northern inner layer should last indefinitely because it receives no ultraviolet rays or abuse from weather.

When changing the outer layer of film on the dome's southern side, you have to remove much of its inner layer for access. And though the inner layer will not need replacement, it may be a good idea to do so; if you plan to reuse it, you'll have to remove the film carefully from the struts, staple by staple, in order not to rip it. This takes time. You may prefer to remove both southern layers of film quickly and easily for fast replacement, despite the extra cost.

When cutting film from an uninsulated southern triangle that shares a strut with an insulated northern one, make sure to leave enough of the old film draped over the strut to wrap around it, then cover it later with a seam from the new film.

Having removed all film from the dome's southern side, carefully inspect the frame for signs of decay, loose bolts and misaligned hubs. In addition to correcting any problems, you should recoat this entire side of the frame twice with redwood stain preservative, and let it dry completely before installing new film.

Changing the outer layer of film on the dome's northern side should coincide with the second replacement of the southern side's covering. So, remove all film from the dome as before, again deciding if you want to reuse or replace the inner layers. Remove all the insulation too, and mark it so you know in which triangle it belongs when repacking.

Inspect the entire frame and correct any flaws. Check all bolts (whenever film has been removed) to see if they need tightening. Then coat the northern side of the frame twice with redwood stain. If you feel ambitious, also re-preserve the dome's southern side, although it may not be needed yet.

When the wood is dry, re-cover the dome's outer layer, then repack the insulation and, finally, re-cover the inner layer, using new film or the old film if it was handled carefully.

REPLACING STRUTS AND HUBS

A well-preserved frame can easily last ten years or more, but check it for signs of decay each time the wood is uncovered. When you find an affected hub or strut, simply remove it and replace it, as done originally. No special techniques are needed.

The strength of the structure is unaffected by the temporary removal of one strut. In fact, the dome remains rigid with as many as one-fourth of its struts removed.

But changing a hub is a bit trickier. Before you can remove one, each of its surrounding hubs must be supported by ladders or people holding them in place. Once you are certain the struts won't change position, remove the decayed hub and replace it.

It is helpful to know why this wood decayed. If it is a base hub or strut, contact with soil probably caused the decay. Check the condition of the rest of the dome base. If the wood decayed because pockets of water accumulated between film layers, check other hubs and struts exposed to the same conditions.

PART THREE: HANDLING EMERGENCIES

Extremely heavy snows and hurricanes are natural hazards to the dome, just as they endanger all structures. Vandalism and careless accidents are other possible causes of occasional emergency repairs.

In general, snow seldom accumulates on the dome's smooth surfaces, especially when there's a light wind. Snow that does accumulate, usually melts and falls from the warm, spherical structure quickly. The Fordham dome withstood, with no difficulties, a 13-inch snowfall, followed a week later by another 17 inches.

But a long succession of cloudy days preceding the storm will result in dome temperatures too low to immediately melt snow on its outer shell. And, despite winds, some snow may accumulate on the structure, particularly if it's a quick-falling snow or blizzard. Even so, the dome can usually handle a snow load of up to twelve inches before showing signs of stress.

In situations like this, prevent the snow from collecting further. When a large storm is predicted, increase the dome's warmth by turning on its heater about an hour or two before the storm's anticipated beginning, and leave it on until the storm abates. If you haven't been using a heater, bring in a space heater temporarily.

If you don't care to use a heater, use a brush at the end of a long stick to wipe snow off the dome during the storm, or, from within the dome, gently bang the covering with poles to dislodge any snow that may have collected. Be very careful not to puncture the film.

If a hurricane is approaching, probably one of the last things you'll think about is the dome. And that's okay because the only needed preparation is to secure the door and vent shut to deny wind an entry point. The dome will be susceptible to damage (like everything else in the storm's path), but should remain relatively unaffected by high winds because its spherical shape deflects even extreme gusts.

Objects tossed about in the wind could damage the dome. Sticks or rocks could puncture the film. There's nothing you can do to prevent this, but the dome's ease of repair should be a small consolation.

On the other hand, the dome is obviously quite vulnerable to vandalism; although the film covering is resilient, it offers little resistance to a knife. Perhaps the best protection against vandalism is a watchful eye and a high fence.

Although this should not be a concern for most people, it was for members of a group who built a dome in New York City. Housing Conservation Coordinators, a neighborhood housing group on the west side of Manhattan, surrounded their dome with a locked fence, but kept the dome itself unlocked. Their street-wise philosophy was: If someone wanted to enter the structure and took the trouble to mount the fence, it was better to let him in rather than have him destroy the film covering trying to enter. In fact, there has been little problem with vandals because neighbors watch the dome carefully.

Chapter 9: Raising Food in the Dome

PART ONE: GARDENING

It would be presumptuous to think we could adequately describe the many gardening methods used today. Entire books have been written on the subject. And many readers may have already established preferred ways to raise vegetables. You might use an organic method or a more conventional one; you might garden in single rows or wide rows, or use a combination of these. Whichever is used, growing food in a dome won't differ much from doing it outside, except there are adjustments for year-round gardening.

In this chapter, we'll describe the intensive gardening methods used by the FUSES team at Fordham. We'll tell you how to develop a thriving dome garden, regardless of the method selected. And, we'll discuss other books that address specific facets of gardening particularly well.

INTENSIVE GARDENING

An adaptation of the French Intensive organic gardening method, a way to produce large yields in a small space, was used at Fordham. This method was developed in the late 19th century for growing cantaloupes on the hills outside Paris. It's well-suited for the dome, which has only about 416 square feet of ground space. The French Intensive method is strongly recommended.

Vegetables are grown in beds of organically rich soil tilled, by hand, to a depth of two feet. These beds are actually more like sculptured mounds of soil, raised nearly a foot above the garden pathways to offer more surface for air and moisture penetration and to better protect the soil from accidental trampling and compaction.

Any soil is fine, but it must be fortified with plant nutrients to make it fertile. The nutrients also should create a soil with a good consistency, one that can retain a favorable balance of moisture and air. Fertile soil, moisture and air are key ingredients for a successful organic garden.

The soil is tilled to a depth of two feet so vegetable plant roots can grow down into it easily; lateral growth and competition for space is less likely. This means vegetables may be planted close together in four-foot wide rows, rows that require little space for pathways. For example, tomato plants are staggered 16 to 18 inches apart instead of the suggested three to four feet, and lettuce plants are four to five inches apart instead of the often suggested eight to ten inches. Up to four times more vegetables can be grown in this garden than in most conventional row gardens.

Another advantage of intensive gardening is that overlapping leaves of neighboring plants act as a living mulch, shading the soil to keep it cool and moist. Obviously, this means less watering is required. And, the

Lush vegetables spill over the edges of a pathway in the geodesic dome.

close plants, particularly in a mature garden, crowd out weeds, which rarely have a chance to start growing in an intensive garden.

As for insects, any garden will have them; they'll never be entirely eliminated. But, with healthy plants in an enclosed environment, it's relatively simple to control pests using natural predators only. The FUSES team members chose this way to keep their garden natural and free of potentially harmful chemicals.

ORGANIC VS. CONVENTIONAL GARDENING METHODS

Organic gardening, the method used in the FUSES dome, involves the use of natural fertilizers and large amounts of compost to fortify the soil. But chemical fertilizers used in more conventional gardens perform the same function.

Basically, both types of fertilizer have the same elements (nitrogen, potassium and phosphorus), although in different forms. And these elements are used in the same manner by plants. The elements supplied by organic fertilizers are in no way any better or worse than those of chemical fertilizers. However, there are a few differences between the nutrients supplied by compost and those of chemical fertilizers:

Compost is made of animal and plant wastes; chemical fertilizers are derived from scarcer fossil fuels.

Compost, because it is made of decayed plant scraps, will almost certainly provide nutrients in the proper balance for new plant growth when returned to the soil. It also helps condition the soil to hold a good balance of air and moisture, which chemical fertilizers don't do unless additives are mixed in. And compost makes soil preparation easier, because a heavily composted garden rarely lacks trace elements or needs pH (acidity) adjustment.

A small backyard gardener can choose between organic and conventional methods, whereas a commercial farmer is pretty much bound to the latter because of space and time considerations. The same reasoning applies when choosing a natural or chemical method of insect control: An enclosed environment is ideal for using insect predators, removing the need for insecticides, while a large-scale outdoor grower could not find this method practical.

SOIL PREPARATION

The most important step toward a thriving garden is to prepare the soil properly. So, whichever method you use, have a soil sample analyzed at the nearest Extension Service office. Learn the condition of the soil and, if you discover problems, correct them. Or, you might buy an inexpensive kit and do the soil samples yourself. It takes only a few minutes.

If you want to use the gardening method adopted by the FUSES team, start by tilling your dome gardening beds. First, dig out one foot of soil, turn it over and pile it on the sides of the beds. Then turn over an additional foot of soil within each bed. and shovel back the first foot, mixing in any required soil additives.

Again, if you're gardening organically, the additives will include compost and other nutrients the soil analysis indicates are needed. If gardening conventionally, add chemical fertilizers, peat moss, fortifiers and other additives to make the soil fertile and to give it a good consistency.

After loosening the soil and mixing in additives, these

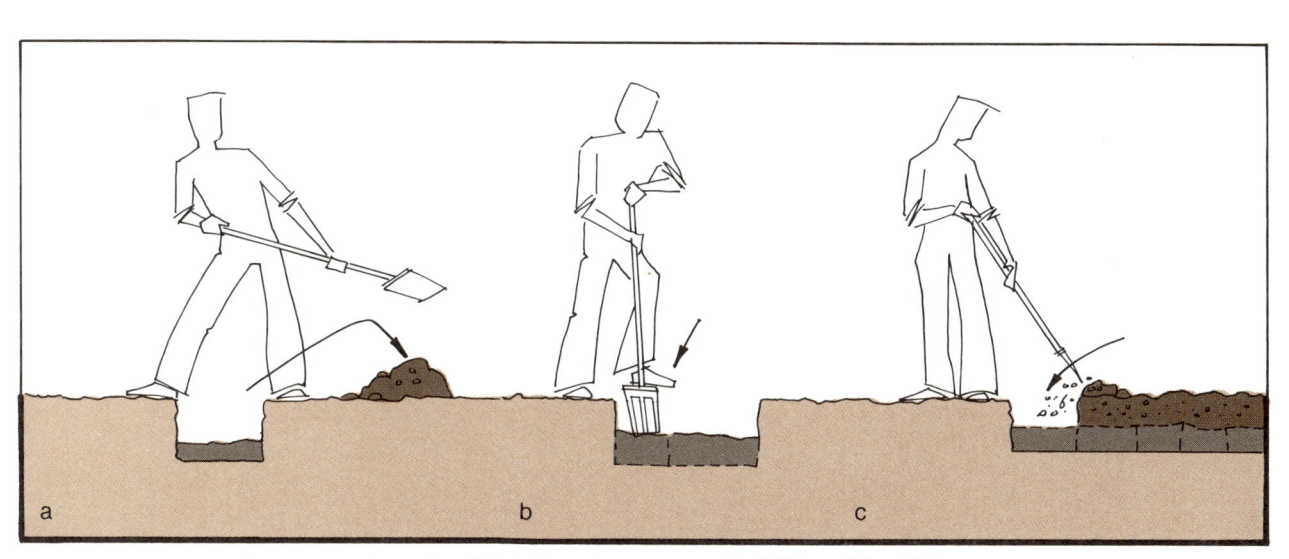

Figure 9-1. First, dig out one foot of soil (a); then turn over an additional foot (b); and, last, shovel back the first foot and mix in soil additives (c).

beds should be about four inches above the ground. To raise them further, dig down the pathways and spread this top soil over the elevated beds. Then the beds will be well-defined, about 6 inches above the pathways and ready for planting.

SETTING UP GARDEN BEDS

Whether you plant narrow, single rows or wide rows, the garden beds should allow for semi-circular paths or steps that conform to the dome's shape. This permits easy access and the best use of available space. Three suggested garden configurations follow.

Wide-Row with Steps

In this configuration, (Figure 9-2), access to the plants is by small, intermittent steps, rather than paths. And, this means the configuration provides the greatest amount of gardening space. Vegetables may be planted all the way from the water storage containers on the dome's northern side to the frame on the southern side.

If planting near the frame, the coldest part of the dome, grow only hardy vegetables that have shallow roots because the underground polyethylene is only about six inches below the surface.

Between the steps, plant vegetables that remain low to the ground, such as lettuce, or you'll have to be a high jumper to get around inside the dome. If you're willing to

Figure 9-2. Here, recessed steps permit access to the garden bed. Small circles indicate positions of heat storage drums.

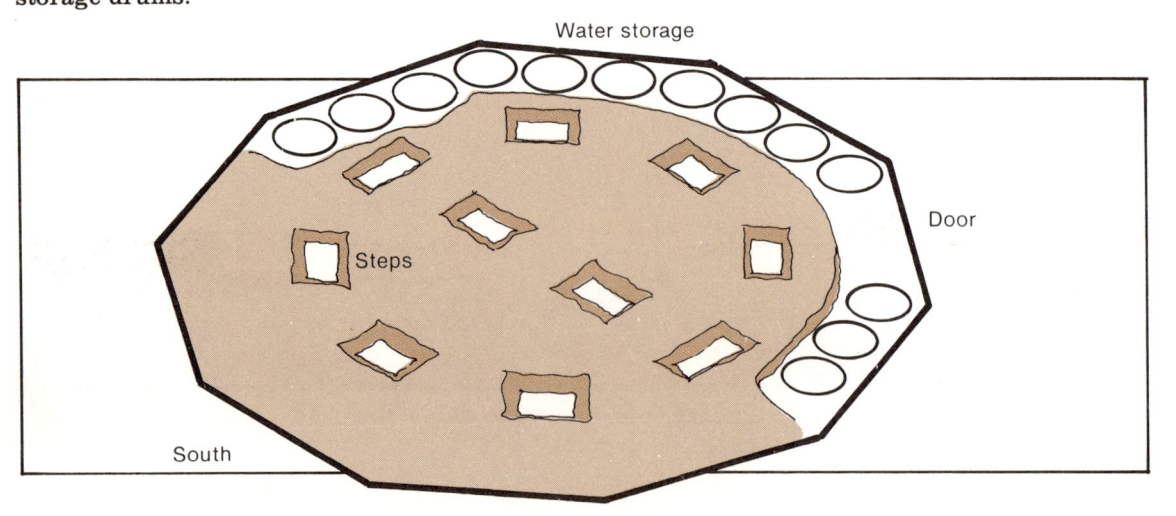

put up with a little awkwardness to gain more gardening space, place the steps as far apart as your stride will permit. The steps should measure 12 x 18 inches; they should be recessed in the garden beds.

Wide-Row with Paths

If you want to leave space in your dome for seedling benches, house plants or other things, or if you want a roomier, more comfortable set-up, consider a wide-row configuration (Figure 9-3).

Plant within a few inches of the water storage containers, the warmest part of the dome where vegetables grow best in winter, or leave a three-foot wide pathway there for seedling benches. Continue the beds until within one foot of the southern side of the frame, where there's a pathway around the dome's perimeter.

Figure 9-3. A more comfortable gardening arrangement is this one — a wide row with narrow paths.

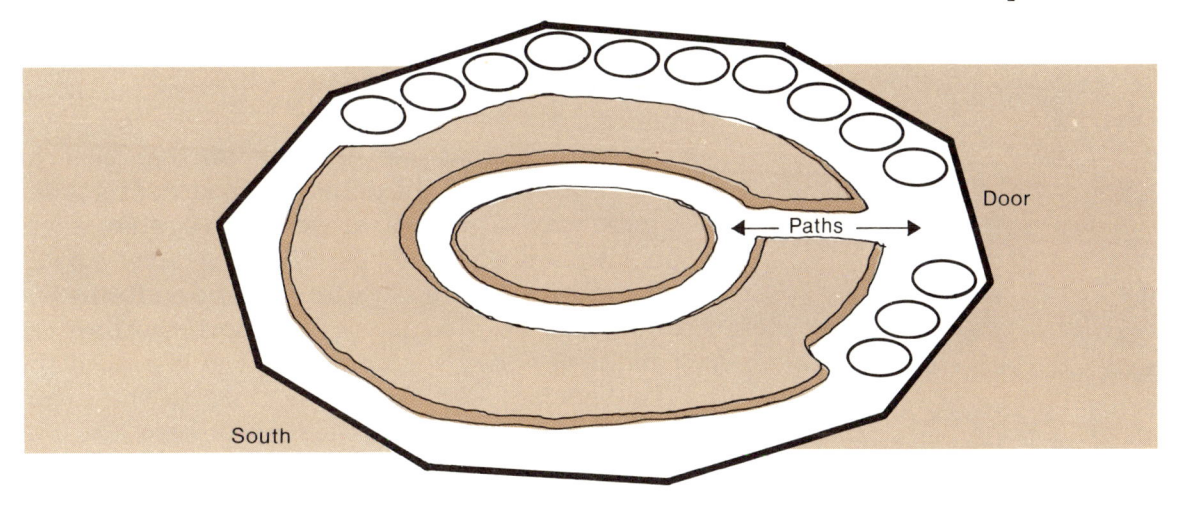

Generally, beds should be as wide — and paths as narrow — as possible while remaining comfortable to use. Working from paths on both sides of a bed, you should be able to reach the entire planting area. The FUSES dome has had beds as wide as six feet and paths as narrow as one foot.

Conventional Row

Conventional, narrow rows can be used in the dome. You may want to make the rows semi-circular to

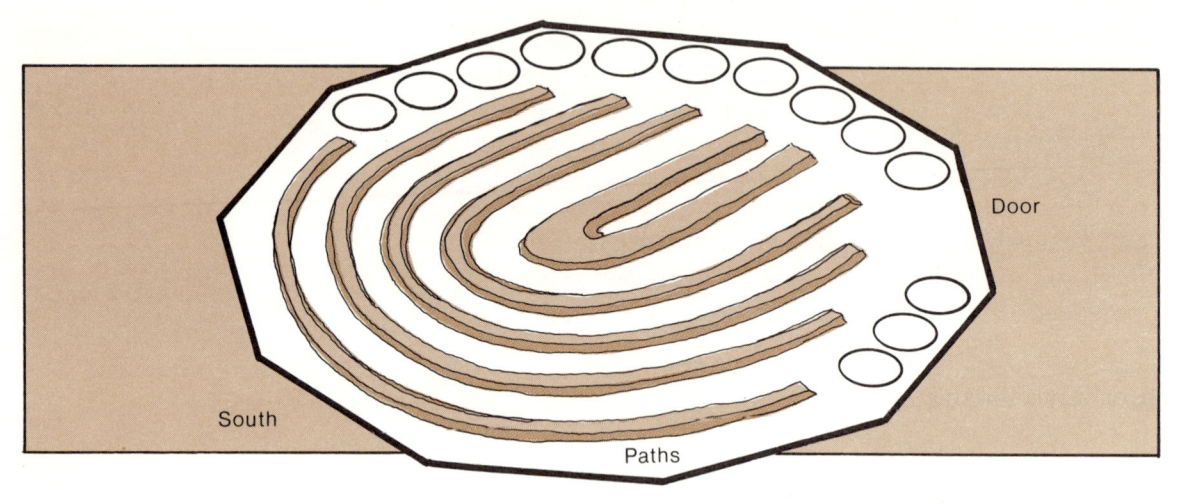

Figure 9-4. Conventional, narrow rows arranged in a semicircular pattern may also be used in the dome.

maximize available space (Figure 9-4). Otherwise, set them up as you would if they were outdoors.

MORE GARDENING IDEAS

To enhance the dome's lush and tropical appearance is not hard at all. The moisture and heat are already there; all you need to add are some full, well-grown house plants hung from eye bolts or hooks on the inner hub plates.

Seedlings may be grown on benches and then transplanted into the dome or an outdoor garden. This is a good way to give warm-weather vegetables a head start on summer. The benches should be narrow so they cause minimum shading of water storage containers, and they should be painted black to absorb sunlight. Place the benches so they conform with the layout of the drums. The benches also should be close to the drums so the seedlings benefit from the drums' heat.

Another idea for your dome: add a small table for working on seedlings or other gardening chores.

GEARING YOUR GARDEN TO THE SEASONS

Working in a dome does away with seasonal restrictions. You'll be able to garden four seasons a year, not just between spring and fall frosts; and you can design your own planting and harvesting schedules, as long as you follow one general rule — grow the **right** vegetables at the right time of the year. During winter, grow cool-weather crops; during summer, grow warm-weather crops. (See lists of these vegetables in Appendix 5.)

Based on your climate, you'll have to decide how late in winter to start planting summer vegetables, and how far into early winter they'll continue to thrive. Your schedule also will be influenced by your particular vegetable preferences.

Here's a sample planting schedule, based on the experiences of the FUSES team at Fordham University in New York City:

• In the fall, begin growing seedlings for cool-weather crops. Transplant these into the dome before the first frosts. The seedlings will develop into fresh vegetables in the late fall and winter. Some successive plantings may be desirable.
• By the beginning of March, start introducing warm-weather vegetables, such as tomatoes and peppers, into the dome. You may simply reseed the garden beds after cool-weather crops are pulled from the ground. Or, if you have propagated seedlings in your home, transplant these into the dome garden.
• About late February or early March, start propagating warm-weather seedlings in the dome for later transplanting to outdoor gardens, perhaps for friends or for sale to a local retailer.
• In later winter and spring, ventilate the dome adequately to prevent bolting (going to seed) of cool-weather crops. Sunny daytime temperatures within the structure can exceed 100°F., even in late winter. How diligent you are at ventilating largely determines how late into the spring these cool-weather crops can grow.
• The garden should be completely turned over to warm-weather vegetables by the start of June. This may seem late, but it's not when you consider warm-weather vegetables should thrive in the dome until mid-December. If you live in a mild climate, they may produce year round.

At Fordham, the FUSES team harvested tomatoes from the dome through late December and, with more water storage or a small amount of electric heat, year-round tomato production might have been possible.

During the fall, begin the cycle again by planting cool-weather crops.

This sample schedule is intended as a starting point for your own experimentation. You'll probably want to implement many of your own ideas for this flexible, four-season dome.

When determining your planting schedule, remember there's no rule that says you have to plant vegetables in all garden beds at the same time. Some outdoor gardeners do this when trying to grow a lot in a short season. In

Warm weather crops, such as these cucumbers, may be planted so they travel along the base of the dome.

Rhonda Pavese stretches through lush, oversized vegetation to reach a cucumber at the Fordham dome.

the dome, four-season gardening is possible and it's probably wise to stagger plantings so you can harvest crops throughout the year.

Also, keep in mind that leaf and root crops (most of the cool-weather crops) are most vulnerable to conditions of low light during the first few weeks of their growth. If you discover that vegetables planted in December and January grow slowly and are spindly, insufficient light may be the problem. One solution is to plant most cool-weather crops in October and early November. They will then be mature or approaching maturity when sunlight diminishes in December and January. Mature vegetables also will be better prepared to withstand winter's lower temperatures.

LOOKING AFTER YOUR GARDEN

Maintaining a dome garden is similar to outdoor gardening, but there are differences:

Growing Seedlings

Because of the year-round growing season in the dome and the use of staggered plantings, there is a continual need for new plants. These can be grown from seeds planted directly in the gardening bed or transplanted as seedlings into the beds when they are needed. The seedlings can be grown on benches set up near the water storage containers.

During most times of the year the dome will provide an ideal environment for growing seedlings, but in harsh climates the dome may not be able to support the germination of seeds during the coldest few weeks of winter. During this period, any needed seedlings can be grown in a south-facing window of your home. During the times of the year when seedlings are needed most, the dome can support their germination and growth. These times include the end of February and March, when seedlings should be grown for use in your outdoor garden or for sale.

Planting

During the winter, when the sun is at a low angle, plant shading is a problem. Therefore, crops that grow low to the ground should be planted near the southern end of the dome and taller plants toward the north. Vegetables like peas, which are trellised to save ground space, should be in the dome's northernmost growing area. Even in this area, don't trellis them more than three feet high, to avoid shading water storage drums.

Cultivation

Weeds should not be a serious problem in the dome because sod is removed from the gardening beds during site preparation.

Weed growth may be deterred by simply scratching the soil surface about once every week or so. Mulch coverings accomplish the same purpose, although they're unnecessary if a wide-row planting method is used. If the sole purpose of mulch is to cover paths, you might want to use bricks or well-leached (no salt) clam shells instead. These produce an attractive garden.

Pollination

Because the dome garden is in an enclosed environment, there are few insects and no wind to pollinate veg-

John Fontanetta, center, uses a small brush to pollinate vegetables. Other members of the Fordham Urban Solar EcoSystem (FUSES) team looking on are, from left, Jim McGurk, George Dale (advisor), Don Devey and Barbara Ann Devey.

etable blossoms. To compensate for this, you can use either of two methods:

During late morning, when the dome is warm and most vegetable blossoms are open, turn on a fan and direct it to different parts of the garden. As the blossoms and leaves rustle, pollen moves among them and first pollination and then fruit-setting occurs.

A much more effective method is to pollinate by hand: Dab the center of each blossom in turn quickly with a fine, camel-haired artist's brush.

One of these methods must be used. Any flower, excluding some hybrid plant varieties, that is not pollinated will not produce fruit, even though the plant matures.

Companion Planting

Many gardeners favor companion planting, or the close planting of vegetables beneficial to each other. Companion planting can be helpful in a dome because compatible plants may be intermingled, thereby saving space. Antagonistic plants should be kept apart. A good reference is **Secrets of Companion Planting for Successful Gardening** by Louise Riotte.

Radishes are good companions for many plants. They

may be planted amidst other plants that are slower to mature. When the quickly maturing radishes are removed, they leave air holes and good growing space for their companions.

Watering

As a general rule, in the summer, the dome garden needs as much, if not more, water than an outdoor plot. But the winter garden needs little water because the dome is closed tightly, trapping moisture inside. The high humidity in the dome and the garden's heavy leaf cover help to slow evaporation from the soil. And water inside the dome continually evaporates and recondenses, like a small, continuous rain. All this produces enough moisture so that the garden may be left unattended for as long as two weeks with no ill effects.

But, sooner or later, watering will be necessary and, whether you use a sprinkler, watering can or hose, you'll need a way to supply water to the dome.

One option, a permanent, underground water line, involves a lot of work. To prevent it from winter freezing, you must dig a trench below the frost line (about three feet), from the water source to the dome, and the line should surface at least one foot inside the dome. If the dome is in your backyard and the nearest water source is your home, you may have to drill through the foundation to run the new water line into the basement and connect with an existing line.

The underground lines may be made of metal or polyethylene. Polyethylene is less expensive than metal and it's sold at plumbing distributorships and hardware stores in one-piece rolls. Polyethylene saves time and effort because you generally don't have to screw sections together. Elbows and Ts of polyvinyl chloride can be used for sharp bends in the pipe layout. Each component must be rodent resistant.

Another, and probably the most practical, option is to run a hose to the dome whenever water is needed. This will be inconvenient in the winter, but water is seldom needed then. If you use a 32-gallon plastic garbage can in the dome as a storage tank, you'll need to run water through the hose only once every two to three weeks.

Also, by watering your garden from this container

Using a watering can, garden hose or spray can are some of the ways to provide moisture to the dome plants.

BUILDING AND USING A SOLAR-HEATED GEODESIC GREENHOUSE

(which should be black to absorb solar energy) of solar-warmed water, you'll help keep soil temperatures warm and encourage plant growth. It's a good idea to fill the container in advance so it has plenty of time to warm.

The container belongs on top of the drum left uncovered for this purpose. With the container in this position, you'll be able to use gravity to help water the garden: Make a siphon hose of 30 feet of garden hose or ½-inch surgical tubing. Extend one end of the hose to the bottom of the container and coil the rest on a wire hook at the container's handle.

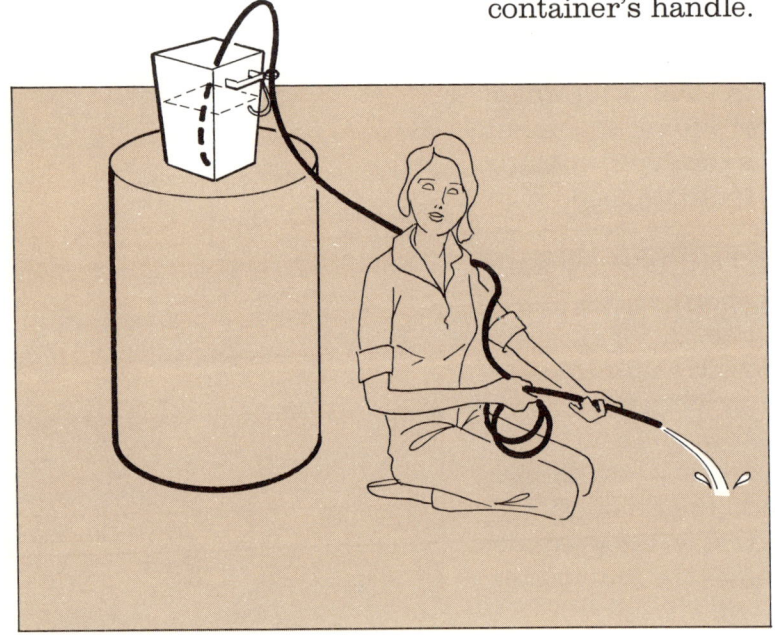

Figure 9-5. Use a siphon hose and water from a plastic garbage can to moisten plants. Dome heat keeps the water warm during winter.

To start the water flow, uncoil the hose a bit and suck on its end as if it were a straw. The water will continue running as long as this end remains lower than the water level inside the container; if you stop the flow accidentally, simply suck on the end again to restart it. By pinching the hose and keeping it low, you can start and stop the flow at will. Water should be applied directly to soil around the plant roots — not to the leaves, since water on leaves evaporates quickly.

However, leaves should be misted or rinsed periodically, particularly the undersides through which plants breathe. Rain cleanses outdoor plants naturally; in the dome, you can run the hose over the plants, but this method wastes water, causes mud splash and sometimes moisture doesn't reach all leaf parts. Or, preferably, you could use an inexpensive pressure sprayer, such as the Melnor Spray Safe Pressure Sprayer. To use it, simply fill its two-gallon canister with water, pump the handle a few times to create pressure, aim the wand where you want the mist to go, and squeeze the trigger. It's probably the most convenient and effective way to mist all parts of the plant leaves. (This sprayer is also a neat, safe way to apply insecticides because it pinpoints the spray, making it easy for you to avoid contact with the spray yourself.)

A sprinkler is not recommended for either watering or misting because it consumes too much water and wets everything in its path, creating a muddy garden.

Insect Control

Because the garden is so easily maintained in its enclosed environment, we strongly suggest that you try organic methods of insect control, rather than chemical insecticides. There will be some insects in your garden and healthy plants can tolerate them in small numbers. There's no need to sterilize the entire garden with insecticides.

To help foster effective organic control of pests, keep your garden clean. Use bricks and clam shells in paths rather than mulch, and keep compost piles outside. And whenever you see pests, crush them. By taking these steps, you may avoid uncontrollable infestations.

To combat insect infestation you may wish to introduce natural predators or "good bugs." Ladybugs and other predators and suppliers are listed in Appendix 6. Lacewings and praying mantises are some of the other predatory insects; predatory animals include toads, frogs, salamanders, chameleons, garden snakes and lizards.

One serious problem is acquiring predators when they're needed. Most suppliers ship them only between spring and fall frosts, when temperatures are warm. If you want continuous, year-round protection, be sure to order a supply in late fall and another in early spring. It's a good idea to seek the advice of suppliers as to the number of predators needed.

When "good bugs" are first introduced to the garden, don't be surprised to see many of them move away to other areas of the dome and die. Either they're upset by

NATURAL vs. CHEMICAL INSECTICIDES

The terms "natural insecticides" and "chemical insecticides" should not be taken literally, since everything, including ourselves, is chemical in nature. The simple distinctions between the two are:

Natural insecticides are toxic chemicals, usually made of plant extracts, that degrade quickly after application. A chemical synthesized in a laboratory to share these characteristics could also be called "natural."

Chemical insecticides are man-made substances that remain highly toxic for long periods.

the crowding from so many of their own kind in the confined area, or they've already eaten their fill. But, don't worry: for every "good bug" that dies, hundreds of bad ones go too.

If you don't want to use "good bugs" to control the bad ones, you might try natural insecticides. These are usually made of plant products and they remain toxic for only a short time. One commonly used by organic gardeners — rotenone — must be handled in strict accordance with directions on the container label because it remains mildly toxic for 48 hours before degrading into a non-toxic form. During this period, rotenone can be harmful to fish raised in the dome or to some beneficial predatory insects. (Natural insecticides and their uses are listed in Appendix 6.)

Chemical insecticides such as DDT are harmful to many more forms of life and remain so for long periods. These are not recommended for use in the dome; if they are used, they must be handled and applied with extreme caution. Wash all vegetables carefully before eating. Follow label instructions carefully.

If predatory insects are used, fresh vegetables may be picked and eaten right from the dome garden.

THE FUSES TEAM WINTER GARDEN

A large variety of cool-weather crops have been grown in the Fordham dome: some were high-yielding, others not; some grew well, but used too much space. Overall, the dome garden produced so many crops that there was no need to worry about using every square foot. Here's a description of how some crops performed for the FUSES team:

Leaf lettuce. Although different varieties were tried, Black-Seeded Simpson was grown most often, and yielded crisp, tasty lettuce throughout the winter. Best yields were achieved when the crop was cut back continually, allowing quick reproduction of new leaves. Aphids were only a minor problem and seemed to prefer other vegetables more.

Peas. Burpeeana early peas thrived, producing bountiful yields of a sweet, tasty vegetable, often eaten fresh off the vine, pod and all.

Radishes. Early Scarlet Globe is an excellent choice for the dome garden: not only do they grow quickly into delicious radishes, but they also tolerate close spacing to other vegetables very well.

Carrots. The two varieties used — Nantes and Chantenay — grew into extremely sweet-tasting carrots. But, because one seed develops into just one carrot and because carrots don't grow as fast as other vegetables, the garden space allotted to them could have been more productive if used for leaf or fruiting vegetables.

Spinach. Much garden space was used for this good-tasting vegetable, which gave excellent yields despite its attractiveness to aphids.

Collards. Although not among the team members' favorite-tasting vegetables, the plants yielded excellent, robust collards.

Cabbages. Large, tasty heads were grown, but not quickly enough, or in a small enough space, to consider cabbage a very good vegetable for dome gardens.

Rhonda Pavese and John Fontanetta harvested a fine crop of peas from these vines at the Fordham dome.

A dome garden must have adequate ventilation and air circulation in the summer to produce good, fresh vegetables. At Fordham, an open door or large open triangle was not used for ventilation because of possible unwanted entry. Instead, one large vent and a smaller cut-out vent was used. The result was high temperatures, sometimes in excess of 100°F., and fast-growing plants that bore little fruit.

Hopefully, your dome is in an area where you can leave the door and large vents open to provide the ventilation the garden needs. Moderate temperatures make for flourishing warm-weather crops. (For additional discussion of dome ventilation, consult Chapter 8.)

Some observations on the FUSES team summer garden follow:

Cucumbers. Burpee Hybrid cucumbers gave the best yields of all the warm-weather crops grown in the dome because they tolerated heat well. But, even with this vege-

THE FUSES TEAM SUMMER GARDEN

Sometimes excessive plant growth occurs when dome temperatures are high. Ventilate to minimize this problem.

table, yields were best in late summer to early fall, when temperatures were lower.

Eggplant and Squash. Both plants grew to extremely large sizes, and shaded other crops. But, fruit yields were not very high because of the heat. These vegetables are not suggested for the dome.

Tomatoes. Tomatoes also grew very large with smaller than average fruit because of the heat. If you anticipate ventilation problems in your dome, you can probably grow large tomatoes by using seeds genetically designed to produce plants that fruit after reaching a certain height.

GARDENING REFERENCES

Here is a short list of suggested readings to help you garden in your dome.

The Postage Stamp Garden Book by Duane G. Newcomb (J.P. Tarcher, Inc., 1975). This book describes and presents strong justifications for French Intensive gardening. It also describes how to compost, how to prepare soil and how to form gardening beds. The book was one of the sources relied upon most by the FUSES team during early work on the dome.

Secrets of Companion Planting for Successful Gardening by Louise Riotte (Garden Way Publishing, 1975). This book details how to use biological methods of insect control and, naturally, tells how to companion plant. Since some vegetables can deter growth of others if planted next to each other, it's important to be aware of such pairings, particularly in a closely-spaced, wide-row garden.

Wide-Row Planting: The Productive Miracle by Dick Raymond (Garden Way Publishing, 1977). This inexpensive booklet describes the methods and benefits of wide-row planting.

The Gardener's Bug Book by Cynthia Westcott (Doubleday, 1973). This is a massive reference work on identifying and combating all insect pests.

The Bug Book by Helen and John Philbrick (Garden Way Publishing, 1974). This book tells how to identify and control pests organically. It includs many bio-dynamic recipes as well as untested but traditional remedies from old gardening books.

Uncountable books have been published on every aspect of gardening. The few cited above should help you develop a thriving year-round vegetable garden, but don't hesitate to consult other sources when unfamiliar situations arise.

PART TWO: AQUACULTURE

The FUSES team is trying to develop a small scale aquaculture system that could be placed in the dome and provide an economical way of producing a high protein food source. Most fish raising around the world is done in ponds or lakes (natural environments).

The difficulty with developing small-scale systems with synthetic environments is that to produce a large number of fish in a relatively small volume of water requires intense filtration. Filtration of the tank water is expensive and complex, and this drives up the cost of producing the fish. The FUSES team is trying to develop an alternative — a passive system requiring little or no filtration to maintain conditions for fish growth. Ideally, this system would be simple to operate and would require little energy and money to maintain.

The researchers are looking for a species of fish that subsists on little or no outside food other than algae produced in the tank, and can thrive in a small-scale simulation of its natural environment. Tilapia aurea, a tropical fish native to Africa and Asia that is raised in pond aquaculture systems of these two continents, has been tried.

TILAPIA

Tilapia are by nature **herbivorous** fish, meaning that they consume plants and algae. They also survive in crowded conditions, and even among high concentrations of their own waste; and they survive in widely fluctuating temperatures, from 55°-95°F. These are all conditions they were subjected to in the Fordham dome, although it doesn't seem these would be ideal growth conditions for anything.

The FUSES team had been led to believe that the fish would thrive in the 725-gallon cylindrical fiberglass tank, subsisting mainly on the algae developed in it by absorption of sunlight; that they would grow well despite their large numbers (250 at a time) in a confined space having little or no filtration; and that, to keep the system productive, 50 gallons of sludge would have to be siphoned from the bottom of the tank each week.

This seemed too good to be true, since this sludge could be used to help fertilize the garden. As an initial experiment, 150 tilapia were placed in the fiberglass fish tank in the dome. The fish tank had a large algae bloom making the water a dark green. Presumably this dense algae would provide ample food for the herbivorous fish so only a small amount of garden by-products (mainly tops of carrots) were added to the tank. Fifty gallons of water was siphoned off the bottom of the tank once a week as a passive method of purification. This water was then used to fertilize the garden.

The theoretical basis for this method of tank maintenance is that sludge on the bottom of the tank has large numbers of bacteria in it. These bacteria are the number one cause of low oxygen and fouled water. If these are removed and 50 gallons of fresh water are added to the tank, the water conditions can be maintained at an acceptable level.

Six months of observation and data collection indicated that, although no fish were dying, they were not growing quickly enough. Two experiments were then conducted to determine why the growth rate of the tilapia was so slow.

Anatomical studies were made, revealing that the fish's widely-spaced gill rakers do not allow them to filter free-floating algae from the water; this prevents the algae from being swallowed in amounts large enough to provide a primary food source. And the tilapia's short gut length is uncharacteristic of a fish that subsists primarily on algae.

The tilapia also were grown in the laboratory under conditions of active filtration and with the use of a commercial feed. Under these conditions they grew quickly. Further experiments attempted to determine the best feeding schedules for tilapia.

The early experiments point out a number of conclusions. Tilapia cannot subsist primarily on algae and be expected to grow quickly enough to be economically feasible. The team found tilapia can survive in close quarters in heavy concentrations of their own waste, but they'll not grow quickly under these conditions. And they found that dense algae in the tank acts as more than a potential

STARTING DENSE ALGAE

While raisers of tropical fish in aquariums dislike having algae in their tanks because it darkens the water and detracts from their hobby's aesthetics, its growth should be encouraged in a food-producing system like the dome. This is particularly so if fish are in your tank; but even when they're not, a dense algae bloom in the tank will help its water absorb solar energy readily to retain warmth in the structure.

To start algae growth, simply add a handful of nitrogen fertilizer to the water. This will darken it, help it absorb sunlight and, within a few days, start the algae bloom you desire. If adding fish to your tank, the nitrogen in their waste will continually encourage any further growth you may want.

food source: it helps the tank absorb solar energy more effectively, and it helps to oxygenate the water and dissipate some of the wastes.

The research team is trying to develop a filtering system that will take advantage of the algae in the tank and also not be expensive to build or operate. This plus the addition of a correct feeding schedule of either commercial feed or some other types of feed (the team is experimenting with duckweed and earthworms) will allow tilapia to be grown quickly and inexpensively.

We recommend that if you raise fish you do it only for pleasure and experimentation. Certainly do not expect to gain a favorable return on your investment. You can grow many different types of fish in aquaculture. We feel tilapia has the best promise of an economic return, but trout, catfish and many others are used. If you would like more information on the possibilities of raising fish in your dome, here are a few good references:

Aquaculture: The Farming and Husbandry of Freshwater and Marine Organisms by John E. Bardach, John H. Ryther, and William O. McLarney (John Wiley & Sons, Inc., 1972).

Fish and Invertebrate Culture: Water Management in Closed Systems by Stephen H. Spotte (John Wiley & Sons, Inc., 1970).

Chapter 10: Using the Dome to Earn and Save Money

Aside from saving money by growing your own food, there are other productive ways to use your dome. And, aside from having the pleasure of picking fresh vegetables from your own four-season garden, there are other satisfactions. This chapter describes some of these ways to stir your imagination and to help you use and enjoy your dome to its fullest potential.

SELLING VEGETABLES

There is, of course, a good market for freshly picked, insecticide-free vegetables in the winter. Supermarket and small store owners might be convinced to put your fresh vegetables on their shelves.

You may want to improve your prospects by growing more expensive, high-yielding crops in the winter, such as lettuce and spinach. By using your entire wide-row garden for these vegetables, you may be able to grow up to 90 pounds a month. In a few months, you may be able to pay back the initial investment for your dome.

GROWING SEEDLINGS FOR SALE

Growing seedlings in the dome can be profitable, especially if you live in the north where demand for them is often high. For example, by using only about 50 square feet of gardening space for a six to eight week period starting in late February, you can grow more than 1,000 seedlings that are in high demand during April and May. These can be sold to outdoor gardeners who want to get a head start on summer.

Seedling prices vary, depending on where they're sold.

A single, healthy, eight-week-old tomato seedling can retail in a New York City nursery for as much as $1. Outlets elsewhere undoubtedly charge less.

Some seedlings will be more popular than others in your vicinity; these are the ones to grow the most of. Investigate local demand first, and then, if you decide to produce seedlings on a large scale, keep these suggestions in mind:

• Plan the distribution of the seedlings, even before growing them. Visit local nurseries, country stores, small department stores and even supermarkets to determine the vegetable preferences in the area. Contact owners of these retail stores and agree on a volume and price for your seedlings. Another possibility: post a sign by your home and sell them right out of the dome.

• Prepare peat pots for the seedlings, then set the pots in plastic trays. Don't water the seedlings directly; instead, fill their trays with water that will be absorbed by the plants.

• To maintain the seedlings at correct temperatures — and avoid possible damage from low temperatures — you may want to connect a heater to a thermostat preset at a comfortable level for them.

• Guard the seedlings closely against disease and insects. Although a mild disease or small infestation may not pose a serious threat to the plants, either will reduce their marketability.

USING THE DOME FOR HOME HEAT

The dome stays warm in the winter because it is a passive solar collector. And most days during the year, particularly in late spring, summer and early fall, it retains more heat than needed to raise vegetables. Even when outside temperatures are only about 40°F., ventilation is necessary to remove excess heat.

You can direct this excess into your home, if it's located near the dome. And, of course, this reduces your dependence on costly home heating sources, such as oil, gas and electricity.

To transfer the dome's warmth to your home, connect the dome to the basement, using two well-insulated air ducts. The ducts should be brought into the dome at ground level through holes in the plastic next to the hubs and be screwed or strapped onto the struts to prevent movement. Secure the film to the ducts with tape to create a weathertight seal. One of the ducts should then travel

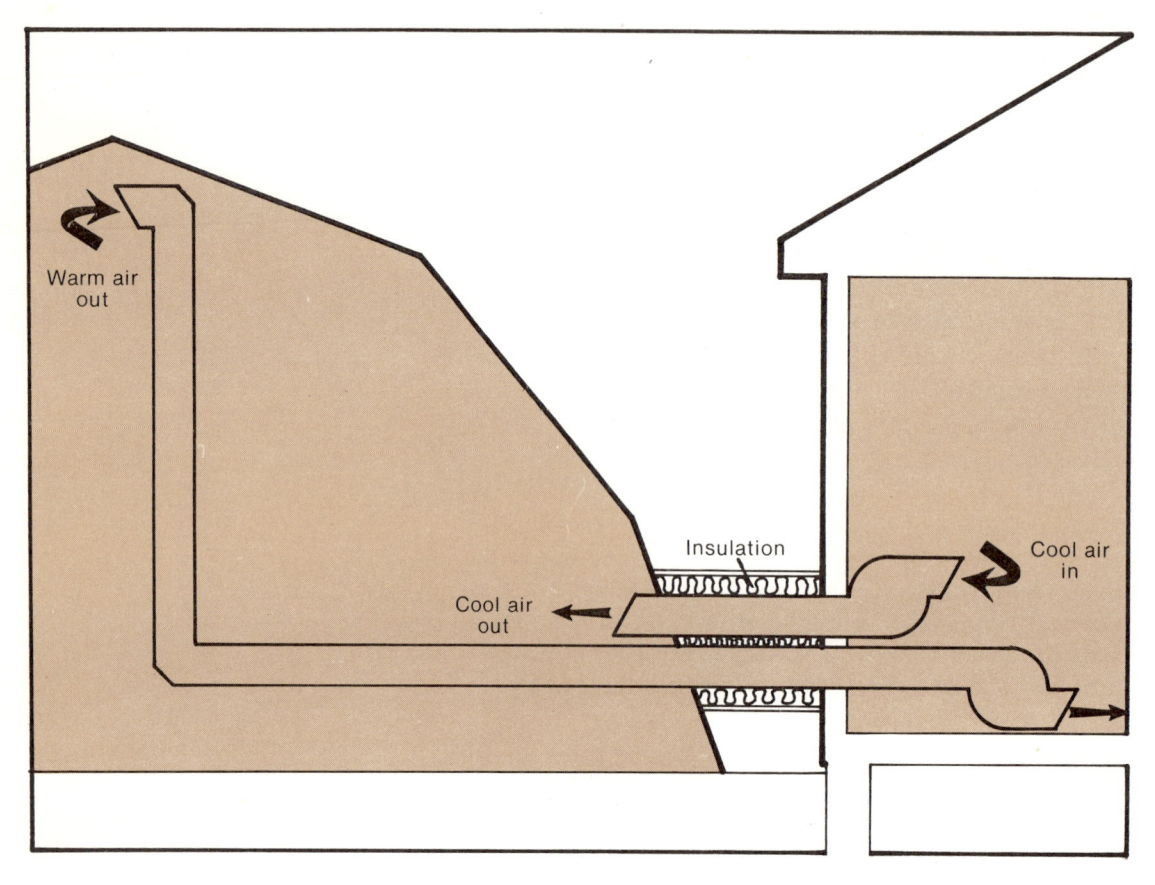

Figure 10-1. Use two well-insulated ducts to transfer dome heat to your home. The ducts may enter above ground level, but ideally the ducts should enter through the basement.

inside the dome to a point near the dome top. Support or hang this duct by wire. Using a fan in the upper duct, draw the dome's hot, humid air into the basement. Sometimes, this air may be 100°F. or more.

To make the system better, connect the fan to a thermostat inside the dome that will turn the fan on at a pre-selected temperature and turn it off when enough hot air has been drawn out of the dome. To obtain maximum home heat, set the thermostat as low as possible, while still retaining sufficient heat in the dome to raise good, healthy vegetables. To determine the best settings, it's a good idea to experiment and to make periodic temperature checks in the dome.

Because the dome air is quite humid, it is circulated in the basement (preferably unfinished), rather than a higher level of the home. As the air rises, it loses some of its moisture. If you have a finished basement, or if you have **no** basement, you may want to operate a dehumidifier where the air enters your home to reduce dampness.

USING THE DOME TO PRE-HEAT WATER

Since the dome is often warmer than necessary, there may be excess heat stored in its solar energy-absorbing containers. You can save money by using some of this excess heat to pre-heat water before it enters your hot-water heater. If you use the dome to do this, or to help heat your home, there's another benefit: you may qualify for energy tax credits. Check your federal income tax return instructions for details.

The temperature of water supplied to a home during winter can sometimes drop to 40°F., but the hot water homeowners need is 120°–180°F. Increasing the temperature of water from 40° to 120°F. creates a huge energy demand from a hot-water heater. But, this demand can, for example, be cut in half by pre-heating the incoming water to 80°F. There's no mystery to doing this, either.

From a water line, or other water source in your home, extend a pipe into the dome and connect it to copper tubing. About 30 feet of tubing is a good length to try at first. Coil this length and submerge it in three 55- or 30-gallon drums. To the other end of the tubing, connect another pipe that returns to your hot water heater's inlet valve. This completes a closed loop pre-heating system.

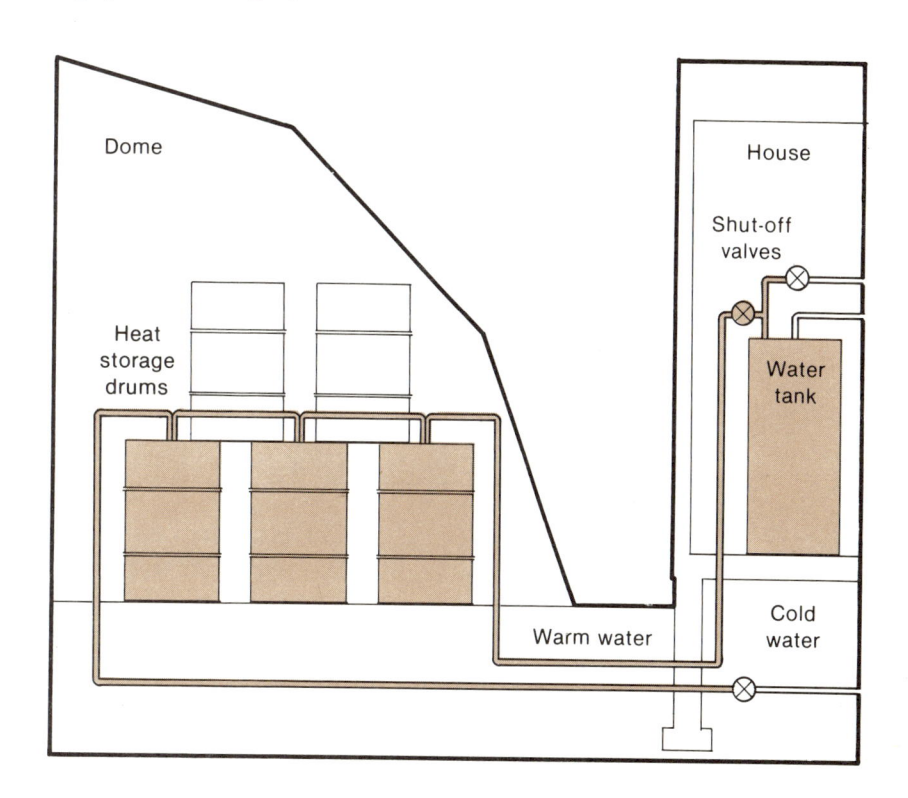

Figure 10-2. Cold water from the house travels to coils in the dome drums. After warming, the water returns to the house to enter the hot water tank.

There should already be a valve on the heater's inlet, so add another valve to the new pipe just before it connects to the heater's inlet valve, then use a T-connection to join the new pipe to the heater. By closing the heater's old inlet valve and opening the new one, you'll divert water through the closed loop for pre-heating before it enters the hot-water heater.

Naturally, the pipes from your house to the dome must be well insulated. But, even this will not prevent water standing in the pipes from freezing unless they are buried in trenches below the frost line. Or, if you decide against using the system in the winter, drain the outdoor pipes to prevent freezing. It's not necessary to drain the coiled copper tubing because it remains warm year round. To drain the outdoor pipes, shut off the water flow to the dome and either use a gravity drain or blow them out.

Even if you don't use the pre-heating system in the winter, you'll save energy because hot water is needed all seasons of the year.

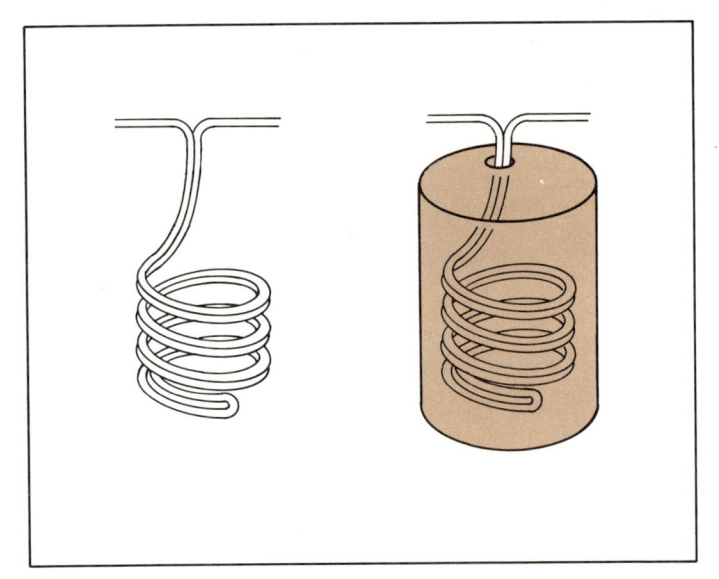

Figure 10-3. Coil copper tubing, then submerge it in a dome drum. Do this three times, so a single 30-foot length passes through three drums.

The length of tubing and number of drums to place it in will vary with the amount of hot water you use. Ideally the water leaving the copper coil should be at or near the temperature of the water in the drums. By experimenting with the length of tubing and number of drums, you can determine the combination that will work best for you.

When operating this system, be careful not to endanger the dome environment by drawing off too much heat. This can be done by keeping an eye on the temperatures in the dome and drums and shutting off the system when temperatures fall too low.

This closed loop system also can be made completely automatic by using two electronic valves at the hot-water heater that would be controlled by a thermostat with a probe, submerged in one of the 30- or 55-gallon drums. These valves are inexpensive and generally available at retail stores. The thermostat should be set to shut off the loop and open the old inlet to your hot water heater when temperatures in the drum fall to a dangerous level.

Temperatures inside these drums can top 100°F. on a sunny day, a substantial heat contribution. And since the water is circulated through your hot-water heater before it is used, you won't notice a difference in the temperature or availability of the hot water you ultimately use. Only lower hot water bills will be noted.

And, by adding a spigot within this loop inside the dome, you have a source of water available for gardening at least three seasons a year, and four, if you dig trenches to bury the pipes.

COMMUNITY GARDENS

A dome may be the focal point for a community garden. Urban, suburban and even rural areas are developing an increasing number of community garden sites.

The Fordham dome in New York City was built with the idea of community gardening in mind. In fact, Beth Smith of the Gannett News Service called the dome a "genesis for what could be the community garden of the future." Two domes have been built in Manhattan, as focal points for neighborhood community gardening projects. Others are planned.

EDUCATIONAL AID

The dome can be an excellent showplace for teaching the basics of gardening, ecology, and solar energy. Public and private schools, special educational facilities, and even a prison in upstate New York have contacted the FUSES team about possible applications for the dome. Twin domes in Gateway National Park in Jamaica Bay, New York were built for educational purposes.

A COVER FOR YOUR SWIMMING POOL OR HOT TUB

One of the dome's more unusual uses is as a covering for an above-ground circular swimming pool or hot tub to keep it warm enough for year round enjoyment. Of course, you won't want it over the pool during summer, and that's where its lightweight frame comes in handy. Once disconnected from its securing posts and underground insulation, it can be moved aside — then replaced again in the fall.

If the dome is used to cover a pool or tub, there must be enough room inside for the water storage drums. If there's sufficient additional room, a small plot might be cultivated; if space is tight, plants may be hung from hub plates to give a tropical appearance.

Chapter 11: Domes of Other Sizes

There are many different geodesic dome designs. The one chosen at Fordham is known as the **two frequency icosa alternate.** Its frame requires only two different sized struts and these form triangles, also of only two different sizes. It was selected because it's easy to construct.

The two-frequency design is unsuited for large, multi-story domes because its struts would have to be too long and would have to be made of much stronger materials than those used at Fordham. The design and construction methods described in this book are suited for domes as large as 25 feet in diameter. Diameters smaller than 16 feet are practically useless because they result in insufficient floor space and ceiling height.

Floor space of a dome is derived by finding the radius (half the diameter), squaring this number, and then multiplying it by 3.14. This means, for example, that a 23-foot diameter dome like the one at Fordham has 416 square feet of floor space, while a 16-foot dome has less than half that amount. If you want more floor space, using the relatively simple two frequency dome design, it's easier and costs less to build two domes rather than one large structure.

The larger dome is more difficult to erect and cover because of its height, and it requires a more complex design and more difficult woodworking techniques. Twin 23-foot domes at Gateway National Park in New York, standing adjacent to each other and connected by a short, above-ground tunnel, are a good example of two structures built to gain extra floor space. These domes are used as educational aids and, therefore, need a lot of floor space to accommodate student visitors.

When choosing a dome size, another major concern is

the efficient, economical use of materials. The 23-foot size requires two different sized frame struts that can be cut from one 12-foot length of 2 x 2 with just a seven-inch piece of waste. The film covering comes on a 14-foot wide roll that neatly covers level four and the triads of levels two and three with little waste.

If you want to try a dome of another size, those with 16- to 23-foot diameters are the most convenient, efficient and cost-effective.

THE FRAME

Whatever size dome is built, hub sizes remain the same; the door and vent are built the same way; and construction and woodworking techniques remain the same, with three minor exceptions:

During woodworking, jigs must be made to the new or appropriate strut size; during site preparation, the length of wire used to lay out base hubs is one-half the dome's new diameter; and, during erection of the frame, level four is raised to a new height, other than 11½ feet.

After selecting a dome diameter, use these formulas to determine the size struts you need:

Long strut length,
in inches = (diameter, in inches) × (0.309) − 12.5

Short strut length,
in inches = (diameter, in inches) × (0.273) − 12.5

MATERIALS

Use the guidelines below to help choose a size for a dome that can be built with minimal waste of materials.

Lumber. Wood is usually sold in 8-, 10-, 12- and 16-foot lengths; obviously, what you buy will be dictated by the dome size you select.

Whatever size that is, keep in mind the following: that wood used for hubs and securing posts remains the same; that there are more long than short struts to be cut, and many hub struts, too; that enough wood must be left to build your door and vent; and that it's not a bad idea to have a few extra wood lengths in case others are damaged or warped.

There are many combinations of wood sizes that work

DOMES OF OTHER SIZES

well for domes of different diameters. For example, if strut lengths are 46.8 and 39.9 inches as in a 16-foot diameter dome, then one long, one short and one hub strut can be cut from an 8-foot length of wood with only about two inches waste; or two long struts can be cut from an 8-foot length with about the same waste. If these lengths are unavailable, simply cut a 16-foot length in half.

It's usually not a good idea to calculate sizes so closely that there's no waste at all; for example, don't try to form two struts with a single cut. Although this procedure seems simple, it often can lead to struts of incorrect sizes because, when wood is cut, it is reduced in size a bit more than the thickness of the saw blade. Particularly when making multiple cuts in a wood length, leave a little margin for waste.

Underground polyethylene. An 8-foot **wide** roll is needed, regardless of the size dome built, because this material is used and positioned the same way in all domes. But, determine the **length** of the material to buy according to this formula:

Length of roll,
in feet = (3.14) × (diameter of dome, in feet) + 8

You may have to buy a larger roll than necessary because only certain sizes are available. One consolation is that this material is inexpensive and can be used for many purposes.

Above-ground polyethylene covering. Monsanto "602" is available in many different size rolls — 100 x 14, 100 x 16, 100 x 20, 100 x 24, 100 x 32 and 100 x 40; or 150 x 40. (All figures indicate feet.) By choosing the roll you need, you can avoid wasting material and spending extra time cutting. There's also less chance for cutting errors.

Unless the dome you build is one of a few sizes, you probably won't find the exact size roll you need. Instead, it will be necessary to buy the next largest size and accept more waste, or to buy a roll that is twice the width you need and cut it in half. This second option can add to the likelihood of miscutting film because more cutting is required.

To determine the size roll you need for above-ground covering, use the following formulas:

Width of roll,
in inches = (2) × (length of short strut, in inches) + 37

Length of roll,
in inches = [(4.46) × (length of short strut, in inches)] + [(8.66) × (length of long strut, in inches)] + 276

Fiberglass insulation (3½-inch thick). Use the following formula to determine the amount of insulation needed for your size dome; it allows for enough extra material to compensate for a few cutting errors:

$$\text{Number of rolls needed} = \frac{[(4.3) \times (\text{length of short strut, in inches} + 12.5) \times (\text{length of long strut, in inches} + 12.5)] + [(1.8) \times (\text{length of long strut, in inches} + 12.5)^2]}{7500}$$

The West 46th Street dome.

A 16-FOOT DOME

A dome built in New York City, on West 46th St., has a 16-foot diameter. If you were to duplicate this dome and determine your material needs based on the formulas presented in this chapter, your key dimensions and requirements would be:

Vital Statistics:
Diameter = 16 feet
Length of short strut = 39.9 inches
Length of long strut = 46.8 inches

Suggested Material Sizes:
Lumber = fifty 8-foot lengths
Underground polyethylene = 8 x 58.4 feet; you'd probably need to buy 8 x 75.
Above-ground covering = 10 x 72 feet; you'd need to buy two 14 x 100-foot rolls (one 4 mil, one 6 mil) or a 20 x 100-foot roll (6 mil) used for both inside and outside layers, causing less waste.
Insulation = 3 rolls

Appendix

Appendix 1: Solar Altitude and Azimuth

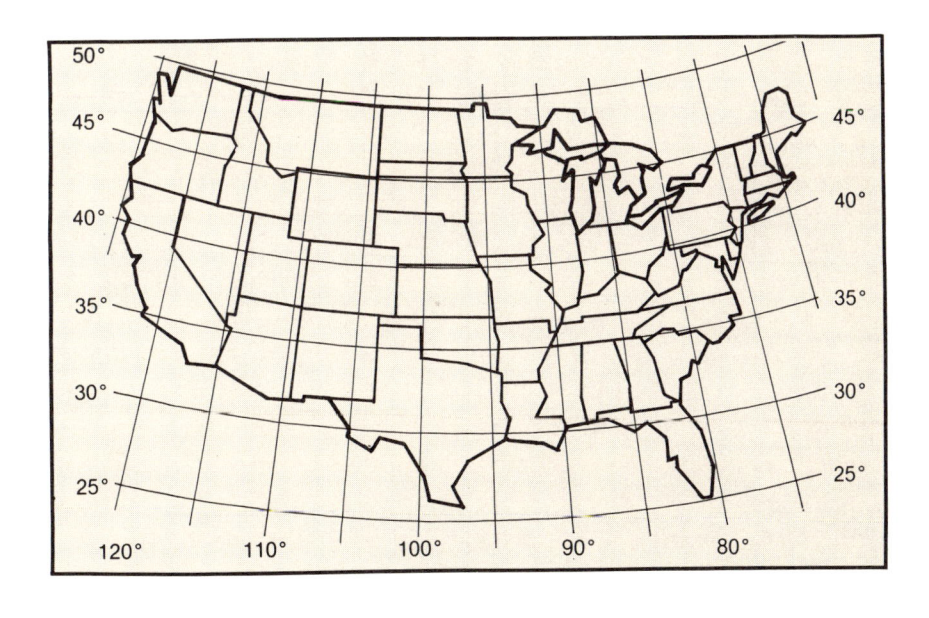

The tables on the following pages (166 through 168) give solar altitudes and azimuths for the 21st day of each month of the year, at five different latitudes in the United States.

Find the table with the latitude closest to the location of your proposed dome site. If a table with your latitude is not included, simply interpolate, using appropriate latitude tables that are presented. For example, if you live along the 28° north latitude, solar altitudes and azimuths for your site are approximately mid way between readings for the 24° and 32° north latitudes.

Take the altitude and azimuths you establish for each dome site obstruction and compare these figures to the altitudes and azimuths in the appropriate tables. By making this comparison, you can determine approximately when shading will occur at your site.

If, for example, at 40 north latitude, the top of a tree has an altitude of 40 and its azimuths are 35° to 40°, the table, "Latitude

Use this map to determine your latitude. If your location is between two latitudes, interpolate as necessary.

165

BUILDING AND USING A SOLAR-HEATED GEODESIC GREENHOUSE

166

BRITISH THERMAL UNITS
Solar radiation intensity is measured in various units. The measurement used in this book is British Thermal Units per square foot (Btu/ft²). A British Thermal Unit (Btu) is the amount of heat required to raise the temperature of one pound of distilled water 1°F. at or near 39.2°F.

North 40", shows that a dome facing this obstruction will be shaded from about 9:30 A.M. to 10 A.M., from October to March.

Although "solar times" are presented in the tables and although these will not be the actual times for your location, solar times are adequate references for the purpose of determining approximate shading. Conversion from solar to local time is not necessary.

In the far right column of the tables, the direct normal irradiation (expressed in British Thermal Units per square foot) indicates the amount of energy transmitted to a spot on earth (your dome), when that spot is in a perpendicular plane to the sun's rays.

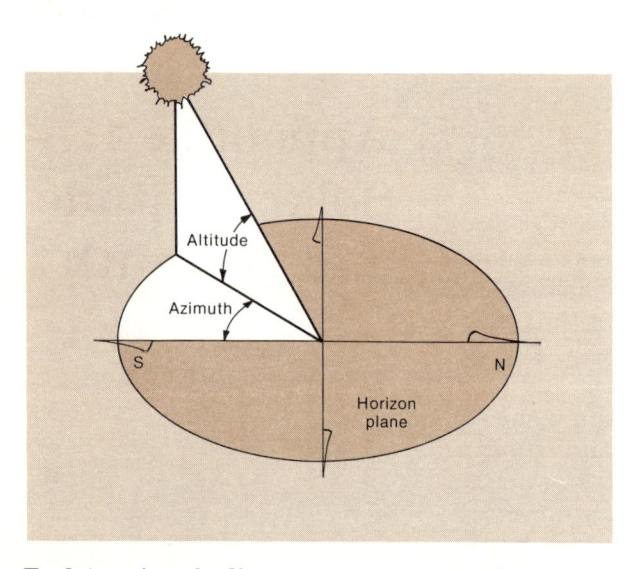

To determine shading, compare an obstacle's altitude and azimuth with the sun's.

Latitude North 24°

Date	Solar Time A.M.	Solar Time P.M.	Alt.	Azimuth	Direct Normal Irradiation, Btuh/sq ft
Jan 21	7	5	4.8	65.6	70
	8	4	16.9	58.3	239
	9	3	27.9	48.8	287
	10	2	37.2	36.1	308
	11	1	43.6	19.6	317
	12	12	46.0	0.0	320
Feb 21	7	5	9.0	73.9	153
	8	4	21.9	66.4	261
	9	3	33.9	56.8	297
	10	2	44.5	43.5	313
	11	1	52.2	24.5	321
	12	12	55.2	0.0	323
Mar 21	7	5	13.7	83.8	194
	8	4	27.2	76.8	267
	9	3	40.2	67.9	295
	10	2	52.3	54.8	308
	11	1	61.9	33.4	315
	12	12	66.0	0.0	317

Latitude N. 24°

Latitude North 24°

Date	Solar Time A.M.	Solar Time P.M.	Alt.	Azimuth	Direct Normal Irradiation, Btuh/sq ft
Apr 21	6	6	4.7	100.6	40
	7	5	18.3	94.9	203
	8	4	32.0	89.0	257
	9	3	45.6	81.9	281
	10	2	59.0	71.8	293
	11	1	71.1	51.6	298
	12	12	77.6	0.0	300
May 21	6	6	8.0	108.4	85
	7	5	21.2	103.2	203
	8	4	34.6	98.5	248
	9	3	48.3	93.6	269
	10	2	62.0	87.7	280
	11	1	75.5	76.9	286
	12	12	86.0	0.0	287
June 21	6	6	9.3	111.6	97
	7	5	22.3	106.8	200
	8	4	35.5	102.6	242
	9	3	49.0	98.7	262
	10	2	62.6	95.0	273
	11	1	76.3	90.7	279
	12	12	89.5	0.0	280
July 21	6	6	8.2	109.0	81
	7	5	21.4	103.8	195
	8	4	34.8	99.2	239
	9	3	48.4	94.5	261
	10	2	62.1	89.0	272
	11	1	75.7	79.2	278
	12	12	86.6	0.0	279
Aug 21	6	6	5.0	101.3	34
	7	5	18.5	95.6	186
	8	4	32.2	89.7	240
	9	3	45.9	82.9	265
	10	2	59.3	73.0	277
	11	1	71.6	53.2	283
	12	12	78.3	0.0	285
Sept 21	7	5	13.7	83.8	172
	8	4	27.2	76.8	248
	9	3	40.2	67.9	277
	10	2	52.3	54.8	292
	11	1	61.9	33.4	298
	12	12	66.0	0.0	301
Oct 21	7	5	9.1	74.1	137
	8	4	22.0	66.7	246
	9	3	34.1	57.1	284
	10	2	44.7	43.8	300
	11	1	52.5	24.7	308
	12	12	55.5	0.0	311
Nov 21	7	5	4.9	65.8	66
	8	4	17.0	58.4	232
	9	3	28.0	48.9	281
	10	2	37.3	36.3	302
	11	1	43.8	19.7	311
	12	12	46.2	0.0	314
Dec 21	7	5	3.2	62.6	29
	8	4	14.9	55.3	225
	9	3	25.5	46.0	281
	10	2	34.3	33.7	304
	11	1	40.4	18.2	314
	12	12	42.6	0.0	317

Latitude N. 24°

APPENDIX

Latitude North 32°

Date	Solar Time A.M.	Solar Time P.M.	Alt.	Azimuth	Direct Normal Irradiation, Btuh/sq ft
Jan 21	7	5	1.4	65.2	1
	8	4	12.5	56.5	202
	9	3	22.5	46.0	269
	10	2	30.6	33.1	295
	11	1	36.1	17.5	306
	12	12	38.0	0.0	309
Feb 21	7	5	6.7	72.8	111
	8	4	18.5	63.8	244
	9	3	29.3	52.8	287
	10	2	38.5	38.9	305
	11	1	44.9	21.0	314
	12	12	47.2	0.0	316
Mar 21	7	5	12.7	81.9	184
	8	4	25.1	73.0	260
	9	3	36.8	62.1	289
	10	2	47.3	47.5	304
	11	1	55.0	26.8	310
	12	12	58.0	0.0	312
Apr 21	6	6	6.1	99.9	66
	7	5	18.8	92.2	206
	8	4	31.5	84.0	256
	9	3	43.9	74.2	278
	10	2	55.7	60.3	290
	11	1	65.4	37.5	296
	12	12	69.6	0.0	298
May 21	6	6	10.4	107.2	118
	7	5	22.8	100.1	211
	8	4	35.4	92.9	249
	9	3	48.1	84.7	269
	10	2	60.6	73.3	279
	11	1	72.0	51.9	285
	12	12	78.0	0.0	286
June 21	6	6	12.2	110.2	130
	7	5	24.3	103.4	209
	8	4	36.9	96.8	244
	9	3	49.6	89.4	263
	10	2	62.2	79.7	273
	11	1	74.2	60.9	278
	12	12	81.5	0.0	280
July 21	6	6	10.7	107.7	113
	7	5	23.1	100.6	203
	8	4	35.7	93.6	241
	9	3	48.4	85.5	261
	10	2	60.9	74.3	271
	11	1	72.4	53.3	277
	12	12	78.6	0.0	278
Aug 21	6	6	6.5	100.5	59
	7	5	19.1	92.8	189
	8	4	31.8	84.7	239
	9	3	44.3	75.0	263
	10	2	56.1	61.3	275
	11	1	66.0	38.4	281
	12	12	70.3	0.0	283
Sep 21	7	5	12.7	81.9	163
	8	4	25.1	73.0	240
	9	3	36.8	62.1	272
	10	2	47.3	47.5	287
	11	1	55.0	26.8	294
	12	12	58.0	0.0	296
Oct 21	7	5	6.8	73.1	98
	8	4	18.7	64.0	229
	9	3	29.5	53.0	273
	10	2	38.7	39.1	292
	11	1	45.1	21.1	301
	12	12	47.5	0.0	304
Nov 21	7	5	1.5	65.4	1
	8	4	12.7	56.6	196
	9	3	22.6	46.1	262
	10	2	30.8	33.2	288
	11	1	36.2	17.6	300
	12	12	38.2	0.0	303
Dec 21	8	4	10.3	53.8	176
	9	3	19.8	43.6	257
	10	2	27.6	31.2	287
	11	1	32.7	16.4	300
	12	12	34.6	0.0	304

↑ P.M. Latitude N. 32°

Latitude North 40°

Date	Solar Time A.M.	Solar Time P.M.	Alt.	Azimuth	Direct Normal Irradiation, Btuh/sq ft
Jan 21	8	4	8.1	55.3	141
	9	3	16.8	44.0	238
	10	2	23.8	30.9	274
	11	1	28.4	16.0	289
	12	12	30.0	0.0	293
Feb 21	7	5	4.3	72.1	55
	8	4	14.8	61.6	219
	9	3	24.3	49.7	271
	10	2	32.1	35.4	293
	11	1	37.3	18.6	303
	12	12	39.2	0.0	306
Mar 21	7	5	11.4	80.2	171
	8	4	22.5	69.6	250
	9	3	32.8	57.3	281
	10	2	41.6	41.9	297
	11	1	47.7	22.6	304
	12	12	50.0	0.0	306
Apr 21	6	6	7.4	98.9	89
	7	5	18.9	89.5	207
	8	4	30.3	79.3	253
	9	3	41.3	67.2	275
	10	2	51.2	51.4	286
	11	1	58.7	29.2	292
	12	12	61.6	0.0	294
May 21	5	7	1.9	114.7	1
	6	6	12.7	105.6	143
	7	5	24.0	96.6	216
	8	4	35.4	87.2	249
	9	3	46.8	76.0	267
	10	2	57.5	60.9	277
	11	1	66.2	37.1	282
	12	12	70.0	0.0	284
June 21	5	7	4.2	117.3	21
	6	6	14.8	108.4	154
	7	5	26.0	99.7	215
	8	4	37.4	90.7	246
	9	3	48.8	80.2	262
	10	2	59.8	65.8	272
	11	1	69.2	41.9	276
	12	12	73.5	0.0	278
July 21	5	7	2.3	115.2	2
	6	6	13.1	106.1	137
	7	5	24.3	97.2	208
	8	4	35.8	87.8	241
	9	3	47.2	76.7	259
	10	2	57.9	61.7	269
	11	1	66.7	37.9	274
	12	12	70.6	0.0	276
Aug 21	6	6	7.9	99.5	80
	7	5	19.3	90.0	191
	8	4	30.7	79.9	236
	9	3	41.8	67.9	259
	10	2	51.7	52.1	271
	11	1	59.3	29.7	277
	12	12	62.3	0.0	279
Sep 21	7	5	11.4	80.2	149
	8	4	22.5	69.6	230
	9	3	32.8	57.3	263
	10	2	41.6	41.9	279
	11	1	47.7	22.6	287
	12	12	50.0	0.0	290
Oct 21	7	5	4.5	72.3	48
	8	4	15.0	61.9	203
	9	3	24.5	49.8	257
	10	2	32.4	35.6	280
	11	1	37.6	18.7	290
	12	12	39.5	0.0	293
Nov 21	8	4	8.2	55.4	136
	9	3	17.0	44.1	232
	10	2	24.0	31.0	267
	11	1	28.6	16.1	283
	12	12	30.2	0.0	287
Dec 21	8	4	5.5	53.0	88
	9	3	14.0	41.9	217
	10	2	20.7	29.4	261
	11	1	25.0	15.2	279
	12	12	26.6	0.0	284

↑ P.M. Latitude N. 40°

Latitude North 48°

Date	Solar Time A.M.	Solar Time P.M.	Alt.	Azimuth	Direct Normal Irradiation, Btuh/sq ft
Jan 21	8	4	3.5	54.6	36
	9	3	11.0	42.6	185
	10	2	16.9	29.4	239
	11	1	20.7	15.1	260
	12	12	22.0	0.0	267
Feb 21	7	5	1.8	71.7	3
	8	4	10.9	60.0	180
	9	3	19.0	47.3	247
	10	2	25.5	33.0	275
	11	1	29.7	17.0	288
	12	12	31.2	0.0	291
Mar 21	7	5	10.0	78.7	152
	8	4	19.5	66.8	235
	9	3	28.2	53.4	270
	10	2	35.4	37.8	287
	11	1	40.3	19.8	295
	12	12	42.0	0.0	297
Apr 21	6	6	8.6	97.8	108
	7	5	18.6	86.7	205
	8	4	28.5	74.9	247
	9	3	37.8	61.2	269
	10	2	45.8	44.6	281
	11	1	51.5	24.0	287
	12	12	53.6	0.0	289
May 21	5	7	5.2	114.3	41
	6	6	14.7	103.7	162
	7	5	24.6	93.0	218
	8	4	34.6	81.6	248
	9	3	44.3	68.3	264
	10	2	53.0	51.3	274
	11	1	59.5	28.6	279
	12	12	62.0	0.0	280
June 21	5	7	7.9	116.5	77
	6	6	17.2	106.2	172
	7	5	27.0	95.8	219
	8	4	37.1	84.6	245
	9	3	46.9	71.6	260
	10	2	55.8	54.8	269
	11	1	62.7	31.2	273
	12	12	65.4	0.0	275
July 21	5	7	5.7	114.7	42
	6	6	15.2	104.1	155
	7	5	25.1	93.5	211
	8	4	35.1	82.1	240
	9	3	44.8	68.8	256
	10	2	53.5	51.9	266
	11	1	60.1	29.0	271
	12	12	62.6	0.0	272
Aug 21	6	6	9.1	98.3	98
	7	5	19.1	87.2	189
	8	4	29.0	75.4	231
	9	3	38.4	61.8	253
	10	2	46.4	45.1	265
	11	1	52.2	24.3	271
	12	12	54.3	0.0	273
Sep 21	7	5	10.0	78.7	131
	8	4	19.5	66.8	215
	9	3	28.2	53.4	251
	10	2	35.4	37.8	269
	11	1	40.3	19.8	277
	12	12	42.0	0.0	280
Oct 21	7	5	2.0	71.9	3
	8	4	11.2	60.2	165
	9	3	19.3	47.4	232
	10	2	25.7	33.1	261
	11	1	30.0	17.1	274
	12	12	31.5	0.0	278
Nov 21	8	4	3.6	54.7	36
	9	3	11.2	42.7	178
	10	2	17.1	29.5	232
	11	1	20.9	15.1	254
	12	12	22.2	0.0	260
Dec 21	9	3	8.0	40.9	140
	10	2	13.6	28.2	214
	11	1	17.3	14.4	242
	12	12	18.6	0.0	250

Latitude N. 48°

Latitude North 56°

Date	Solar Time A.M.	Solar Time P.M.	Alt.	Azimuth	Direct Normal Irradiation, Btuh/sq ft
Jan 21	9	3	5.0	41.8	77
	10	2	9.9	28.5	170
	11	1	12.9	14.5	206
	12	12	14.0	0.0	216
Feb 21	8	4	6.9	59.0	115
	9	3	13.5	45.6	207
	10	2	18.7	31.2	245
	11	1	22.0	15.9	262
	12	12	23.2	0.0	267
Mar 21	7	5	8.3	77.5	127
	8	4	16.2	64.4	215
	9	3	23.3	50.3	253
	10	2	29.0	34.9	272
	11	1	32.7	17.9	281
	12	12	34.0	0.0	284
Apr 21	5	7	1.4	108.8	0
	6	6	9.6	96.5	122
	7	5	18.0	84.1	201
	8	4	26.1	70.9	240
	9	3	33.6	56.3	261
	10	2	39.9	39.7	273
	11	1	44.1	20.7	279
	12	12	45.6	0.0	280
May 21	4	8	1.2	125.5	0
	5	7	8.5	113.4	92
	6	6	16.5	101.5	175
	7	5	24.8	89.3	219
	8	4	33.1	76.3	244
	9	3	40.9	61.6	259
	10	2	47.6	44.2	268
	11	1	52.3	23.4	273
	12	12	54.0	0.0	275
June 21	4	8	4.2	127.2	21
	5	7	11.4	115.3	121
	6	6	19.3	103.6	185
	7	5	27.6	91.7	221
	8	4	35.9	78.8	243
	9	3	43.8	64.1	256
	10	2	50.7	46.4	264
	11	1	55.6	24.9	268
	12	12	57.4	0.0	270
July 21	4	8	1.7	125.8	0
	5	7	9.0	113.7	91
	6	6	17.0	101.9	169
	7	5	25.3	89.7	212
	8	4	33.6	76.7	236
	9	3	41.4	62.0	251
	10	2	48.2	44.6	260
	11	1	52.9	23.7	265
	12	12	54.6	0.0	267
Aug 21	5	7	2.0	109.2	1
	6	6	10.2	97.0	112
	7	5	18.5	84.5	186
	8	4	26.7	71.3	224
	9	3	34.3	56.7	245
	10	2	40.5	40.0	257
	11	1	44.8	20.9	263
	12	12	46.3	0.0	265
Sep 21	7	5	8.3	77.5	107
	8	4	16.2	64.4	194
	9	3	23.3	50.3	233
	10	2	29.0	34.9	253
	11	1	32.7	17.9	263
	12	12	34.0	0.0	266
Oct 21	8	4	7.1	59.1	103
	9	3	13.8	45.7	192
	10	2	19.0	31.3	230
	11	1	22.3	16.0	247
	12	12	23.5	0.0	252
Nov 21	9	3	5.2	41.9	75
	10	2	10.1	28.5	164
	11	1	13.1	14.5	200
	12	12	14.2	0.0	210
Dec 21	9	3	1.9	40.5	5
	10	2	6.6	27.5	113
	11	1	9.5	13.9	165
	12	12	10.6	0.0	180

Latitude N. 56°

APPENDIX

169

Appendix 2: Degree Days Across the United States

Degree day is a measurement originally used by oil companies to anticipate consumer need for oil in various parts of the country. It is the number of degrees between 65°F., assumed to be the average home temperature, and the mean temperature of a particular day. For example, if the mean outside temperature is 30°F. on a given day, then the number of degree days for that day is 35.

By using January figures for the listed city nearest you in the following tables, and the information given in Chapter 2, you'll have a good idea of how well your dome will perform.

STATE AND STATION	JULY	AUG.	SEP.	OCT.	NOV.	DEC.	JAN.	FEB.	MAR.	APR.	MAY	JUNE	ANNUAL
ALA. BIRMINGHAM	0	0	6	93	363	555	592	462	363	108	9	0	2551
HUNTSVILLE	0	0	12	127	426	663	694	557	434	138	19	0	3070
MOBILE	0	0	0	22	213	357	415	300	211	42	0	0	1560
MONTGOMERY	0	0	0	68	330	527	543	417	316	90	0	0	2291
ALASKA ANCHORAGE	245	291	516	930	1284	1572	1631	1316	1293	879	592	315	10864
ANNETTE	242	208	327	567	738	899	949	837	843	648	490	321	7069
BARROW	803	840	1035	1500	1971	2362	2517	2332	2468	1944	1445	957	20174
BARTER IS.	735	775	987	1482	1944	2337	2536	2369	2477	1923	1373	924	19862
BETHEL	319	394	612	1042	1434	1866	1903	1590	1655	1173	806	402	13196
COLD BAY	474	425	525	772	918	1122	1153	1036	1122	951	791	591	9880
CORDOVA	366	391	522	781	1017	1221	1299	1086	1113	864	660	444	9764
FAIRBANKS	171	332	642	1203	1833	2254	2359	1901	1739	1068	555	222	14279
JUNEAU	301	338	483	725	921	1135	1237	1070	1073	810	601	381	9075
KING SALMON	313	322	513	908	1290	1606	1600	1333	1411	966	673	408	11343
KOTZEBUE	381	446	723	1249	1728	2127	2192	1932	2080	1554	1057	636	16105
MCGRATH	208	338	633	1184	1791	2232	2294	1817	1758	1122	648	258	14283
NOME	481	496	693	1094	1455	1820	1879	1666	1770	1314	930	573	14171
SAINT PAUL	605	539	612	862	963	1197	1228	1168	1265	1098	936	726	11199
SHEMYA	577	475	501	784	876	1042	1045	958	1011	885	837	696	9687
YAKUTAT	338	347	474	716	936	1144	1169	1019	1042	840	632	435	9092
ARIZ. FLAGSTAFF	46	68	201	558	867	1073	1169	991	911	651	437	180	7152
PHOENIX	0	0	0	22	234	415	474	328	217	75	0	0	1765
PRESCOTT	0	0	27	245	579	797	865	711	605	360	158	15	4362
TUCSON	0	0	0	25	231	406	471	344	242	75	6	0	1800
WINSLOW	0	0	6	245	711	1008	1054	770	601	291	96	0	4782
YUMA	0	0	0	0	148	319	363	228	130	29	0	0	1217
ARK. FORT SMITH	0	0	12	127	450	704	781	596	456	144	22	0	3292
LITTLE ROCK	0	0	9	127	465	716	756	577	434	126	9	0	3219
TEXARKANA	0	0	0	78	345	561	626	468	350	105	0	0	2533
CALIF. BAKERSFIELD	0	0	0	37	282	502	546	364	267	105	19	0	2122
BISHOP	0	0	42	248	576	797	874	666	539	306	143	36	4227
BLUE CANYON	34	50	120	347	579	766	865	781	791	582	397	195	5507
BURBANK	0	0	6	43	177	301	366	277	239	138	81	18	1646
EUREKA	270	257	258	329	414	499	546	470	505	438	372	285	4643
FRESNO	0	0	0	78	339	558	586	406	319	150	56	0	2492
LONG BEACH	0	0	12	40	156	288	375	297	267	168	90	18	1711
LOS ANGELES	28	22	42	78	180	291	372	302	288	219	158	81	2061
MT. SHASTA	25	34	123	406	696	902	983	784	738	525	347	159	5722
OAKLAND	53	50	45	127	309	481	527	400	353	255	180	90	2870
POINT ARGUELLO	202	186	162	205	291	400	474	392	403	339	298	243	3595
RED BLUFF	0	0	0	53	318	555	605	428	341	168	47	0	2515
SACRAMENTO	0	0	12	81	363	577	614	442	360	216	102	6	2773
SANDBERG	0	0	30	202	480	691	778	661	620	426	264	57	4209
SAN DIEGO	6	0	15	37	123	251	313	249	202	123	84	36	1439
SAN FRANCISCO	81	78	60	143	306	462	508	395	363	279	214	126	3015
SANTA CATALINA	16	0	9	50	165	279	353	308	326	249	192	105	2052
SANTA MARIA	99	93	96	146	270	391	459	370	363	282	233	165	2967
COLO. ALAMOSA	65	99	279	639	1065	1420	1476	1162	1020	696	440	168	8529
COLORADO SPRINGS	9	25	132	456	825	1032	1128	938	893	582	319	84	6423
DENVER	6	9	117	428	819	1035	1132	938	887	558	288	66	6283
GRAND JUNCTION	0	0	30	313	786	1113	1209	907	729	387	146	21	5641
PUEBLO	0	0	54	326	750	986	1085	871	772	429	174	15	5462
CONN. BRIDGEPORT	0	0	66	307	615	986	1079	966	853	510	208	27	5617
HARDFORT	0	6	99	372	711	1119	1209	1061	899	495	177	24	6172
NEW HAVEN	0	12	87	347	648	1011	1097	991	871	543	245	45	5897
DEL. WILMINGTON	0	0	51	270	588	927	980	874	735	387	112	6	4930

STATE AND STATION	JULY	AUG.	SEP.	OCT.	NOV.	DEC.	JAN.	FEB.	MAR.	APR.	MAY	JUNE	ANNUAL
FLA. APALACHICOLA	0	0	0	16	153	319	347	260	180	33	0	0	1308
DAYTONA BEACH	0	0	0	0	75	211	248	190	140	15	0	0	879
FORT MYERS	0	0	0	0	24	109	146	101	62	0	0	0	442
JACKSONVILLE	0	0	0	12	144	310	332	246	174	21	0	0	1239
KEY WEST	0	0	0	0	0	28	40	31	9	0	0	0	108
LAKELAND	0	0	0	0	57	164	195	146	99	0	0	0	661
MIAMI BEACH	0	0	0	0	0	40	56	36	9	0	0	0	141
ORLANDO	0	0	0	0	72	198	220	165	105	6	0	0	766
PENSACOLA	0	0	0	19	195	353	400	277	183	36	0	0	1463
TALLAHASSEE	0	0	0	28	198	360	375	286	202	36	0	0	1485
TAMPA	0	0	0	0	60	171	202	148	102	0	0	0	683
WEST PALM BEACH	0	0	0	0	6	65	87	64	31	0	0	0	253
GA. ATHENS	0	0	12	115	405	632	642	529	431	141	22	0	2929
ATLANTA	0	0	18	127	414	626	639	529	437	168	25	0	2983
AUGUSTA	0	0	0	78	333	552	549	445	350	90	0	0	2397
COLUMBUS	0	0	0	87	333	543	552	434	338	96	0	0	2383
MACON	0	0	0	71	297	502	505	403	295	63	0	0	2136
ROME	0	0	24	161	474	701	710	577	468	177	34	0	3326
SAVANNAH	0	0	0	47	246	437	437	353	254	45	0	0	1819
THOMASVILLE	0	0	0	25	198	366	394	305	208	33	0	0	1529
IDAHO BOISE	0	0	132	415	792	1017	1113	854	722	438	245	81	5809
IDAHO FALLS 46W	16	34	270	623	1056	1370	1538	1249	1085	651	391	192	8475
IDAHO FALLS 42NW	16	40	282	648	1107	1432	1600	1291	1107	657	388	192	8760
LEWISTON	0	0	123	403	756	933	1063	815	694	426	239	90	5542
POCATELLO	0	0	172	493	900	1166	1324	1058	905	555	319	141	7033
ILL. CAIRO	0	0	36	164	513	791	856	680	539	195	47	0	3821
CHICAGO	0	0	81	326	753	1113	1209	1044	890	480	211	48	6155
MOLINE	0	9	99	335	774	1181	1314	1100	918	450	189	39	6408
PEORIA	0	6	87	326	759	1113	1218	1025	849	426	183	33	6025
ROCKFORD	6	9	114	400	837	1221	1333	1137	961	516	236	60	6830
SPRINGFIELD	0	0	72	291	696	1023	1135	935	769	354	136	18	5429
IND. EVANSVILLE	0	0	66	220	606	896	955	767	620	237	68	0	4435
FORT WAYNE	0	9	105	378	783	1135	1178	1028	890	471	189	39	6205
INDIANAPOLIS	0	0	90	316	723	1051	1113	949	809	432	177	39	5699
SOUTH BEND	0	6	111	372	777	1125	1221	1070	933	525	239	60	6439
IOWA Burlington	0	0	93	322	768	1135	1259	1042	859	426	177	33	6114
DES MOINES	0	9	99	363	837	1231	1398	1165	967	489	211	39	6808
DUBUQUE	12	31	156	450	906	1287	1420	1204	1026	546	260	78	7376
SIOUX CITY	0	9	108	369	867	1240	1435	1198	989	483	214	39	6951
WATERLOO	12	19	138	428	909	1296	1460	1221	1023	531	229	54	7320
KANS. CONCORDIA	0	0	57	276	705	1023	1163	935	781	372	149	18	5479
DODGE CITY	0	0	33	251	666	939	1051	840	719	354	124	9	4986
GOODLAND	0	6	81	381	810	1073	1166	955	884	507	236	42	6141
TOPEKA	0	0	57	270	672	980	1122	893	722	330	124	12	5182
WICHITA	0	0	33	229	618	905	1023	804	645	270	87	6	4620
KY. COVINGTON	0	0	75	291	669	983	1035	893	756	390	149	24	5265
LEXINGTON	0	0	54	239	609	902	946	818	685	325	105	0	4683
LOUISVILLE	0	0	54	248	609	890	930	818	682	315	105	9	4660
LA. ALEXANDRIA	0	0	0	56	273	431	471	361	260	69	0	0	1921
BATON ROUGE	0	0	0	31	216	369	409	294	208	33	0	0	1560
BURRWOOD	0	0	0	0	96	214	298	218	171	27	0	0	1024
LAKE CHARLES	0	0	0	19	210	341	381	274	195	39	0	0	1459
NEW ORLEANS	0	0	0	19	192	322	363	258	192	39	0	0	1385
SHREVEPORT	0	0	0	47	297	477	552	426	304	81	0	0	2184
MAINE CARIBOU	78	115	336	682	1044	1535	1690	1470	1308	858	468	183	9767
PORTLAND	12	53	195	508	807	1215	1339	1182	1042	675	372	111	7511
MD. BALTIMORE	0	0	48	264	585	905	936	820	679	327	90	0	4654
FREDERICK	0	0	66	307	624	955	995	876	741	384	127	12	5087
MASS. BLUE HILL OBSY	0	22	108	381	690	1085	1178	1053	936	579	267	69	6368
BOSTON	0	9	60	316	603	983	1088	972	846	513	208	36	5634
NANTUCKET	12	22	93	332	573	896	992	941	896	621	384	129	5891
PITTSFIELD	25	59	219	524	831	1231	1339	1196	1063	660	326	105	7578
WORCESTER	6	34	147	450	774	1172	1271	1123	998	612	304	78	6969
MICH. ALPENA	68	105	273	580	912	1268	1404	1299	1218	777	446	156	8506
DETROIT (CITY)	0	0	87	360	738	1088	1181	1058	936	522	220	42	6232
ESCANABA	59	87	243	539	924	1293	1445	1296	1203	777	456	159	8481
FLINT	16	40	159	465	843	1212	1330	1198	1066	639	319	90	7377
GRAND RAPIDS	9	28	135	434	804	1147	1259	1134	1011	579	279	75	6894
LANSING	6	22	138	431	813	1163	1262	1142	1011	579	273	69	6909
MARQUETTE	59	81	240	527	936	1268	1411	1268	1187	771	468	177	8393
MUSKEGON	12	28	120	400	762	1088	1209	1100	995	594	310	78	6696
SAULT STE. MARIE	96	105	279	580	951	1367	1525	1380	1277	810	477	201	9048
MINN. DULUTH	71	109	330	632	1131	1581	1745	1518	1355	840	490	198	10000
INTERNATIONAL FALLS	71	112	363	701	1236	1724	1919	1621	1414	828	443	174	10606
MINNEAPOLIS	22	31	189	505	1014	1454	1631	1380	1166	621	288	81	8382
ROCHESTER	25	34	186	474	1005	1438	1593	1366	1150	630	301	93	8295
SAINT CLOUD	28	47	225	549	1065	1500	1702	1445	1221	666	326	105	8879
MISS. JACKSON	0	0	0	65	315	502	546	414	310	87	0	0	2239
MERIDIAN	0	0	0	81	339	518	543	417	310	81	0	0	2289
VICKSBURG	0	0	0	53	279	462	512	384	282	69	0	0	2041
MO. COLUMBIA	0	0	54	251	651	967	1076	874	716	324	121	12	5046
KANSAS	0	0	39	220	612	905	1032	818	682	294	109	0	4711
ST. JOSEPH	0	6	60	285	708	1039	1172	949	769	348	133	15	5484
ST. LOUIS	0	0	60	251	627	936	1026	848	704	312	121	15	4900
SPRINGFIELD	0	0	45	223	600	877	973	781	660	291	105	6	4561

STATE AND STATION	JULY	AUG.	SEP.	OCT.	NOV.	DEC.	JAN.	FEB.	MAR.	APR.	MAY	JUNE	ANNUAL
MONT. BILLINGS	6	15	186	487	897	1135	1296	1100	970	570	285	102	7049
GLASGOW	31	47	270	608	1104	1466	1711	1439	1187	648	335	150	8996
GREAT FALLS	28	53	258	543	921	1169	1349	1154	1063	642	384	186	7750
HAVRE	28	53	306	595	1065	1367	1584	1364	1181	657	338	162	8700
HELENA	31	59	294	601	1002	1265	1438	1170	1042	651	381	195	8129
KALISPELL	50	99	321	654	1020	1240	1401	1134	1029	639	397	207	8191
MILES CITY	6	6	174	502	972	1296	1504	1252	1057	579	276	99	7723
MISSOULA	34	74	303	651	1035	1287	1420	1120	970	621	391	219	8125
NEBR. GRAND ISLAND	0	6	108	381	834	1172	1314	1089	908	462	211	45	6530
LINCOLN	0	6	75	301	726	1066	1237	1016	834	402	171	30	5864
NORFOLK	9	0	111	397	873	1234	1414	1179	983	498	233	48	6979
NORTH PLATTE	0	6	123	440	885	1166	1271	1039	930	519	248	57	6684
OMAHA	0	12	105	357	828	1175	1355	1126	939	465	208	42	6612
SCOTTSBLUFF	0	0	138	459	876	1128	1231	1008	921	552	285	75	6673
VALENTINE	9	12	165	493	942	1237	1395	1176	1045	579	288	84	7425
NEV. ELKO	9	34	225	561	924	1197	1314	1036	911	621	409	192	7433
ELY	28	43	234	592	939	1184	1308	1075	977	672	456	225	7733
LAS VEGAS	0	0	0	78	387	617	688	487	335	111	6	0	2709
RENO	43	87	204	490	801	1026	1073	823	729	510	357	189	6332
WINNEMUCCA	0	34	210	536	876	1091	1172	916	837	573	363	153	6761
N. H. CONCORD	6	50	177	505	822	1240	1358	1184	1032	636	298	75	7383
MT. WASH. OBSY.	493	536	720	1057	1341	1742	1820	1663	1652	1260	930	603	13817
N. J. ATLANTIC CITY	0	0	39	251	549	880	936	848	741	420	133	15	4812
NEWARK	0	0	30	248	573	921	983	876	729	381	118	0	4859
TRENTON	0	0	57	264	576	924	989	885	753	399	121	12	4980
N. MEX. ALBUQUERQUE	0	0	12	229	642	868	930	703	595	288	81	0	4348
CLAYTON	0	6	66	310	699	899	986	812	747	429	183	21	5158
RATON	9	28	126	431	825	1048	1116	904	834	543	301	63	6228
ROSWELL	0	0	18	202	573	806	840	641	481	201	31	0	3793
SILVER CITY	0	0	6	183	525	729	791	605	518	261	87	0	3705
N. Y. ALBANY	0	19	138	440	777	1194	1311	1156	992	564	239	45	6875
BINGHAMTON (AP)	22	65	201	471	810	1184	1277	1154	1045	645	313	99	7286
BINGHAMTON (PO)	0	28	141	406	732	1107	1190	1081	949	543	229	45	6451
BUFFALO	19	37	141	440	777	1156	1256	1145	1039	645	329	78	7062
CENTRAL PARK	0	0	30	233	540	902	986	885	760	408	118	9	4871
J. F. KENNEDY INT	0	0	36	248	564	933	1029	935	815	480	167	12	5219
LAGUARDIA	0	0	27	223	528	887	973	879	750	414	124	6	4811
ROCHESTER	9	31	126	415	747	1125	1234	1123	1014	597	279	48	6748
SCHENECTADY	0	22	123	422	756	1159	1283	1131	970	543	211	30	6650
SYRACUSE	6	28	132	415	744	1153	1271	1140	1004	570	248	45	6756
N.C. ASHEVILLE	0	0	48	245	555	775	784	683	592	273	87	0	4042
CAPE HATTERAS	0	0	0	78	273	521	580	518	440	177	25	0	2612
CHARLOTTE	0	0	6	124	438	691	691	582	481	156	22	0	3191
GREENSBORO	0	0	33	192	513	778	784	672	552	234	47	0	3805
RALEIGH	0	0	21	164	450	716	725	616	487	180	34	0	3393
WILMINGTON	0	0	0	74	291	521	546	462	357	96	0	0	2347
WINSTON SALEM	0	0	21	171	483	747	753	652	524	207	37	0	3595
N. DAK. BISMARCK	34	28	222	577	1083	1463	1708	1442	1203	645	329	117	8851
DEVILS LAKE	40	53	273	642	1191	1634	1872	1579	1345	753	381	138	9901
FARGO	28	37	219	574	1107	1569	1789	1520	1262	690	332	99	9226
WILLISTON	31	43	261	601	1122	1513	1758	1473	1262	681	357	141	9243
OHIO AKRON	0	9	96	381	726	1070	1138	1016	871	489	202	39	6037
CINCINNATI	0	0	54	248	612	921	970	837	701	336	118	9	4806
CLEVELAND	9	25	105	384	738	1088	1159	1047	918	552	260	66	6351
COLUMBUS	0	6	84	347	714	1039	1088	949	809	426	171	27	5660
DAYTON	0	6	78	310	696	1045	1097	955	809	429	167	30	5622
MANSFIELD	9	22	114	397	768	1110	1169	1042	924	543	245	60	6403
SANDUSKY	0	6	66	313	684	1032	1107	991	868	495	198	36	5796
TOLEDO	0	16	117	406	792	1138	1200	1056	924	543	242	60	6494
YOUNGSTOWN	6	19	120	412	771	1104	1169	1047	921	540	248	60	6417
OKLA. OKLAHOMA CITY	0	0	15	164	498	766	868	664	527	189	34	0	3725
TULSA	0	0	18	158	522	787	893	683	539	213	47	0	3860
OREG. ASTORIA	146	130	210	375	561	679	753	622	636	480	363	231	5186
BURNS	12	37	210	515	867	1113	1246	988	856	570	366	177	6957
EUGENE	34	34	129	366	585	719	803	627	589	426	279	135	4726
MEACHAM	84	124	288	580	918	1091	1209	1005	983	726	527	339	7874
MEDFORD	0	0	78	372	678	871	918	697	642	432	242	78	5008
PENDLETON	0	0	111	350	711	884	1017	773	617	396	205	63	5127
PORTLAND	25	28	114	335	597	735	825	644	586	396	245	105	4635
ROSEBURG	22	16	105	329	567	713	766	608	570	405	267	123	4491
SALEM	37	31	111	338	594	729	822	647	611	417	273	144	4754
SEXTON SUMMIT	81	81	171	443	666	874	958	809	818	609	465	279	6254
PA. ALLENTOWN	0	0	90	353	693	1045	1116	1002	849	471	167	24	5810
ERIE	0	25	102	391	714	1063	1169	1081	973	585	288	60	6451
HARRISBURG	0	0	63	298	648	992	1045	907	766	396	124	12	5251
PHILADELPHIA	0	0	60	291	621	964	1014	890	744	390	115	12	5101
PITTSBURGH	0	9	105	375	726	1063	1119	1002	874	480	195	39	5987
READING	0	0	54	257	597	939	1001	885	735	372	105	0	4945
SCRANTON	0	19	132	434	762	1104	1156	1028	893	498	195	33	6254
WILLIAMSPORT	0	9	111	375	717	1073	1122	1002	856	468	177	24	5934
R. I. BLOCK IS.	0	16	78	307	594	902	1020	955	877	612	344	99	5804
PROVIDENCE	0	16	96	372	660	1023	1110	988	868	534	236	51	5954
S. C. CHARLESTON	0	0	0	59	282	471	487	389	291	54	0	0	2033
COLUMBIA	0	0	0	84	345	577	570	470	357	81	0	0	2484
FLORENCE	0	0	0	78	315	552	552	459	347	84	0	0	2387
GREENVILLE	0	0	0	112	387	636	648	535	434	120	12	0	2884
SPARTANBURG	0	0	15	130	417	667	663	560	453	144	25	0	3074

APPENDIX

171

STATE AND STATION	JULY	AUG.	SEP.	OCT.	NOV.	DEC.	JAN.	FEB.	MAR.	APR.	MAY	JUNE	ANNUAL
S. DAK. HURON	9	12	165	508	1014	1432	1628	1355	1125	600	288	87	8223
RAPID CITY	22	12	165	481	897	1172	1333	1145	1051	615	326	126	7345
SIOUX FALLS	19	25	168	462	972	1361	1544	1285	1082	573	270	78	7839
TENN. BRISTOL	0	0	51	236	573	828	828	700	598	261	68	0	4143
CHATTANOOGA	0	0	18	143	468	698	722	577	453	150	25	0	3254
KNOXVILLE	0	0	30	171	489	725	732	613	493	198	43	0	3494
MEMPHIS	0	0	18	130	447	698	729	585	456	147	22	0	3232
NASHVILLE	0	0	30	158	495	732	778	644	512	189	40	0	3578
OAK RIDGE (CO)	0	0	39	192	531	772	778	669	552	228	56	0	3817
TEX. ABILENE	0	0	0	99	366	586	642	470	347	114	0	0	2624
AMARILLO	0	0	18	205	570	797	877	664	546	252	56	0	3985
AUSTIN	0	0	0	31	225	388	468	325	223	51	0	0	1711
BROWNSVILLE	0	0	0	0	66	149	205	106	74	0	0	0	600
CORPUS CHRISTI	0	0	0	0	120	220	291	174	109	0	0	0	914
DALLAS	0	0	0	62	321	524	601	440	319	90	6	0	2363
EL PASO	0	0	0	84	414	648	685	445	319	105	0	0	2700
FORT WORTH	0	0	0	65	324	536	614	448	319	99	0	0	2405
GALVESTON	0	0	0	0	138	270	350	258	189	30	0	0	1235
HOUSTON	0	0	0	6	183	307	384	288	192	36	0	0	1396
LAREDO	0	0	0	0	105	217	267	134	74	0	0	0	797
LUBBOCK	0	0	18	174	513	744	800	613	484	201	31	0	3578
MIDLAND	0	0	0	87	381	592	651	468	322	90	0	0	2591
PORT ARTHUR	0	0	0	22	207	329	384	274	192	39	0	0	1447
SAN ANGELO	0	0	0	68	318	536	567	412	288	66	0	0	2255
SAN ANTONIO	0	0	0	31	207	363	428	286	195	39	0	0	1549
VICTORIA	0	0	0	6	150	270	344	230	152	21	0	0	1173
WACO	0	0	0	43	270	456	536	389	270	66	0	0	2030
WICHITA FALLS	0	0	0	99	381	632	698	518	378	120	6	0	2832
UTAH MILFORD	0	0	99	443	867	1141	1252	988	822	519	279	87	6497
SALT LAKE CITY	0	0	81	419	849	1082	1172	910	763	459	233	84	6052
WENDOVER	0	0	48	372	822	1091	1178	902	729	408	177	51	5778
VT. BURLINGTON	28	65	207	539	891	1349	1513	1333	1187	714	353	90	8269
VA. CAPE HENRY	0	0	0	112	360	645	694	633	536	246	53	0	3279
LYNCHBURG	0	0	51	223	540	822	849	731	605	267	78	0	4166
NORFOLK	0	0	0	136	408	698	738	655	533	216	37	0	3421
RICHMOND	0	0	36	214	495	784	815	703	546	219	53	0	3865
ROANOKE	0	0	51	229	549	825	834	722	614	261	65	0	4150
WASH. NAT'L. AP.	0	0	33	217	519	834	871	762	626	288	74	0	4224
WASH. OLYMPIA	68	71	198	422	636	753	834	675	645	450	307	177	5236
SEATTLE	50	47	129	329	543	657	738	599	577	396	242	117	4424
SEATTLE BOEING	34	40	147	384	624	763	831	655	608	411	242	99	4838
SEATTLE TACOMA	56	62	162	391	633	750	828	678	657	474	295	159	5145
SPOKANE	9	25	168	493	879	1082	1231	980	834	531	288	135	6655
STAMPEDE PASS	273	291	393	701	1008	1178	1287	1075	1085	855	654	483	9283
TATOOSH IS.	295	279	306	406	534	639	713	613	645	525	431	333	5719
WALLA WALLA	0	0	87	310	681	843	986	745	589	342	177	45	4805
YAKIMA	0	12	144	450	828	1039	1163	868	713	435	220	69	5941
W. VA. CHARLESTON	0	0	63	254	591	865	880	770	648	300	96	9	4476
ELKINS	9	25	135	400	729	992	1008	896	791	444	198	48	5675
HUNTINGTON	0	0	63	257	585	856	880	764	636	294	99	12	4446
PARKERSBURG	0	0	60	264	606	905	942	826	691	339	115	6	4754
WIS. GREEN BAY	28	50	174	484	924	1333	1494	1313	1141	654	335	99	8029
LA CROSSE	12	19	153	437	924	1339	1504	1277	1070	540	245	69	7589
MADISON	25	40	174	474	930	1330	1473	1274	1113	618	310	102	7863
MILWAUKEE	43	47	174	471	876	1252	1376	1193	1054	642	372	135	7635
WYO. CASPER	6	16	192	524	942	1169	1290	1084	1020	657	381	129	7410
CHEYENNE	19	31	210	543	924	1101	1228	1056	1011	672	381	102	7278
LANDER	6	19	204	555	1020	1299	1417	1145	1017	654	381	153	7870
SHERIAN	25	31	219	539	948	1200	1355	1154	1054	642	366	150	7683

Appendix 3: The Nature of Sunlight

An understanding of solar energy, though not vital to the effective operation of the dome, should enhance your appreciation of the dome's major working force: the sun.

Solar energy is radiated from the sun in the form of electromagnetic radiation. It is energy traveling in packets, called photons, which emanate from a source in pulsating fashion. The higher the energy level, the greater the frequency of these energy packets.

Electromagnetic radiation is often thought of as traveling in waves. Forms of it we all know include radio and television waves, radar, infrared rays, visible light, ultraviolet and x-rays. Their energy levels differ: radio and TV waves are low frequency, x-rays are much higher frequencies.

The sun primarily emanates the medium-to-high levels of radiation: infrared rays, visible light and ultraviolet rays. Infrared radiation we perceive as heat; visible light is the radiation we see; and ultraviolet is the radiation that burns us on the beach and fades and decays most cloths and plastics exposed to the sun.

Appendix 4: The Time It Takes to Build Your Dome

One of the dome's major advantages is its ease of construction. This means it may be built in a relatively short time. In fact, using the figures below as general guidelines, you can see that one person working eight hour days can complete all steps in just 10 to 15 days — unless slowed by foul weather or a delayed purchase order.

Some steps are basically one-person jobs, such as woodcutting. Although a second person may ease the task, it will not be completed in half the time.

Other steps, like preserving wood and digging trenches, are completed twice as fast with two people, three times quicker with a third person, and so on. Covering the dome is easier and considerably faster with two or more people.

Here is a list of the approximate time needed to complete each task:

Site Survey — Total time will depend on the number of sites you survey, and how many obstructions to the sun's path are present. A survey of one site should require no more than 45 minutes.

Woodworking — Times given here are for two people working; one person alone will not take much longer, nor will a third cut time substantially, except in wood-preserving. These times also include set-up of the work area and the building of all jigs.

Cutting long, short and hub struts	2 hours
Cutting plywood plates	3 hours
Drilling all holes	3 hours
Preserving all wood	2 hours
	(excluding drying time)
Assembling hubs	4 hours
Total:	14 hours

Site Preparation — Times are for two people working; one alone will take twice the time, while three or more will save time proportionately.

Laying out base struts	1 hour
Digging trenches and installing polyethylene	16 hours
Installing securing posts	2 hours
Preparing garden beds	3 hours
Total:	22 hours

Erecting Frame — Times are for two people working; three or more people will make a small time difference.

Erection	2 hours
Realigning and tightening hubs	1 hour
Building door and vent	2 hours
Total:	5 hours

Covering the Dome — Times are for two people working; one alone will take almost twice as long, while three will save considerable time.

Installing outer film layer	5 hours
Installing fiberglass insulation	3 hours
Installing inner film layer	3 hours
Covering and hanging door and vent	2 hours
Total:	13 hours

Appendix 5: Vegetables for Different Seasons

Vegetables listed below are categorized for the seasons in which they grow best, and are shown with their probable time to harvest and spacing recommendations for wide-row and conventional gardens.

During winter, grow your hardiest cool-weather crops near the door and southern perimeter of the dome, the coolest spots within the structure. During summer, use your thermometers to determine your dome's warmest spots, where the hardiest warm-weather crops should be grown.

Generally, plants should be spaced so their mature leaves will barely touch each other, creating a living mulch over the entire garden bed.

APPENDIX

SUGGESTED DOME VEGETABLES

Vegetables	Wide-Row Spacing* (inches)	Conventional Spacing (inches)	Days to Harvest
WINTER-HARDY CROPS			
Asparagus	10	12–18	2 years
Beets	2	3–4	50–65
Broccoli	12	18–24	50–80 from transplant
Brussels sprouts	12	18–24	65–75 from transplant
Cabbage	10	18–24	60–90 from transplant
Kale	8	8–12	50–65
Mustard	3–4	6	35–45
New Zealand Spinach	6	18–24	70
Onions	2	4	25–35
Radishes	1	1	25–35
Rutabagas	6	6–8	80–90
Spinach	2–4	2–4	40–50
Turnips	3–4	6–8	40–60
WINTER CROPS			
Carrots	1	2–3	55–80
Cauliflower	18–24	18–24	65–80
Endive	12–18	12–18	80–90
Lettuce, butterhead	4	3–6	75
Lettuce, head	9	10–18	90
Lettuce, leaf	5	8–10	45
Peas (trellised)	1–3	2–3	50–80
Rhubarb	24	30–36	1 year
Swiss chard	3–4	6–8	45–55
SUMMER CROPS			
Beans, bush	4	4–6	50–60
Beans, pole	8	18–36	60–70
Corn	8	8–12	60–95
Cucumbers (trellised)	4	12	50–70
Eggplant	22	24–30	80–90
Melons (supported)	24	36	75–100
Okra	12	18–24	50–55
Peppers	12	18–24	60–100
Squash (winter)	16	36–48	85–120
Tomatoes (trellised)	18	24–36	55–90

*Wide-row spacing recommendations are based upon gardening experiences at the Fordham University dome. You may decide to space plants differently, depending upon your own experiences, the planting methods used and the vegetable varieties selected.

Appendix 6: Organic Methods of Insect Control

While natural insecticides can be used sporadically or whenever a problem arises, beneficial insect predators should be introduced to your dome environment periodically. One of the most effective of these is the attractive ladybug. It does quite a job on aphids and other small insects, and should be brought into your dome three or four times a year for continued protection. A small container of them will do wonders to solve most common problems.

But other "good bugs" abound, and can be used to handle other pest problems. If you're ever unsure of how to handle an infestation, take an affected plant or leaf to your county agricultural agent or cooperative extension. They can identify your bug problem and recommend a solution. The following discussion of beneficial insects and natural insecticides is from **The Complete Greenhouse Book** by Peter Clegg and Derry Watkins.

BENEFICIAL INSECTS

Aphid lions. See **Lacewings.**

Braconid wasps. Small wasps which lay their eggs in caterpillars. The larvae make tiny white cocoons which stick out all over the caterpillar like fat spines. The caterpillar gradually is eaten alive by the wasp larvae, which then hatch out and go on to lay their eggs in other caterpillars.

Damsel flies. See **Dragonflies.**

Dragonflies. Like their smaller relatives the damsel flies, dragonflies are skilled hunters. They catch other insects in midair or swoop them from the surface of the water. They are especially fond of mosquitos.

Encarsia formosa. A tiny parasitic wasp that can decimate the white fly population in a few months. It lays its eggs in the white fly larvae, turning them black. They are so effective that sometimes they starve themselves out by eradicating all the white flies. Probably more worthwhile in a large greenhouse. It is worth keeping one badly infested plant elsewhere to be sure the wasps will have enough white flies to reproduce in, especially during the winter when white flies breed more slowly.

Fireflies. Besides being the delight of summer evenings, fireflies eat slugs and snails for you, and their larvae eat cutworms. So if your children catch any of these dull, black elongated beetles with their phosphorescent green taillights, ask them to release their fireflies in your greenhouse. They may not stay long, but they might eat a few pests on their way out.

Hover flies. (syrphid flies). Their larvae look like small green slugs and eat enormous quantities of aphids. It might be worth planting convolvulus tricolor (a small relative of the morning glory) near the greenhouse to feed the adult hover flies so they will lay their eggs among your aphids.

Ichneumon flies. Really a long slender delicate wasp (up to two inches long.) It looks like it might sting but it does not; it uses what looks like its stinger to lay eggs in many kinds of caterpillars. The larva eats the caterpillar from within.

Lacewing flies. These flies look like gauzy, pale green flies with golden eyes. Their larvae, nicknamed **aphid lions,** are small ferocious-looking creatures which eat aphids and many other small insects with gusto. Available from: Rincon-Vitova Insectaries, Box 95, Oak View, California 93022; or Vitova Insectary, Box 475, Rialto, California 92376; or Insect Pest Advisory Service, 762 South First St., Kerman, California 93630.

Ladybugs. The prime predator of small soft-bodied insects, especially aphids. Their cheerful red shells with black spots are a common and welcome feature of most gardens and many greenhouses. Less well known, but almost equally voracious, are their larvae — like small black crocodiles with yellow or orange spots down their backs. Ladybug eggs are bright yellow and come in clusters, usually on the underside of the leaves. Ladybugs should be protected and encouraged in every way. They are available from: Bio-Control Co., 10180 Ladybird Ave., Auburn, California 95603; Greenberg Control Co., Route 4, Box 1891, Oroville, California 95603; Insect Pest Advisory Service, 762 South First St., Kerman, California 93630; Lakeland Nursery, Hanover, Pennsylvania 17331; H.A. Mantyla, Route 2, Box 2407, Auburn, California 95603; Montgomery Ward, 618 West Chicago Ave., Chicago, Illinois 60610; G.C. Quick, 367 East Virginia Ave., Phoenix, Arizona 85000; Robert Robbins, 424 North Courtland, East Stroudsburg, Pennsylvania 18301; L.E. Schnoor, Box 114, Rough & Ready, California 95975; or World Garden Products, 2 First St., East Norwalk, Connecticut 06855.

Phytoseiulus persimilis. A tiny mite that is a predator on the red spider mite. Both nymphs and adults eat spider mite eggs. The predatory mite reproduces rapidly and keeps the greenhouse spider mite population well under control. Available from Rincon-Vitova Insectaries, Box 95, Oak View, California 93022.

Praying mantises (walking stick insect). A large awkward-looking insect, two to five inches long, surprisingly able to blend into surroundings and look like a twig. Has a long stiff body, long legs and big green eyes. Eats many varieties of insects. The egg cases can be bought in winter. They should be attached to the stem of a large plant or to an out-of-the-way part of the greenhouse and left alone. In spring they will hatch out and begin foraging. Available from: Ted P. Bank, 608 Eleventh St., Pitcairn, Pennsylvania 15140; Burnes, 109 Kohler St., Bloomfield, New Jersey 07003; Bio-Control Co., 10180 Ladybird Ave., Auburn, California 95603; H.P. Comeaux, Route 2, Box 259, Lafayette, Louisiana 70501; Eastern Biological Control Co., Route 4, Box 482, Jackson, New Jersey 08527; Gothard Inc., Box 370, Canutillo, Texas 79835; Lakeland Nurseries Sales, Insect Control Division, Hanover, Pennsylvania 17331; Little Gem Farm, Box 9024, Huntington, West Virginia 25704; Mantis Unlimited, Glenhardie Farm, 625 Richards Road, Wayne, Pennsylvania 19087; Mincemoyer, 104 Hackensack St., Wood Ridge, New Jersey 07075; L.R. Murray, Aguila, Arizona 85320; Robert Robbins, 424 N. Courtland St., East Stroudsburg, Pennsylvania 18301; or Sidney A. Schwartz, The Mantis Man Inc., East Northport, New York 11731. Several commercial seed houses also offer praying mantis cases.

Spiders. Very useful in catching endless small flying insects. Unless you can't bear the untidy look, their webs should be left alone.

Syrphid flies. See **Hover flies.**

Tachnid flies. Look like large house flies but move more quickly. They lay their eggs in many species of caterpillar, in Japanese beetles, earwigs and grasshoppers, so are decidedly helpful.

Trichogramma wasps. Minute wasps, 1/50 of an inch long, which are parasitic on the eggs of most varieties of caterpillars. The larvae of trichogamma wasps can be bought, but they are probably more useful out of doors unless you are subject to severe attacks of caterpillars. One packet contains up to 4,000 wasp larvae and should be able to control an area of several acres. Ideally, wasps should be released at the time the moths are laying eggs. Available from: Rincon-Vitova Insectaries, Box 95, Oak View, California 93022; or Gothard Inc., Box 370, Canutillo, Texas 79835, or Insect Pest Advisory Service, 762 South First St., Kerman, California 93630.

NATURAL INSECTICIDES

Ammonia. Household ammonia is a good fumigant to get rid of wood lice and earwigs in a greenhouse. Simply shut all the vents, sprinkle ammonia liberally over the floor and leave the greenhouse shut up tight overnight.

Bacillus Thuringiensis (Thuricide or Biotrol.) A bacterial disease that affects several varieties of caterpillars. It is long-lasting, effective, and harmful only to caterpillars, but is probably more useful in the garden than in the greenhouse.

It is available from many of the major seed companies, including Farmer Seed and Nursery Co., Faribault, Minnesota 55021, and Joseph Harris Co., Moreton Farm, Rochester, New York 14624, as well as the following: Eastern States Farmers Exchange Inc., 26 Central St., West Springfield, Massachusetts 01089; Grain Processing Corp., Muscatine, Iowa 52761; International Minerals and Chemical Corp, Crop Aids Department, 5401 Old Orchard Road, Skokie, Illinois 60076; Hubbard-Hall Chemical Co., Box 233, Portland, Connecticut 05480; Pennsalt Chemical Corp., Philadelphia, Pennsylvania 19100; and Thompson-Hayward Chemical Co., Box 2383, Kansas City, Missouri 66110.

Ced-o-Flora. A natural insect repellent made of pine oils and other plant essences. Very effective against aphids and mealy bugs. Available from most garden shops.

Derris. The roots of a South American plant which is the main ingredient in rotenone. Good against chewing and sucking insects but harmful to fish, nesting birds and some beneficial insects, including bees and lady bug larvae. Effective for about forty-eight hours. Available from garden shops.

Diatomaceous earth (Tripoli). The fine silica remains of the skeletons of millions of prehistoric one-celled creatures. Kills on contact, probably by dehydration after the silica pierces the insect's body. Very effective and harmless to other creatures, including earthworms. Can be sprinkled on, or diluted with water and sprayed on. Available from: Desert Herb Tea Co., 736 Darling St., Ogden, Utah 84400; Perma-Guard Division, Bower Industries Inc., 1701 East Elwood St., Box 21024, Phoenix, Arizona 85036.

Garlic and red pepper. The organic gardener's standby. Many combinations are possible, but a typical recipe would be:

- 3 cloves of garlic or 1 tablespoon garlic powder
- 1 large onion
- 1 tablespoon ground cayenne, or two whole hot red peppers, or 1 tablespoon tabasco sauce
- 1/2 ounce soft soap or 1 tablespoon liquid detergent (see **Soft Soap**)
- 1 quart water

Blend, strain and use immediately, or store in a glass or plastic container in the refrigerator. Mustard, or mint or horseradish leaves are sometimes added. Deters most insects.

Hot water. Potted plants can be dipped in hot (140-150°F.) water for five minutes to kill aphids, scale and most other pests, but it may damage the plant as well. It is best to try this only when the plant is relatively dormant.

Nettle tea. An old biodynamic recipe, useful both as a fertilizer and as insect repellent. Fill a bucket with stinging nettles and cover with water (preferably rain water). Cover it and leave in the sun to ferment. In about a week the nettles will have rotted to a slimy mass and the brew will smell terrible. Dilute it one to five and spray on plants or drench the soil around them. Excellent against aphids and flea beetles, also good stimulant for sickly plants.

Nicotine. See **Tobacco.**

Pyrethrum. The dried flowers of a plant closely related to chrysanthemums. Good against many insects including thrips and whitefly, but harmful to fish, bees and ladybugs. Harmless to warm-blooded animals except that some people are allergic to it. It is best to grind up the flowers yourself. This can be dusted directly over the plant, or a spray can be made by steeping one teaspoon of ground flowers in one quart of hot water for three hours. Strain, add a half ounce of soft soap, and spray. Loses its potency twelve hours after the flowers are ground up. Pyrethrum may be grown outdoors near the greenhouse.

Seeds are available from George W. Park Seed Co., Greenwood, South Carolina 29646. The dried flowers are often available in garden shops, if not, write to the Pyrethrum Information Center, 744 Broad St., Newark, New Jersey 07102, for the name and address of a source near you.

Quassia. The ground-up wood of a South American tree with an intensely bitter taste. Makes a good spray against aphids, thrips, slugs and small caterpillars. Soak two ounces of quassia in one gallon of water for three days. Then simmer slowly for three hours. Strain and mix with two ounces of soft soap. Available from: Desert Herb Tea Co., 736 Darling St., Ogden, Utah 84400; Indiana Botanic Gardens, Box 5, Hammond, Indiana 46320; Meer Corporation, 318 West 46 St., New York, New York 10036; George W. Park Seed Co., Greenwood, South Carolina 29646; or Charles Siegel & Son, 5535 North Lynch Ave., Chicago, Illinois 60630.

Red pepper. See **Garlic and red pepper.**

Rotenone. See **Derris.**

Rubbing alcohol. Effective against mealy bugs and almost all other insects. Individual pests can be executed with a Q-tip dipped in pure rubbing alcohol (or turpentine or kerosene), but be careful not to get any on the plant. In a heavy infestation, the plant can be sprayed with a mixture of one tablespoon rubbing alcohol in one pint of water. A teaspoon of camphor dissolved in the alcohol will make it even more effective.

Salt. Effective dry sprinkled on slugs, and it can also be used in a weak solution (one teaspoon salt to one quart water) sprayed on brassicas against cabbage worms or on other plants to combat spider mites. Be careful not to get too much salt on the soil because it reduces fertility.

Soft soap. Fels Naptha, ordinary hand soap (chopped up or leftover slivers), green soap, or Ivory Flakes left in enough water to cover for a few days will form a jelly-like solution that can be added to other aromatic ingredients to form a spray that adheres better and will penetrate the protective coating of many insects. If you are in a hurry, you can boil up the soap and it will liquefy faster. Liquid detergent could be used instead, but many people think it may be harmful to plants. Diluted with water (two ounces per gallon), soft soap can be used by itself as a spray. Or small potted plants can be dipped in the suds; cover the soil and turn the pot upside down, swishing the plant through the suds, rinse well afterwards. Good against aphids and cabbage worms, moderately effective against scale and mealy bugs.

Tobacco. Every form of tobacco is an effective insecticide. It is also highly toxic to most other creatures including humans, so use with care. Do not breathe it in or get it on your skin or in your eyes, and be sure to wash your hands after using. Fortunately, its toxicity dissipates gradually and is pretty much gone in two or three days. It is especially useful against caterpillars and it does no harm to ladybugs. Nicotine is the active ingredient in tobacco and can be bought in concentrated form. Nicotine sulphate **(Blackleaf 40)** is less powerful but longer lasting.

You can extract the nicotine yourself by steeping tobacco dust, tobacco stems, chopped up plug tobacco or even cigarette butts in boiling water. Leave them twenty-four hours, then strain and dilute with four parts of water to one part tobacco extract. This can be used as is or a quarter ounce soft soap per quart can be added for a more penetrating spray. Tobacco dust can also be shaken directly over the plants. Nicotine fumigation is effective at getting into all the nooks and crannies of a greenhouse where pests lurk unseen waiting to reinfest a plant after you have cleaned it up.

Nicotine fumigants are available from: California Spray Chemical Corp., Richmond, California 94800, or Fuller System, 226 Washington St., Woburn, Massachusetts 01801. Nicotine sulphate is available from most garden supply stores. Tobacco dust is available from: Odlin Organics, 743 Dennison Drive, Southbridge, Massachusetts 01550; or Quaker Lane Products, Box 100, Pittstown, New Jersey 08867. Tobacco stem meal is available from: Brookside Nurseries, Darien, Connecticut 06820.

Water. A good hard jet of plain water will remove a proportion of the insects on a plant, will remove dust and dirt that have accumulated on its leaves and seems to have a stimulating overall effect. Hosing the undersides of leaves is especially important since insects congregate there, so cover the soil and turn the plant upside down to get a better aim. Rain water is better than tap water both for watering and for making sprays. Some plants resent the residues from hard water; others resent water-softening chemicals.

Glossary

Air duct. A thin-walled metal pipe or duct work used to convey air.

Air lock. An air space between two doors for entrance to or exit from a structure without permitting a large exchange of air.

Algae. Any group of chiefly aquatic nonvascular plants with chlorophyll often masked by a brown or red pigment.

Altitude. See **Solar altitude.**

Aluminum conduit. An aluminum pipe used to protect electric wires.

Angle of incidence. The angle between perpendicular and the direction light strikes a surface.

Aphid. A small parasitic insect that sucks juices from plant stems and leaves, causing wilting and distorted growth.

Aquaculture. The cultivation of fish and other natural produce of water.

Attachments. Methods of securing inner and outer layers of film to the frame. Three types are used: seam, temporary and wrap-around.

Azimuth. The angle in a horizontal plane between true south and the sun's position in the sky.

Batt. A piece of insulation of specific width to fit within a structure's frame.

Bolting. A plant's production of seeds, causing it to become bitter-tasting and often inedible.

British Thermal Unit (Btu). The amount of heat required to raise the temperature of one pound of water one degree Fahrenheit at or near 39.2°F., its temperature of maximum density.

Cement footing. Cement poured around a securing post to hold it in place.

Compost. A mixture of decayed organic matter used for fertilizing and conditioning soil.

Conduction. The transfer of heat through an object from an area of warmer temperatures to one of cooler temperatures.

Dead air space. The insulating two-inch space between the inner and outer layers of glazing.

Deciduous trees. Trees that shed their leaves seasonally.

Degree day. A unit used to measure the difference between 65°F. and the mean daily outside temperature, used primarily to gauge the fuel requirements.

Diameter. The length of a straight line through the center of a circle, drawn from perimeter to perimeter.

Electromagnetic radiation. Energy traveling in packets, called photons, which emanate from a source in pulsating fashion.

Extension Service. An agency providing agricultural and other types of information to the public.

Fertile. Capable of sustaining abundant plant growth.

Foil vapor barrier. Barrier attached to insulation to redirect sunlight back towards the garden, and to prevent the flow of moisture into the insulation, which would impair its effectiveness.

Fossil fuels. Fuels derived from underground stores of fossilized plants and animals, such as natural gas, oil, coal.

Foundation. Base onto which a structure is built.

Free-standing frame. Any of a number of greenhouses that stand by themselves with no other support. Term is most commonly used to describe a solar greenhouse with a sloped southern wall and an upright or partially sloped northern wall.

FUSES. Acronym for the Fordham Urban Solar EcoSystem research team.

Geodesic dome. A dome made of light, straight structural elements in triangular formations to relieve as much stress as possible. Two frequency icosa alternate is the type of dome used in the FUSES solar-heated dome greenhouse.

Germination. Sprouting of seeds.

Glazing. A clear or translucent covering over a greenhouse frame that allows light to pass through to heat the structure and encourage plant growth.

Heat conduction. See **Conduction**.

Hub. Component of the frame to which struts are secured to maintain the dome's triangular elements. Three types are used in the dome: pent, hex and base hubs.

Infiltration. The entrance of cool air into the dome through small gaps near the door and vent.

Infrared radiation. Lower levels of electromagnetic radiation found in sunlight, perceived by us as heat.

Insulation (thermal). A barrier to the flow of heat, made of a relatively nonconductive material.

Intensive gardening. A method of gardening using special techniques to result in higher yields. French Intensive and wide-row are two examples, often used in small gardens.

Irradiation. A giving off of rays of light; the emission of radiant energy.

Jig. A device used to maintain proper position of a piece of work during cutting and assembly.

Lean-to. A greenhouse that shares a common wall with the house to which it is attached.

Leach. To wash with water to remove an unwanted chemical (i.e. — leaching salt from clam shells or seaweed).

Level. In a plane perpendicular to an imaginary line drawn to the center of the earth.

Level (relative). A term used in site preparation indicating that all components of the dome's base are in the same plane, even though it may not be level to the center of the earth.

Magnetic deviation. The difference between magnetic north as read off a compass and true north on the earth's surface. Amount of deviation varies throughout the earth.

Magnetic north. The northerly direction in the earth's magnetic field as indicated by the magnetic needle of a compass.

Magnetic south. South as read off a compass, as opposed to true south.

Mulch. A protective covering spread or left on the ground to slow evaporation, maintain even soil temperature, prevent erosion, control weeds and enrich the soil.

Night blanket. Also known as night curtain and thermal blanket. A blanket draped over the outside of a greenhouse's clear surface, or supported just inside it, to slow heat loss through this part of the structure at night.

Organic gardening. Any method of gardening that employs natural fertilizers and large amounts of compost to fortify soil.

Peat moss. A soil additive used to create a proper balance of air and moisture. It is a type of moss that grows in wet, acid areas.

Peat pots. Small flower pots made of compressed peat moss. Seedlings planted in them can be transplanted, pot and all, into the soil; their roots grow through the pot, which breaks up in the soil.

Perimeter. A continuous line around the boundary of a closed object.

Photons. Small increments of radiant energy.

Photosynthesis. The forming of carbohydrates from carbon dioxide and water in chlorophyll-containing cells exposed to light.

Photovoltaic cells. Silicone-derived substances that convert sunlight directly into electricity.

Pickax. A heavy iron or steel tool pointed at one or both ends and often curved, wielded by means of a long wooden handle.

Plumb line. A weighted line hung from an object to determine a vertical direction.

Pollination. Fertilizing plants so they'll bear fruit.

Polyethylene film. A lightweight plastic film generally resistant to chemicals and moisture.

Polyethylene Monsanto "602". A resilient polyethylene film specially treated for resistance to harmful ultraviolet rays from the sun.

Polyethylene pipe. A semi-rigid plastic pipe that is used mainly for underground sprinkler systems.

Polystyrene. A rigid transparent plastic that has good insulating properties.

Polyurethane. A polymer used chiefly in making flexible and rigid foams, and resins for coatings and adhesives.

Pressure sprayer. A spraying device whose canister is pressurized by pumping a handle. It gives a continuous, well-directed fluid spray.

Quonset hut. A tunnel-shaped structure, framed of aluminum conduit, and usually set on a cement foundation.

R-value. The resistance of a material to the flow of heat through it.

Sod. The upper layer of soil filled with grass and grass roots.

Solar altitude. The angle between the earth's surface (horizon) and the position of the sun in the sky, measured in a vertical plane.

Solar collector. Any device that transforms solar energy into another useful form of energy for a specific purpose.

Solar collector (active). A device that utilizes some energy in order to gain energy from the sun (i.e. a flat-plate collector which often uses a pump to circulate water).

Solar collector (passive). A device that gains the sun's energy by being warmed passively.

Solar energy. Energy derived from the sun.

Solar time. A time used in solar altitude and azimuth tables to calculate the sun's position in the sky.

Spade. An implement for turning soil that resembles a shovel, adapted for being pushed into the ground by foot via its heavy, usually flat and oblong, blade.

Strut. A major component of the dome's frame, made of 2 x 2 pieces of lumber of different lengths.

Submersible heater. A heater that can operate safely while submerged in water or other fluids.

Sun survey. Surveying a possible site for your dome to determine the amount of shading it will receive at various times of the year.

Thermostat. An automatic device for regulating temperature.

Tilapia aurea. A tropical fish native to Africa and Asia, of the cichlid family.

Till. To turn soil to prepare for seeding.

Translucent. A physical property of glazing materials that allows diffused light to pass through, although objects behind this material cannot be clearly distinguished.

Transplant. To move a plant or seedling from one place to another.

Trellis. A structure or frame of latticework used as a screen or as a support for climbing plants.

Triad. An area of the dome consisting of two small triangles on either side of one large triangle.

True south. Geographic south, bearing no relation to the earth's magnetic fields.

Ultraviolet light. The highest energy levels found in sunlight, a relatively high level form of electromagnetic radiation. It is invisible, but we perceive it by the suntans it gives us.

Walmanize. A way of preserving wood by permeating it with a pressurized salt solution.

Wide-row. A method of gardening using wide rows rather than conventional narrow rows for higher yields in the same amount of space.

Wide-row with steps. A type of gardening used in the dome. Designed to maximize space-saving and vegetable growth.

Wood piling foundation. A base made of heavy pieces of wood, such as railroad ties and telephone poles.

Acknowledgments

There are many people without whose foresight and encouragement the Fordham Urban Solar EcoSystem (FUSES) research project would not have been possible. We are especially grateful to: Frank R. Borchardt, assistant dean; Rev. James C. Finlay, president; Paul J. Reiss, executive vice president; Rev. Robert J. Roth, dean, Fordham College; The late Rev. Harry Sievers, dean, Graduate School of Arts and Sciences; Prof. Grace M. Vernon and Prof. E. Ruth Witkus.

Others contributed valuable insights and advice, including Prof. George Dale, Rev. G. Richard Dimler, Prof. Joseph Shapiro, Prof. Gerald Shattuck and Prof. Stanislaus Skalski.

And many others aided the FUSES project with their research and hard work, notably Douglas Crozier, James Cruess, John Fuscia, Patrick Jacob, Chris LaVigna, Roxanne MacDonald, James Manousos, Mike Mercado, John Pappas, and Laura Schneider.

We would also like to acknowledge those who assisted the FUSES project in many different ways: Robert M. Brown, Georgie Calia, Thomas J. Courtney, Ken Davies, Margaret Donovan, Marianne Kristoff, Robert A. Mahan, Mary Jane O'Connell and, especially, Ralph DeLuca, Martin King, Rhonda Pavese, Austin Richardson, William E. Rodger and Fred Stetson.

And a special thanks to Marilyn Heller, and the rest of our families and friends who have been so patient and supportive during the writing of this book.

Index

Advantages of FUSES dome, 1–6
Air ducts, 153–54
Air lock, 124–25 and *illus.*
   definition, 183
Air space as insulation, 4, 17, 18 and
   illus., 21–22, 123
Algae in fish tank, 150
Aluminum conduit:
   as framing material, 22
American Vegetable Grower magazine, 25
Aquaculture, 149–51
   definition, 183
Assembly:
   ease of, 3–4
   frame, 71–88 and *illus.*
Attachments, *see* Film (plastic): attachments
Azimuth (solar), 11–12 and *illus.*, 165,
   tables 166–68
   definition, 183

Barrels, *see* Drums
Base circle:
   components, 71
   trouble-shooting, 55–56
Base hubs, *see* Hubs: base
Brace Research Institute, McGill University, Montreal, 19
Bracket:
   to secure posts to base hubs, 67–68 and
     illus.
British Thermal Units (Btu), 166
   definition, 184
Building-code restrictions, 7
Bunching film, 98

Cap, *see* Dome: levels: four
Ceiling (for insulation), 123–24 and
   illus.
Cement footings, 24
   definition, 184
Cleaning dome, 128
Community garden, 157
Companion planting, 142–43
Conduction:
   definition and formula, 17, 184
Containers for water storage, 26–28
   combinations possible, 114–18, *illus.*
     116, *illus.* 117
   selection, 114
Cooling strategies, 125–26
   see also Ventilation

Cost of:
   drums, 31–32
   fish tank, 29
   hardware, 32–33
   insulation, 20, 30
   lumber, 31
   Monsanto "602" film, 24–25, 30
   staple gun, 26
   tape, 29–30
Crawford, Charles, 5
Creosote as wood preservative, 22–23

Dead air space as insulation, 4, 17, 18
   and *illus.*, 21–22, 123
   definition, 184
Degree days, 16, *tables* 169–72
   definition, 184
Ditch:
   for drainage, 65
Dome:
   advantages, 1–6
   assembly, *see* Assembly
   base circle, *see* Base circle
   covering, *see* Film (plastic)
   covering process, 89–112 and *illus.*
     door, 108–109 and *illus.*
     inner covering, 107–108
     level four, 93–98 and *illus.*
     level three, 98–102 and *illus.*
     level two, 102–104 and *illus.*
     procedures, 90–91
     vent, 108–109 and *illus.*
   diameter:
     measurement, 53–55
     sixteen-foot, 163
   door, *see* Door
   floor space, *see* Floor space
   frame, *see* Frame
   maintenance, 127–31
   rigidity, 53, 75
   size variations, 159–63
   as source of home heat, 153–54 and
     illus.
   strength, 2, 53
   temperature, *see* Temperature maintenance
   vent, *see* Vent
   wooden parts, *see* Wooden parts
Door:
   construction, 84–88 and *illus.*
   covering with film, 108–109 and *illus.*
   frame, 82–84, *illus.* 83
   hanging, 110–12 and *illus.*
   location, 62, *illus.* 63
   misfit, 110
   protection from infiltration, 118–20
     and *illus.*, 124–25 and *illus.*
   screened, 125–26
Drainage ditch, 65
Drilling holes, 40–41
   for outer plates, 51–52 and *illus.*
   strut holes, 42–43
Drums for water heat storage, *illus.* 26, 27
   positioning, 115–16 and *illus.*
   preparation, 114–15

Drums for water heat storage *(cont'd)*
   purchasing, 31–32
   used with fish tank, 117–18
   used with gallon jugs, 116–17 and
     illus.
   used for home water heating, 155–57
     and *illus.*

Electricity:
   supply, 122–23
Electric line (underground), 66, 122–23
Emergencies, 130–31

Fertilizer, 134
Fiberglass:
   as glazing material, 24
   insulation, *see* Insulation: fiberglass
Film (plastic), 4
   attachments, 91–93 and *illus.*
     seam, 93 and *illus.*
     temporary, 91
     wrap-around, 92
   bunching, 98
   cleaning, 128
   cutting and measuring, 90, 99 and
     illus., 103–104
     troubleshooting, 104
   for domes of various sizes, 161–62
   insufficient supply, 108
   light-transmission, 25
   patching, 104
   pieces required, 89
   protection strategies, 90–91
   purchasing, 30
   replacement procedure, 127–29
   slack, 90–91
   as underground insulation, 20
     amount needed for domes of various
       sizes, 161
     attaching to frame, 68–70
     installation, 64–66, *illus.* 65
     protection, 112
Fish raising, 149–51
Fish tank, 4, 6
   algae in, 150
   for heat storage, 27, 117–18
   purchasing, 29
   timing of installation, 70
Floor space:
   formula, 159
Fordham Urban Solar Eco-System
   (FUSES), 3, 81
Frame, *illus.* 36
   adjustments for various sizes, 160
   assembling, 71–88 and *illus.*
     sequence, 72
   attaching to underground film, 68–70
     and *illus.*
     trouble-shooting, 70
   levels, 71–72 and *illus.*
     four: assembly, 76–77 and *illus.*;
       covering, 93–98 and *illus.*
     three: assembly, 78, *illus.* 79;
       covering, 98–102 and *illus.*

Frame, levels *(cont'd)*
    two: assembly 74–76 and *illus.*;
        covering, 102–104 and *illus.*
    materials, 21–22
    parts enumerated, 36–37
    struts, *see* Struts
    wooden parts, *see* Wooden parts
French Intensive gardening method, 4, 132–34
FUSES, *see* Fordham Urban Solar Eco-System

Garden:
    bed: preparation, 58–59, 133, 135–36
    bibliography, 148
    community project, 157
    companion planting, 142–43
    design, 136–38 and *illus.*
    French Intensive method, 4, 132–34
    organic vs. conventional methods, 134–35
    paths, 136–38 and *illus.*
    pests, 134
        control, 134–35, 145–46, 176–82
        planting and harvesting schedule, 138–40
        sample, 139
    seasons, 138–40, 174–75
    steps, 136–37 and *illus.*
    summer crops, 147–48, 175
    watering, 143–45
    wide rows, 133, 136–37 and *illus.*
    winter crops, 146–47, 175
Gateway National Park, Jamaica Bay, N.Y.:
    domes, *illus.* 21, 157, 159
Glass:
    as glazing material for dome, 24
Glazing:
    definition, 185
    selection and ordering, 24–25
    see also Film (plastic); Monsanto "602"

Hanging door and vent, 110–112 and *illus.*
Hardware, 24
    purchasing, 32–33
    to secure struts to hubs, *illus.* 32
Hazards:
    hurricane, 131
    moisture collection, 127
    snow, 130-31
    vandalism, 127, 131
    wind, 131
    yellowing, 128
Heater (auxiliary), 16
Heating home with dome heat, 153–54 and *illus.*
Heat storage:
    amount required, 27
    by water, 26, 114–20
        containers, 26–28; combinations, 114–18, *illus.* 116, *illus.* 117; selection, 114
Hex hubs, *see* Hubs: hexagonal

Holes: drilling, *see* Drilling holes
Home:
    heating from dome, 153–54 and *illus.*
Hose, 143-44
Hubs:
    assembling, 47-51
    base:
        assembling, 50–51 and *illus.*
        cutting, 45, *illus.* 45–46
        securing to posts, 66–68 and *illus.*
    definition, 185
    hexagonal:
        assembling, 48–50 and *illus.*
        cutting, 43–44 and *illus.*
    misalignment, 79–82
    pentagonal:
        assembling, 50 and *illus.*
        cutting, 44–45 and *illus.*
        misalignment, 127–28
    plates:
        cutting, 43–46
        securing to hubs, 101
    replacing, 130
    securing to struts:
        hardware required, *illus.* 32
Humidity, *see* Moisture in dome
Hurricane hazard, 131

Infiltration:
    definition, 185
    protection from, 118–20 and *illus.*; *see also* Insulation
Insects, *see* Garden: pests
Insulation, 5–6
    above-ground:
        amount required, 19–20
        installation, 104–107 and *illus.*
        selection and ordering, 18–21
        see also Insulation: fiberglass
    dead air space, 4, 17, 18 and *illus.*, 21–22, 123
    definition, 17
    fiberglass, 5 and *illus.*, 17, 18–20 and *illus.*
        amount needed for domes of various sizes, 162
        foil backing, 5, *illus.* 6, 18, *illus.* 19
    purchasing, 30
    selection and ordering, 17–21
    underground, 5–6
        affected by moisture, 8
        cost, 20
        selection and ordering, 20–21 and *illus.*, 30
        trenches, 59–62 and *illus.*
    see also Air lock; Infiltration: protection from; Night blanket
Intensive gardening, 4, 132–34
    definition, 185

Jigs:
    definition, 185
    for drilling holes, 40–42 and *illus.*
    for hub struts, 39
    for long struts, 37–38 and *illus.*
    for short struts, 39

Jugs for water heat storage, *illus.* 26, 27, 28
    preparation, 115
    used with drums, 116–17 and *illus.*

Knots in wood, 39

Levels of dome frame, *see* Frame: levels
Lumber, *see* Wooden parts

Maintenance, 127–31
Martin's latex paint, 28
Materials:
    list and prices, 29–33
    selection and ordering, 17–33 and *illus.*; *see also* individual materials, e.g. Hardware
McNiff, Veronica, 5
Measurement problems:
    base circle of dome, 55–56
    cutting wooden parts, 40
    door, 110
    film, 104, 108
Moisture in dome, 127, 143
Money-earning from dome, 152–58
Monsanto "602" polyethylene film, 4, 89
    advantages, 24–25
    see also Film (plastic)
Mulch, 133, 141

New York magazine, 5
Night blanket (insulating), 123
    definition, 186

Obstructions to sunlight, 13–15
Opaquing compounds, 125
Organic vs. conventional gardening, 134–35
Outer plates, *see* Hubs: plates

Paint:
    solar energy-absorbing, 28
Pent hubs, *see* Hubs: pentagonal
Plastic film, *see* Film (plastic)
Plastic jugs, *see* Jugs for heat storage
Pollination, 141–42
    by hand, 142 and *illus.*
Polyethylene film, *see* Film (plastic)
Post hole digger, 63
Posts, 23–24 and *illus.*
    installation, 62-64 and *illus.*
    securing to base hubs, 66–68 and *illus.*
    walmanized, 3–4, 22
Preservative:
    redwood stain, 3, 23, 47, 85, 110, 129
    toxicity, 22–23
    see also Walmanized wooden parts
Pressure sprayer, 145
    definition, 187
Prices, *see* Cost

Radiation (solar), 166, 172–73
Redwood stain preservative, 3, 23, 47
    door and vent, 85, 110
    recoating frame, 129

192

Replacing film:
  complete layer, 128–29
  individual section, 127
Rigidity, 53, 75
Rod (threaded):
  to secure posts to base hubs, 66–67 and *illus.*
Rust inhibiter, 68

Scotchrap 50 tape, 24, *illus.* 26, 90
  advantages, 25
  purchasing, 29–30
Screen door, 125–26
Seam attachment of film, 93 and *illus.*
Securing posts, *see* Posts
Seedlings, 137, 138, 140–41
  selling, 152–53
Selection of site, 7–16 and *illus.*
Shading, 16
  see also Obstructions to sunlight
Shading cloth, 125
Site:
  drainage, 7–8
  leveling, 8, 56–58 and *illus.*, 81
  preparation, 53–70 and *illus.*
    equipment needed, 53
  selection, 7–16 and *illus.*
  shading, 16
  sunlight available, 9
Snow hazard, 130–31
Soil:
  analysis, 135
  preparation for gardening, 58–59, 133, 135–36
  temperature, 120
  tilling, 135–36 and *illus.*
  as underground insulation, 20 and *illus.*, 21
    protection from water, 70
Solar altitude, 11, *illus.* 12, 165, *tables* 166–68
  definition, 187
  see also Sun: angle
Solar azimuth, 11, *illus.* 12, 165, *tables* 166–68
Solar radiation, 166, 172–73
Solar time, 165–66
South (true):
  to locate from dome site, 13
Sprayer for plants, *see* Pressure sprayer
Staple gun, 24, 26
Steps, in garden, 136–37 and *illus.*
Strength of dome, 2
Struts, 21
  definition, 187
  hub:
    connecting to struts, 73 and *illus.*
    cutting, 39–40

Struts *(cont'd)*
  long:
    connecting to hub struts, 73 and *illus.*
    cutting, 38–39
  misplaced, 82
  replacing, 130
  securing to hubs, 73 and *illus.*
    hardware required, *illus.* 32
  short:
    connecting to hub struts, 73 and *illus.*
    cutting, 39
  size for various dome diameters:
    formula, 160
Sun:
  angle, 10–12 and *illus.*
  position, 9–12
  surveying, 12–15 and *illus.*, 165–66
  definition, 188
  see also Solar . . .
Sunlight:
  obstructions, 13–15
  radiation, 166, 172–73
  requirements, 15–16
Surveying device (homemade), *illus.* 12
  construction, 12–13
  use, 13–15
Swimming pool cover, 158

Tape, 24
  problems in using, 95
  purchasing, 29–30
  uses, 25, 90
Temperature:
  maintenance, 113–27 and *illus.*
    spring and fall, 126–27
    supplementary strategies, 121, 123–25
  measurement, 113–14 and *illus.*
  requirements, 120
Temporary film attachment, 91
Thermometers, 113–14 and *illus.*
Tilapia aurea (fish), 149–51, 188
Tilling soil, 135–36 and *illus.*
Time required for building dome, *tables* 173–74
  covering dome with film, 89, 174
  cutting wooden parts, 34, 173
  erecting dome frame, 71, 174
  site preparation, 53, 174
Toxicity of wood preservative, 22–23
Trellis, 141
  definition, 188
Trenches for underground insulation, 59–62 and *illus.*
Triad:
  definition, 98, 188

Underground insulation, *see* Insulation: underground

Vandalism, 127, 131
Vegetables:
  light requirements, 140
  seedlings, *see* Seedlings
  selling, 152
  summer crops, 147–48, 175
  winter crops, 146–47, 175
  see also Garden
Vent:
  construction, 84–88 and *illus.*
  covering with film, 108–109 and *illus.*
  frame:
    location, 84 and *illus.*
    hanging, 110–112 and *illus.*
    prop, 111 and *illus.*
    protection from infiltration, 118–20 and *illus.*
  supplementary, 125
Ventilation, 125–26
  effect on crops, 139, 147

Walmanized wooden parts, 3–4, 22
  definition, 188
Water:
  drums, *see* Drums
  heat storage, *see* Heat storage: by water
  hot (domestic supply), 155–57
  line (underground), 66, 143
Watering garden, 143–45
Weeds, 134, 141
Wide rows, 133, 136–37 and *illus.*
Wind barriers, 8–9 and *illus.*
Wind hazard, 131
Wire:
  to measure dome diameter, 53, *illus.* 54
Wooden parts:
  assembling, 21; *see also* Frame: assembling
  cutting and drilling, 21, 34–52
    equipment required, 35
    measurement problems, 40
    time required, 34
  damaged lumber, 37
  for domes of various sizes, 160–61
  knots in wood, 39
  organizing for frame assembly, 73–74
  preservation, 22–23
  purchasing, 31
  selection and ordering, 21–22
  see also Frame; Hubs; Posts; Struts
Woodlife as preservative, 22–23
Wrap-around film attachment, 92

Other Garden Way Books You Will Enjoy

The Complete Greenhouse Book, by Peter Clegg and Derry Watkins. Quality paperback, 288 pages, $9.95; hardcover, $14.95. A thorough "how-to" book on using the sun to heat glass-enclosed spaces — from cold frames to "sunspace" living areas. Includes greenhouse gardening, pests and diseases. Heavily illustrated.

Building and Using Our Sun-Heated Greenhouse, by Helen and Scott Nearing. Quality paperback, 156 pages, $6.95. A close-up, personal view of the Nearings' year-round gardening techniques in an unheated Maine greenhouse.

Designing and Building a Solar House, by Donald Watson, 288 pages, 8½ x 11, quality paperback, $9.95; cloth, $12.95. "A nuts-and-bolts book that brings the sun down to earth," said Alvin Toffler, author of **Future Shock.**

Homemade: 101 Easy-to-Make Things for Your Garden, Home or Farm, by Ken Braren and Roger Griffith. 176 pages, quality paperback, 8½ x 11, $6.95. Plans and instructions for making fences, chairs, birdhouses, potting benches, and scores of other useful items for country living.

Down-to-Earth Vegetable Gardening Know-How, featuring Dick Raymond. 160 pages, deluxe illustrated paperback, $5.95. A treasury of complete vegetable gardening information.

Profitable Herb Growing at Home, by Betty E.M. Jacobs. 240 pages, quality paperback, $5.95. The perfect book for those who wish to expand a home herb garden into a money-making country sideline.

Home Energy for the Eighties, by Ralph Wolfe and Peter Clegg. Quality paperback 8½ x 11, 288 pages, $10.95. How to deal with the energy crisis by turning to solar heat, water power, wind power, and wood. Plus catalog sections on what's available now in these fields.

At Home in the Sun: An Open-House Tour of Solar Homes in the United States, by Norah Davis and Linda Lindsey. Quality paperback, 8½ x 11, 248 pages, $9.95. What it's like to live in a solar house, as told by the owners of thirty-one solar homes around the country.

These books are available at your bookstore, or directly from Garden Way Publishing, Box 171X, Charlotte, Vermont 05445. If ordering by mail and your order is under $10, please enclose 75¢ for postage and handling.